Development Displacement and Rehabilitation of Tribes in Andhra Pradesh

Development Displacement and Rehabilitation of Tribes in Andhra Pradesh

Dr Devath Suresh

KALPAZ

ISBN: 978-93-5128-213-6

Price: ₹ 950

First Published, 2016

Published by

Kalpaz Publications
C-30, Satyawati Nagar,
Delhi – 110052
E-mail: kalpaz@hotmail.com
Ph.: 9212142040

Printed at: G. Print Process, Delhi

Cataloging in Publication Data—DK
Courtesy: D.K. Agencies (P) Ltd. <docinfo@dkagencies.com>

Suresh, Devath, author.
Development, displacement and rehabilitation : with special reference to tribal habitations of Andhra Pradesh / Dr Devath Suresh.
pages cm
Includes bibliographical references.
ISBN 9789351282136

1. Andhra Pradesh (India)—Scheduled tribes—Relocation. 2. Andhra Pradesh (India)—Scheduled tribes—Rehabilitation—Government policy. 3. Economic development projects—Social aspects—India—Andhra Pradesh. I. Title.

HB2100.A53S87 2016 DDC 304.808694095485 23

Contents

Preface and Acknowledgements

Since Displacement was considered to be necessary, rather obvious for Development, the only solace for the displaced lot was to get the meagre compensation decided by the state authorities in accordance with the colonial Land Acquisition Act of 1894. Though, initially the Constitution vested property right as a fundamental right but the same was crippled by the very first Amendment to the Constitution in 1951, by adding Article 31A which provided legitimacy to land acquisition by State but not without payment of compensation that is not less than the existing market rate, and finally in 1978 the Right to Property was omitted from being a fundamental right and was reduced to a mere constitutional right under Article 301A.

Legally speaking all the land acquisitions by the state are lawful, if only the state pays the requisite compensation to the displaced. However, monetary compensation, for the land deprived, to the individual is no compensation at all as the land for him, besides being a property, has emotional, cultural, social, ethical, and economic value for which the mere monetary compensation does not compensate. Hence, the concept of 'Land for land' and provisions for resettlement and rehabilitation of those affected by such acquisitions came into vogue. But these concepts are followed more in violations than in observance.

In a welfare state the State is obliged to take care of the subjects like a parent, and when it is so ensured under the Constitution (Fundamental Rights) it becomes all the more imperative on the state to grant protection. The ill-effects of the displacement induced by development ought to be taken care of by the state and necessary arrangement thereof be made, i.e., the displaced persons be resettled in a safe habitat wherein they can start their life afresh. However, this would require more than mere allocation of certain piece of land for resettlement or mere construction of make-shift camps for temporary settlement. What is needed is the "rehabilitation" of the persons affected by the projects; Rehabilitation means to "restore to the former condition", and thus, all that was lost by displacement, the emotional, cultural, social, political and economic losses must be restored at a priority basis than to the Project itself.

The rehabilitation and resettlement policies are the result of concerns expressed by the social activists, academicians and NGOs. Most of the Pre-1980 projects in India did not have a clear-cut resettlement plans. Resettlement was taken on a case-to-case basis and only a few of the projects offered resettlement in the form of house sites and infrastructure to the displaced. As a result of this ad-hoc approach, many of the displaced were left out of the process. The Rehabilitation and Resettlement (R&R) Policies for the Project Affected Families (PAFs) at the National and Andhra Pradesh State levels were formulated. The Governments (Central and State) did not frame any rehabilitation and resettlement policies prior to1988. It was the lukewarm attitude of the Governments towards the plight of Project Affected Persons (PAPs), even after they were up rooted. The Government of India announced National Rehabilitation Policy for Project Affected Families in February 2004, while the Andhra Pradesh government announced Rehabilitation and Resettlement (R&R) Policy in 2005.

Millions of people since independence have been displaced by various projects in India and Andhra Pradesh in the name of development. Displacement means people forgoing their villages, lands, work, income, culture and the way of life established and accumulated since the time immemorial. It amounts to a total destruction of the existing economy in the process of creating a new one for a new set of people and regions. Consequently, a set of losers and gainers have been created. Losers are those who are displaced and the gainers are those who live in command area of the irrigation projects, the industrialists, bureaucrats and the contractor-politician combine.

The magnitude of displacement is very high in India and takes top in Andhra Pradesh. Michael Cernea, senior advisor, social policy and sociology, World Bank, in one of his papers observed that in the absence of proper Resettlement and Rehabilitation policy, people have been thrown into landlessness; joblessness; marginalisation; increased morbidity and mortality; food insecurity; loss of access to common property and services and community disarticulation this was true in the case of Andhra Pradesh also.

The present study deals with the Resettlement and Rehabilitation policies followed by different political regimes during post-state formation periods (1956-2014) of Andhra Pradesh. The question before any planner is how to rebuild the destroyed economy of the displaced people of a project.

The aim of the present study is to find out what measures have been taken and what policy has been adopted by the governments for displaced tribal people. The focus of analysis is on the concern shown for the displaced and their resettlement and rehabilitation. For the purpose of the study, the tribal habitations affected in irrigation projects are selected in the Warangal district. For the purpose of the present study five Thandas have been taken as samples, viz., Janakamma Banda Thanda located at Moripirala Village of Ryaparthy Mandal, Vidynagar Thanda located at Ryaparthy Mandal, Guguloth Bondalu Thanda and Gyama Thanda which are located at Parvathagiri Mandal and finally Dongachelima Thanda located at Narmetta Manda of Warangal district.

The present study is my Post-Doctoral Work which is financed through the Post-Doctoral Fellowship awarded by University Grants Commission, New Delhi. Regarding my work, I express my warm thanks to Professor V. Bhaskara Rao (Retd), Department of Public Administration & HRM, Kakatiya University, Warangal and to my teacher, Professor P. Narsimha Rao, Department of Public Administration & HRM, Kakatiya University, Warangal.

Dr Devath Suresh

List of Tables

Abbreviations

ADB	:	Asian Development Bank
AIR	:	All India Radio
APL	:	Above Poverty Line
APRRP	:	Andhra Pradesh Rehabilitation and Resettlement Policy
APSADRR	:	Andhra Pradesh Scheduled Areas Debt Relief Regulation
APSALTR	:	Andhra Pradesh State Agency Land Transfer Regulation
APSALTRR	:	Andhra Pradesh State Agency Land Transfer Regulation Rules
APSAMLR	:	Andhra Pradesh Scheduled Areas Money Lenders Regulation
ATILTA	:	Agency Tracts Interest and Land Transfer Act
BC	:	Backward Classes
BHEL	:	Bharat Heavy Electricals Limited
BPL	:	Below Poverty Line
CAPART	:	Council for Advancement of People's Action and Rural Technology
CBO	:	Community Based Organisations
CESS	:	Centre for Economic and Social Studies
CGM	:	Cash Grant Method
CIL	:	Coal India Limited

CIP	:	Coal India Policy
CPRs	:	Common Property Resources
CSR	:	Corporate Social Responsibility
CSWB	:	Central Social Welfare Board
CTDMLV	:	Centre for Tribal Development of the Manikya Lal Verma
CWC	:	Central Water Commission
DDP	:	Desert Development Programme
DPAP	:	District Primary Education Programme
DPs	:	Displaced Peoples
DPs	:	*Displaced Persons*
DRM	:	Disputes Redressal Mechanism
DTP	:	Displaced Tribal People
FC	:	Forward Classes
FDI	:	Foreign Direct Investment
FRL	:	Full Reservoir Level
FTL	:	Full Tank Level
GCC	:	Girijana Cooperative Corporation
GFI	:	General Felicity Index
GOs	:	Government Orders
GRC	:	Grievance Redressal Cell
HIV	:	Human Immunodeficiency Virus
ICDS	:	Integrated Child Development Scheme
ICOLD	:	International Commission on Large Dams
IDPs	:	Internally Displaced Persons
IEC	:	Information, Education and Communication
IFAD	:	International Fund for Agricultural Development
IIPA	:	Indian Institute of Public Administration
IMF	:	International Monetary Fund
IRDP	:	Integrated Rural Development Programme
IRN	:	International Rivers Network
ISRO	:	Indian Space Research Organisation
ITDA	:	Integrated Tribal Development Agency

ITDP	: Integrated Tribal Development Project
LPG	: Liberalisation, Privatisation and Globalisation
MAWs	: Minimum Agricultural Wages
Mcft	: Million Cubic Feet
MDGs	: Millennium Development Goals
MFPs	: Minor Forest Produces
MGNREGA	: Mahatma Gandhi National Rural Employment Guarantee Act
MLA	: Member of Legislative Assembly
MNCs	: Multi National Companies
MP	: Member of Parliament
MW	: Mega Watts
MWL	: Mean Water Level
NEP	: National Forest Policy
NEP	: New Economic Policy
NGOs	: Non Governmental Organisations
NHPC	: National Hydroelectric Power Corporation
NLTA	: Non Lending Technical Assistance
NPRR	: National Policy on Rehabilitation and Resettlement
NPRRPAF	: National Policy on Resettlement & Rehabilitation for Project Affected Families
NREGS	: National Rural Employment Guarantee Scheme
NREP	: Nation Rural Employment Programme
NTPC	: National Thermal Power Company
NWDTA	: Narmada Water Disputes Tribunal Award
PAAs	: Project Affected Areas
PAF	: Project Affected Family
PAP	: Project Affected Persons
PAPs	: Project Affected Persons/Peoples
PDS	: Public Distribution System
PESA	: Panchayat Raj Extension Act to Scheduled Areas
PIL	: Public Interest Litigation
PRIs	: Panchayat Raj Institutions

PRM	:	Physical Rehabilitation Method
PSUs	:	Public Sector Undertakings
R&R	:	Rehabilitation and Resettlement
R&R-PAFERP	:	Resettlement and Rehabilitation, Project Affected Families, Economic Rehabilitation Plan
RLEGP	:	Rural-Landless Employment Guarantee Programme
RRPAFs	:	Resettlement and Rehabilitation for Project Affected Families
SC	:	Schedule Caste
SCs	:	Scheduled Castes
SIA	:	Social Impact Assessment
SMRR	:	State Mission for Resettlement and Rehabilitation
ST	:	Scheduled Tribe
STAs	:	Scheduled Tribal Areas
STs	:	Scheduled Tribes
TBL	:	Tank Balance Level
TISS	:	Tata Institute of Social Sciences
TMC	:	Thousand Million Cubic Feet
UN	:	United Nations
UNDP	:	United Nations Development Programme
USA	:	United States of America
WBEDs	:	World Bank Environment Departments
WCD	:	World Commission on Dames
WRR	:	World Rivers Review

Chapter 1

Introduction

The term "development administration" came into use in the 1950s to represent the aspects of public administration and the changes in public administration, which are needed to carry out policies, projects, and programmes to improve social and economic conditions. During a period of 15 years following the end of World War II, in 1945, colony after colony threw off the imperial yoke. Country after country achieved independence and political autonomy. This new status gave promise of freedom and liberty and self-determination in political systems of representative democracy. It gave hope of greater individual freedom and equality of treatment in the society. And independence created hopes of higher national and per capita income, a rapid rise in standards of living, and an increase in individual opportunity. Even in countries which had not been colonies but had been administered by some other form of authoritarian government, this was a generation of rising and insistent expectations pressing for rapid political, social, and economic change. New governments and their bureaucracies, their administrative agencies and processes, were expected to give reality to these anticipated fruits of independence and liberty. These new functions and demands upon the administration system, were enormous in size and weight, novel and complex in character.[1]

Development administration is that branch of Public Administration which is concerned with the development of a country's economy and society and the system of development administration depends on the socio-political system prevailing in a country. The socio-political system of developed countries is quite different from the socio-political system of underdeveloped countries. The socio-political system of a country depends on various factors. The most important of these is the basic objective for which a society stands. The system also depends on whether a country has adopted the capitalist system of economy or opted for a socialistic pattern. Development administration further varies in countries which have taken to the communist system.[2]

Meaning of Development Administration

Development administration is concerned with plans, policies, programmes and projects which focus on nation building and socio-economic development. It aims at achieving socio-economic goals through the talents and expertise of bureaucrats. Development administration focuses on the results to be achieved rather than the traditionalist view of strict adherence to rules and hierarchy. Strict adherence to rules creates rigidness, delay and procrastination.

- Development per se is oriented towards change in a destined direction. Thus, development administration is change oriented and rejects status quo.
- Every development function has a goal to be achieved. i.e., Economic Development has the goal to improve the quality of life such as better literacy rate, life expectancy and reduction in poverty rates.
- For the goals to be achieved, to relate the means to ends, planning and temporal dimension are salient feature. Planning aids in deciding the resource required for the goal, the time in which it needs to achieve.
- Development administration has an innovative dimension; it is flexible enough to design new methods, procedures, policies which would save time, increase effectiveness and quality.
- Administrators under this concept are required to be committed to the policies, plans and programmes. The commitment is not necessarily to the political parties, who enacts the policies but to the values that an administrator should uphold in his/her profession.

- Development is ultimately aimed at the people, hence it should accord primacy to the public and the administration should be client oriented.
- For the development function to be effective and for it to be people oriented, participation of people is emphasised in formulating plans, implementation and sharing the benefits derived. Thus, Development administration should focus on "planning with people" rather than "planning for people". It should be people centered rather than production centred. i.e., not in maximising production, goods and services but to address the needs of people and empower people.

Development administration has two concepts, administration of development and administrative development. Administrative development is increasing and improving the capabilities of administrative system. It involves modernisation of administrative structure, capabilities of personnel and attitudinal and behavioural changes among the administrators.

Displacement

In the process of economy-driven development, virtually all developmental project within the discourse had taken one thing for granted, i.e. "Displacement" (Displacement is seen as the result of a model of development that enforces certain technical and economic choices without giving any serious consideration to those options that would involve the least social and environmental costs).[3] It is taken to be a natural corollary of development and the public at large is 'forced to believe' that the reason for displacement is in "national" or "public" interest.

Conventionally, there was no question of challenging the displacement or the development paradigm itself as such, moreover, with time the 'Temples' increased in number and categories, from Dam to mines, powerhouses, factories, sanctuaries, urbanisation, tourism project and defence projects became the "public purpose" and displaced people 'normally'. Walter Fernandes *et. al.,* estimated that 30 million people were affected by these projects till 1994, the World Commission on Dams Report (November 2000) estimated the total number of the displaced people by 4500 large dams in India to be 30-40 million.[4]

The figure quoted by Arundhati Roy in her essay 'The Greater Common Good: The Human Cost of Big Dams' reflects the same. It is worth quoting her persuasive reasoning: According to a detailed study of 54 Large Dams done by the Indian Institute of Public Administration, the average number of people displaced by a Large Dam is 44,182. Admittedly 54 Dams out of 3,300 is not a big enough sample. But it's all we have erred on the side of *abundant* caution and take an average of just 10,000 people per Large Dam. 33 million that's what it works out to be. What about those that have been displaced by the thousands of other Development Projects? Fifty million people, I feel, like someone who's just stumbled on a mass grave.[5]

However, the voices of the displaced are no longer extraordinary. Echoed in virtually every displacement situation, be it Tehri, Narmada, Singrauli or Keol Karo, only to name a few which they reveal what it means to be a "displaced lot": Loss of livelihood and traditional lands; demolition of homes; loss of social networks; severance from an eco-system that sustained them earlier and, above all, a feeling of powerlessness and insecurity for the future.

Displacement is a multidimensional phenomenon, which not only confined to physical relocation; it also reduces the "quality of life" of the communities into sub-human conditions. This understanding of displacement highlights: (i) the alienation of the individual and community from legal and customary rights and dislocation of the social and economic organisation, and (ii) the politics of legal and policy instruments that sanctions such disenfranchisement. In this context displacement refers not only to those who are forced to physically relocate in order to make way for the project and its related aspects but also includes those who are displaced from their resource base and livelihoods. It is commonly experienced through the loss of land and the disruption of social and economic relationships.[6]

Ironically, the existing definition of project affected persons (PAPs) did not include the landless, the non-asset class, the seasonal farmers, the fishermen, boatmen, those engaged in the work of art, culture and handicraft, and small shopkeepers in the affected village. Also it did not recognise those affected by the canals, colonies, sanctuaries, catchment area treatment, secondary displacement and displacement through subsidiary and ancillary projects as 'ousters', making the whole process as class biased and only in terms of cash economy.

Ideally, it is to be expected that those likely to be negatively affected by the projects would be consulted and kept informed in such a way as to enable them to best rebuild their ravaged lives. However, it is not the case, rather, from the inception of planning of most projects, through various stages of displacement and resettlement, there is bewilderment and confusion among the resettled in virtually every large project about the extent and intensity of the damage.[7]

Rehabilitation and Resettlement

Since Displacement was considered to be necessary, rather obvious for Development, the only solace for the displaced lot was to get the meagre compensation decided by the state authorities in accordance with the colonial Land Acquisition Act of 1894. Though, initially the Constitution vested property right[8] as a fundamental right but the same was crippled by the very first Amendment to the Constitution in 1951, by adding Article 31A which provided legitimacy to land acquisition by State but not without payment of compensation that is not less than the existing market rate, and finally in 1978 the Right to Property was omitted from being a fundamental right and was reduced to a mere constitutional right under Article 301A.

Legally speaking all the land acquisitions by the state is lawful, if only the state pays the requisite compensation to the displaced. However, monetary compensation for the land deprived to the individual is no compensation, as the land for him, besides being a property, has emotional, cultural, social, ethical, and economic value for which the mere monetary compensation does not compensate. Hence, the concept of 'Land for land' and provisions for resettlement and rehabilitation of those affected by such acquisitions. But these concepts are followed more in violations than in observance.

In a welfare state the State is obliged to take care of the subjects like a parent, and when it is so ensured under the Constitution (Fundamental Rights) it becomes all the more imperative on the state to grant protection. The ill-effects of the displacement induced by development ought to be taken care of by the state and necessary arrangement thereof be made, i.e., the displaced persons be resettled in a safe habitat wherein they can start their life afresh. However, this would require more than mere allocation of certain piece of land for resettlement or mere construction of make shift camps for temporary settlement. What is needed is the "rehabilitation" of the persons affected by the projects; rehabilitation means to "restore to the former condition", and thus, all that was lost by displacement, the emotional, cultural, social, political and economic losses must be restored at a priority basis than to the Project itself, which is the cause of the impoverishment.

Initially, when displacement was considered to be "sacrifice in the nation building" rather, more appropriately, "temple building", the miseries and pains of displaced were ignored with no specific arrangement even for their 'resettlement' leave alone `rehabilitation'. It was only when people started questioning (since the late 70s and 80s) the 'sacredness' of the 'sacrifice' and the 'latent purpose' behind the 'public purpose' unleashing a national debate on the whole issue, the state was compelled to announce resettlement and rehabilitation of the displaced, nonetheless, the practice remained same, rather the intensity of the projects and consequent displacement increased manifold riding high on the fast tracks of 'liberalisation' after the new economic policy of 1991. The irony is that, those already affected were never attended to and on the other hand every new economic project was exposing hundreds of thousands of families to displacement. In the present march of globalisation-induced liberalisation, the development has been proceeding in such an unprecedented manner and unformidable pace that development has become almost synonymous to the term displacement. Wherever there is drum-beat of development, thousands and thousands of people are not only apprehending, but also facing the bulldozer of displacement.

Taken randomly any project that boasts of economic well-being of the nation is not free from this malady of displacement, and in no case the people affected have received the much needed protection of resettlement and rehabilitation. On the contrary, the projects are given a free go-ahead without completion of the resettlement and rehabilitation programmes. The abrupt closing of flood gates of Rihand Dam which left more than 50000 people missing is not just one isolated example, in executing the Maan Irrigation Project of Narmada Valley on 20 July 2002, police forcibly evicted the residents of Khedi Balwari, the first village to be submerged. The sluice gates of the dam were deliberately closed, though the affected persons had not been rehabilitated. The villagers terrified that the police virtually dragged them into buses and took them to rehabilitation sites 45-70 kms away. While pushing people into buses, children the smallest being of a couple of months were separated from their parents and left behind. The women complained that they did not know the whereabouts of their children for over a week. Virtually all developmental projects have one or even more episodes of such ghastly instances to their glory; besides, forced resettlement (in absence of consultation with the people affected by the projects) has been the rule of the day and planned ones being rare exceptions.

A few projects have no rehabilitation policies in India, even on paper. Projects like Tehri and Narmada, which have comprehensive rehabilitation policies in place even if they are most often not implemented are rare. The National Rehabilitation Policy, though captures certain important concerns relating to the experience of displacement, fails to provide appropriate mechanism or framework for the assessment of the necessity of displacement, or the identification or compensation of the 'ousters' with livelihood. The awful situation of resettlement and rehabilitation is same across the developmental projects irrespective of damming, mining, industrialisation, urbanisation, infrastructures and the like including the cases of natural disasters.

The provision of 'land for land' that has been envisaged since the Narmada Project, for the PAP, though a positive step, was rendered unfruitful by the tribunals like *Narmada Water Disputes Tribunal Award* (NWDTA)[9] and not so well founded judgments of the Supreme Court. In the part of resettlement programmes in the country the government has not compensated the displaced in a just manner by their giving an insultingly paltry sum as compensation while appropriating their sources of livelihood. One of the fundamental reasons of dismal record of resettlement and rehabilitation is the biases and prejudices of those who design the projects, for them it is the responsibility of the local authorities and something that is outside the ambit of the project, in other words, an 'external cost' to the project. Most of the time the matter is dealt on an ad-hoc basis, virtually with no practical information, rather based on guess work. Delay in work, involvement of middlemen, corruption and red-tapizm further aggravate the miseries of the poor and vulnerable victims.

The progress and prosperity of a nation is judged from the socio-economic status of its population, especially of the weaker sections of the society suffering from abject poverty, hunger, disease, unemployment, exploitation etc., as well as disadvantaged groups like, women, children, scheduled castes and tribal people etc. It is of prime importance that such segments of the society, mostly living in remote, backward, hilly, rural and tribal areas should receive the serious and earnest attention of policy-makers, planners, social welfare administrators, social scientists and academicians, so that the down-trodden section of the society can also live a decent life ensured by the Constitution of India in 1950 through special provisions in the nature of Fundamental Rights and Directive Principles of the State Policy. This will enable the national endeavour for establishment of a better social order based on equality, liberty and fraternity as mentioned in the Preamble to the Constitution of India and this, in turn, would involve them in the task of national development and modernisation.

Meaning and Definition of Tribes

The English term "Tribe" is derived from the Latin Word "*Tribus*" designating a particular kind of social and political organisation existing in all these societies. Originally, it was used to imply three divisions among the early Romans, later on; it was used to mean the "poor" or the "masses". In English language, the word appeared in the sixteenth century and denoted a community of persons claiming descent from a common ancestor. In India, the term "tribe" has legal and administrative connotations. British census officials-cum-anthropologists first used the term "tribe" for the purpose of enumerating social groups in India and the term was used from 1881 to 1931 censuses. The Government of India Act 1935 used the term "backward tribe". The Indian constitution retained the terminology with slight modification using "Scheduled" in place of "Backward".[10] But the constitution does not contain a precise definition of the term.[11]

The Dictionary of Anthropology mentions a tribe as a social group, usually with a definite area, dialect, cultural homogeneity and unifying social organisation. The term "tribe" in that sense refers to a type of society and designated a stage of evolution in human society.[12] As a type of society, the term signifies a set of characteristic features and as a state evolution; it connotes a specific mode of social organisation. Anthropologists define tribe as a collection of groups of people who share patterns of speech, basic cultural characteristics, and in the traditional sense, a common territory. According to Ghurye, the common features possessed by all the tribal groups in India are as follows:[13]

1. They live away from the civilised world in the inaccessible parts in the forests and hills.
2. They speak the same tribal dialect.
3. They belong either to one of the three stocks-Negiritos, Austroloid or Mongoloids.
4. They profess primitive religion known as animism in which worship of ghosts and spirits is the most important element.
5. They follow primitive occupation such as gleaning, hunting and gathering of forest products.
6. They are largely carnivorous.
7. They live either naked or semi-naked.
8. They have nomadic habits and love for drink and dance.

The assumptions of Lewis has been the ideally tribal societies which are small in scale, restricted in their spatial and temporal range of their social, legal and political relations and possess a morality of religion and world view of corresponding dimensions. This definition, however, does not focus the essential characteristics of a "tribe" and the scope of the definition is restricted to their ideas of tribal societies. Pathy was of the opinion that a tribe is a tribe which is included in the list of Scheduled Tribes.[14]

However, T.B. Naik proposed seven criteria by which a "tribe" can be recognised. They are:[15]

1. Functional interdependence within the community.
2. Economic backwardness.

3. Geographical isolation.
4. Common dialect.
5. Politically one unit under a common tribal authority.
6. Owned traditional laws and
7. Members are averse to change.

Vimal Chandra was of the view that primitiveness and backwardness are the tests applied for specifying a scheduled tribe: The main characteristics common to all the scheduled tribes are:[16]

1. Tribal origin.
2. Primitive way of life.
3. Habitat in remote and less accessible areas and
4. General backwardness in all respects.

According to Stephen Fuchs, "As far as Indian tribes go, the essentials seem to be only a comparatively simple and primitive economy combined with a certain degree of residential instability, a simple, though not always, class of social organisation."[17]

Tribe, as defined by Bellellie is a collection of individuals sharing a common culture. Suresh Chandra Rajora has attempted to cite some basic features of a tribal society like:[18]

1. Tribal society is a whole society.
2. Tribal oral system is a normative binding force.
3. Culture of silence.
4. Tribes have their own specific economic system.
5. Polygamy is an institution of prestige and glory.
6. Clan solidarity and
7. Liquor economy.

Thus, the term itself bears the ideology of self identification.

Definitions

Here are a few definitions of 'tribe' being used as the basis of discussion in the following lines:

"A tribe is a collection of families bearing a common name, speaking a common dialect, occupying or professing to occupy a common territory and is not usually endogamous, though originally it might have been so" – *Imperial Gazetteer of India.*[19]

"A tribe is a group of people in a primitive or barbarous stage of development acknowledging the authority of a chief and usually regarding themselves as having a common ancestor" - *Oxford Dictionary.*[20]

"In its simplest form the tribes are a group of bands occupying a contiguous territory or territories and having a feeling of unity deriving from numerous similarities in culture, frequent contacts, and a certain community of interest" – *Ralph Linton.*[21]

"A tribe is an independent political division of a population with a common culture" – Lucee Mair.[22]

"A tribe is a group united by a common name in which the members take a pride by a common language, by a common territory, and by a feeling those that who do not share this name are outsiders, 'enemies' in fact" – *G.W.B. Muntingford.*[23]

"A tribe is a social group with territorial affiliation, endogamous, with no specialisation of functions, ruled by tribal officers, hereditary or otherwise, united in language or dialect, recognising social distance with other tribes or castes, without any social obloquy attaching to them, as it does in the caste structure, following tribal traditions, beliefs and customs, illiberal of naturalisation of ideas from alien sources, above all conscious of homogeneity of ethnic and territorial integration" – *D.N. Majumdar.*[24]

"Ideally, tribal societies are small in scale, restricted in the spatial and temporal range of their social, legal, and political relations, and possess a morality, a religion, and words-view of corresponding dimensions. Characteristically too, tribal languages are unwritten, and hence, the extent of communication both in time and space is inevitably narrow. At the same time, tribal societies exhibit a remarkable economy of design and have a compactness and self-sufficiency which is lacking in modern society" – *L.M. Lewis.*[25]

Majumdar rightly comments that when one looks into the definitions given by various anthropologists, one is bound to be impressed by the dissimilarity of their views as regards what constitutes a tribe. Kinship ties, common territory, one language, joint ownership, one political organisation, absence of interline strife have all been referred to as the main characteristics of a tribe. Some anthropologists have not only accepted some of the above characteristics, but also stoutly denied some of them to be characteristics of a tribe. Thus, they did not mention habitation in a common territory as a vital feature of tribal organisation, although others like Perry have insisted on it, saying that even nomadic tribes roam about within a definite region. Radcliffe Brown has given instances of one section of a tribe fighting another from his Australian data. The only conclusion one can draw from such diversity of learned opinion is that the views of each anthropologist arise from the type of data with which he is most familiar. One may, therefore, make a list of universal characteristics, some of which would define a tribe any where.[26] Thus, Majumdar claims universal applicability of his definition given in preceding lines.

A major hurdle of defining a tribe is that related with the problem of distinguishing the tribe from peasantry "it is no doubt possible to use the labels 'tribal' and 'peasant' for this type of social organisation and to characterise one by contrasting it with the other. But in spite of all the effort invested by anthropologists in the study of primitive societies, there really is no satisfactory way of defining a tribal society. What this amounts to in the Indian context is that anthropologists have tried to characterise a somewhat nebulous sociological type by contrasting it with another which is almost equally nebulous. Earlier anthropologists had not paid sufficient attention to the definition of tribal society, but tacitly assumed that what they were studying in Australia, Melanesia, and Africa were various forms of tribal society. The tribe was somewhat vaguely assumed to be a more or less homogeneous society having a common government, a common dialect and a common culture. Though not everybody will agree with the assumption of Beitelle but his statement may be cited as one of the many schools of thought grappling with the problem.

The above discussion shows that it is not easy to define a tribe or a tribal society conclusively and any standard definition in this regard is very difficult to obtain. Hence, the regional connotation of the concept of tribe and focus attention on gaining standardisation within the Indian universe to solve our problems. This seems to be quite sensible in the situation when definitions of universal applicability are either very broad and loose or very narrow and restricted. In this context Andre Beitelle[27] aptly remarks that Baigley is perhaps the only anthropologist working in the India field, who has tried to characterise tribes in terms of seminary principles, but the contrast in which he is interested is not between 'tribe' and 'peasant' but between 'tribe' and 'caste'. Further, unlike Baigley, the majority of India anthropologists have not given much serious thought to the problem of creating a definition of tribal society which will be appropriate to the Indian context.

Now let us examine the problem especially in the Indian context. The most accepted definition in the Indian context is given by Professor Majumdar. According to him, "A tribe is a social group with territorial affiliation, endogamous with no specialisation of functions, ruled by tribal officers, hereditary or otherwise, united in language or dialect, recognising social distance from tribes or castes. But without any stigma attached in the case of caste structure, following tribal traditions, beliefs and customs, illiberal of naturalisation of ideas from alien sources, above all, conscious of a homogeneity of ethnic and territorial integration".[28]

T.B. Naik[29] raises the problem in proper perspective by talking of the criteria and indices of the tribal life in specifically Indian setting. What should be the criteria and indices of tribal life? Living in forest? The Dublas of Surat and a host of others do not live in forests. They live in fertile plains; nevertheless they are included in the schedule Primitive religion? But you do not know what primitive religion is in India, there being a continuance from the most abstruse philosophy to the tribal gods and superstitious beliefs in the religion of most of the advanced communities of India. "This index being very fluid and not exact will not do geographical isolation? There are many peasant groups who are living by equally primitive economic system. Thus, Naik goes on to present his own criteria for a tribe which are as follows:

1. A tribe to be a 'tribe' should have the least functional interdependence within the community (the Hindu caste system is an example of high interdependence).

2. It should be economically backward, which means:
   (a) The full import of monetary economics should not be understood by its members.
   (b) Primitive means of exploiting natural resources should be used.
   (c) The tribes economy should be at an underdeveloped stage
   (d) It should have multifarious economic pursuits.
3. There should be a comparative geographic isolation of its people from others.
4. Culturally, members of a tribe should have a common dialect which may be subject to regional variations.
5. A tribe should be politically organised and its community panchayat should be an influential institution.
6. The tribes' members should have the least desire to change. They should have a sort of psychological conservatism making them stick to their old customs.
7. A tribe should have customary laws and its members might have to suffer in a law court because of these laws.

Naik further elaborates that a community to be a 'tribe' must have all these attributes. It might be undergoing acculturation, but the degree of acculturation will have to be determined in the context of its customs, gods, language etc. A very high degree of acculturation will automatically debar it from being a tribe.

The Tata Institute of Social Sciences in its report on the Indian Tribes has also joined those who have been criticising the anthropologist's approach of the problem. It says that the (anthropological) criteria apply to ideal typical tribal communities as conceived by the anthropologists for theoretical purpose. These do not appear to be empirically related to communities that have been included in the list of the scheduled tribes. The logical implication seems to be that communities which do not satisfy the above criteria should not be considered as tribes even though they are included in the list of the scheduled tribes.[30] Arthur Wilke[31] too, like some others, opines that some measure, if not a substantial measure, of the difficulty is inherent in the intellectual legacy of the discipline of anthropology. Aiyappan, provoked by such statements, remarks rather sceptically, reminding us of the well-known definition given by Tata Regan of 'species'. Adopting the definition he said that a tribe is a group which a competent anthropologist considers to be a tribe. If the administrator wants a clear-cut definition which he can apply blindly and get along with, we should tell him that he is just as the zoologist who is not in a position to give a clear-cut, all purpose definition of 'species'.

Despite such theoretic and academic polemics on the problem of definition of tribe, quite a substantial measure of standardisation has been accomplished in designating which people 'are' or 'are not' entitled to particular protection and privilege. This could become possible only due to vigorous academic efforts of the much maligned and misunderstood anthropologists who, with the help of rigorous and painstaking empirical resource, ultimately came out with definite and empirically verifiable ethnographic data to clear the cobwebs of misgiving regarding Indian tribes. Majumdar[32] demonstrates this new mood by emphatically stating the following facts:

1. In Tribal India and Tribe is definitely a territorial group; a tribe has a traditional territory, and emigrants always refer to it as their home. The Santhals working in the Assam tea gardens refer to particular regions of Bihar or Bengal as their home.
2. All members of tribe are not kin of each other, but within every Indian tribe kinship operates as a strong, associative regulative and integrating principle. The consequence is tribal endogamy and the division of a tribe into clans and sub-clans and so on. These clans, etc., being kin groups, are exogamous.
3. Members of an Indian tribe speak one common language, their own or and that of their neighbours. Intra-tribal conflict on a group scale is not a feature of Indian tribes. Joint ownership of property, wherever present, as for instance among the Hoes, is not exclusive. Politically, Indian tribes are under the control of the State Governments, but within a tribe there may be a number of panchayats corresponding to

the heterogeneity, racial and cultural, of the constituent population in a village or in adjacent villages.

4. There are other distinguishing features of Indian tribes. Thus, there are their dormitory institutions; the absence of institutional schooling for boys and girls, distinctive customs regarding birth, marriage, and death; a moral code different from that of Hindus and Muslims; peculiarities of religious beliefs and rituals which may distinguish tribesmen even from low caste Hindus.

To wind up this discussion it seems to be quite apt to refer to Arthur Wilke who opines that even the constraints of bureaucratic decision-making and administration reign supreme, there is a tendency to glass over the rich and at times puzzling mosaic of human affairs. What accounts for in determination in the concept of tribe is likely that the dictates of bureaucratic procedures and the unceasing acculturation going on throughout India and particularly among many identified tribal people make it difficult to apply an idea which is in many respects, an ideal type of formulation.

However, there is no particular definition, which is universally accepted. There are diversities of views of each anthropologist nevertheless; certain characteristic features as discussed above, have been put forward for determining a "tribe" or a "tribal community". In India their comments designate as "Adivasi" (original settlers), Girijan (hill dwellers), Vanyajati (forest caste), Adimjati (primitive castes), Janjati (folk communities), Anusuchitjanjati (scheduled tribes).[33]

Scheduled Tribe Population in India

Schedule Tribe population Census is started in the British Period along with the General Census started in 1981 and it is continuing till now. The scheduled tribe population in India is given below in the following table:

Table 1.1: Schedule Tribe Population in India

Year	*Tribal Population*	*Per cent to General population*	*Per cent of Decadal Growth Rate*	*Sex Ratio (female per 1,000 males*
		British India		
1881	642511	2.57	-	-
1891	9112018	3.26	41.79	992
1901	8184758	2.88	-10.18	1021
1911	9593695	3.17	17.21	1016
1921	9072024	3.00	-7.2	996
1931	7629959	2.45	-15.9	1009
1941	8791354	2.26	6.17	985
		Independent India		
1951	19111498	5.29	41.19	1021
1961	30130184	6.86	33.84	987
1971	38015162	6.94	26.3	982
1981	51628638	7.83	30.8	983
1991	67758380	8.08	31.4	972
2001	84326240	8.20	24.5	978
2011	104,281,034	8.61	23.7	990

Source: For British India figures, Davis (1951), Table 77, p.179; Mamoria (1958), .26; And Natarajan (1971), p. 9. Director, Census Operations, Hyderabad 2011.

Above table reveals about the scheduled tribe population increasing system in India. In British India the scheduled tribe population in 1881 year is 642511 (2.57 per cent), it is increased upto 8791354 in 1941 (2.26 per cent). After Independence the scheduled tribe population is 19111498 in 1951, it is increased upto 8.61 per cent, it means 104,281,034 in 2011.[34]

Tribes in Andhra Pradesh: A Profile

The State of Andhra Pradesh was formed on 1st November 1956 comprising the Telugu Speaking People. Hyderabad is the capital of Andhra Pradesh, situated in the South-East of India. Andhra Pradesh is the biggest state in South India. Andhra Pradesh extends in between 12°37′ and 19°54′ North Latitudes and 76°46′ and 84°46′ East Longitudes. There are 23 districts in Andhra Pradesh and its area is 275,045 sq. kms. Andhra Pradesh occupies fifth place in area among the States of India. Basing on physical, social and economic conditions, Andhra Pradesh is divided into three regions. They are:

1. Telangana,

2. Coastal Andhra,
3. Rayalaseema.

In Andhra Pradesh people have different culture, tradition, history and social status. The people have different types of languages, habits and living conditions. These people are residing in various geographical conditions. Like other states in India, Andhra Pradesh state also had various types of tribal population. They are living in entire Andhra Pradesh. They have different types of languages, customs, culture, traditions and living system. They differ from non-tribal peoples in socio-economic conditions.

Scheduled Tribes and Scheduled Areas in Andhra Pradesh

According to the Clause (1) of Article 342 and 244 (1) of Fifth Schedule of the Constitution of India, the President of India, after consultation with the Andhra Pradesh Governor issued Orders specifying the scheduled tribes and scheduled areas in Andhra Pradesh. According to the orders, 33 scheduled tribes are living in Andhra Pradesh. They are given in the following table:

Table 1.2: Scheduled Tribes in Andhra Pradesh

Sl. No.	*Name of the Scheduled Tribe*
1.	Andh
2.	Bagata
3.	Bhil
4.	Chenchu, Chenchuwar
5.	Gadabas
6.	Gond, Naikpod, Rajgond
7.	Gondu (in the agency tracts)
8.	Konda Reddi
9.	Jatapus
10.	Kammara
11.	Kattunayakan

(*Contd...*)

12.	Kolam, Mannervarlu
13.	Konda Doras
14.	Hill Reddi (Konda Reddis)
15.	Konda Kapus
16.	Kondhs, Kodi, Kodhu, Desaya Kondhs, Dongri Kondhs, Kuttiya Kondhs, Tikiria Kondhs, Yenity Kondhs
17.	Kotia, Bentho Oriya, Bartika, Dhulia, Dulia, Holva, Paiko, Putiya, Sanrona, Sidhopaiko
18.	Koya, Goud, Rajah, Rasha Koya, Lingadhari Koya (Ordinary) Kottu Koya, Bhine Koya, Raj Koya
19.	Kulia
20.	Malis (Excluding Adilabad, Hyderabad, Karimnagar, Khammam, Mahabubnagar, Medak, Nalgonda, Nizamabad and Warangal Districts)
21.	Manna Dhora
22.	Mukha Dhora, Nooka Dhora
23.	Nayaks (in the agency tracts)
24.	Pardhan
25.	Porja, Parangiperja
26.	Reddi Dhoras
27.	Rona, Rena
28.	Savaras, Kapu Savaras, Muliya Savaras, Khutto Savaras
29.	Sugalis, Lambadis
30.	Thoti (in Adilabad, Hyderabad, Karimnagar, Khammam, Mahabubnagar, Medak, Nalgonda, Nizamabad and Warangal Districts)
31.	Valmiki (in the agency tracts)
32.	Yenadis
33.	**Yerukulas**

Source: The Scheduled Castes and Scheduled Tribes (Amendment) Act, 1976, No.108 of 1976 dated 18th September 1976.

Primitive Tribal groups in Andhra Pradesh

In Andhra Pradesh, Government of India have identified 12 Primitive Tribal Groups namely, Chenchus of Ranga Reddy, Karnool, Mahabubnagar, Nalgonda, Prakasham and Guntur districts in the year 1975-76, Kolams of Adilabad and Konda Reddis of East Godavari, West Godavari and Khammam districts in the year 1980. In the year 1982-83 Government of India have also recognised the following communities as Primitive Tribal Groups:

1. Thoti,
2. Bondo Porja,
3. Kond Porja,
4. Parengperja,
5. Dongri Kond,
6. Kuttla Konda
7. Gutob Gadaba
8. Bodo Gadaba
9. Kondasavara,
10. Kolam,
11. Chenchu and
12. Konda Reddy.

Scheduled Areas in Andhra Pradesh

According to the Article 224(1) Fifth Schedule of Constitution of India, the President issued Orders after consultation with the Governor of Andhra Pradesh in 1950. According to these orders Scheduled Areas are identified in Andhra Pradesh. Scheduled Areas in Andhra Pradesh are given in the following lines: The tribals are spread over 30,028 Sq. Kms. area in entire Andhra Pradesh. This is the 11 per cent of the entire area of Andhra Pradesh. Major tribal population is living in Srikakulam, Vishakhapatnam, Vizianagaram, East Godavari, West Godavari, Warangal, Adilabad, Khammam and Mahabubnagar districts in Andhra Pradesh. Sixty-eight per cent tribal populations is living in scheduled areas, remaining 32 per cent tribal population is living in plain areas together with non-tribal people.

The scheduled area extends over 11,595 Sq. Miles sprawling from Skrikakulam district in the North East to Adilabad District in the North West and it forms a circular belt comprising 6,172 Scheduled villages in the districts of Srikakulam, Vizianagaram, Warangal, Adilabad, Visakhapatnam, East Godavari, West Godavari, Khammam, and Mahabubnagar.[35] The schedule areas in Andhra Pradesh are given in the following Table:

Table 1.3: List of Scheduled Areas in Andhra Pradesh

Sl. No.	*Name of the District*	*No. of Scheduled Villages*	*Area in Sq Kms*	*No. of Non-Scheduled Villages*	*No. of TSP Villages*
1.	Adilabad	412	6138.5	164	576
2.	Mahabubnagar	25	1191.9	-	27
3.	Warangal	177	3122.46	77	254
4.	Visakhapatnam	3368	5904.51	96	3464
5.	Vizianagaram	298	1740.98	183	481
6.	Srikakulam	108	1289.32	240	348
7.	Khammam	889	6899.92	8	895
8.	East Godavari	559	4191.95	40	599
9.	West Godavari	102	1006.10	1	103
	Total	**5938**	**31485.64**	**809**	**6747**

Source: Tribal and Tribal areas of Andhra Pradesh (Basic Statistics); TCR & TI, Tribal Welfare Department, Government of Andhra Pradesh, Hyderabad-2004.

In addition to the above-mentioned, the tribal area is also divided into five parts according to their living places and characteristics of groups. They are given in the following table:

Table 1.4: Distribution of Areas in Andhra Pradesh according to tribal areas

Sl.No.	*Name of the area*	*Covered Area*
1.	Gondu-Kolam Area	Tribal areas in Adilabad District
2.	Koya-Konda Reddi Area	Tribal areas of the Godavari River Bank of Karimnagar, Warangal, Khammam, East Godavari, West Godavari Districts.
3.	Kondu-savara Areas	Tribal areas of Visakhapatnam, Vizianagaram, Srikakulam Districts.
4.	Chenchu Areas	Tribal areas of Mahabubnagar, Nalgonda, Karnool, Prakasham, Guntur Districts.

(*Contd...*)

5.	Plain Areas	All Districts in Andhra Pradesh. Yanadi, Yerukalabanjara or Lambada or Sugali is the major tribal population living in this eara. These three tribes are identified as tribe science 1956-1977. After 1977 these three tribes are identified as scheduled tribe in entire Andhra Pradesh

Source: Tribes and Tribal Areas of Andhra Pradesh (Basic Statistics), Publication of Tribal Cultural Research & Training Institute, Tribal Welfare Department, Government of Andhra Pradesh, Hyderabad-2004.

Table 1. 5: Major Scheduled Tribes as District-wise in Andhra Pradesh

Sl. No.	*District*	*Major Scheduled Tribe*
1.	Srikakulam	Savara, Jatopus, Gadaba, Konda Doras
2.	Vizaianagaram	Savara, Jatopus, Gadaba, Konda Doras
3.	Visakhapatnam	Bagata, Gadaba, Kammara, Konda Doras, Kotia, Konds, Maalis, Mannedoras, Mukha Doras, Reddi Roras, Rorjas, Valmikis, Goudu.
4.	East Godavari	Koya, Konda Reddis, Kammara, Konda Doras.
5.	West Godavari	Koya, Konda Reddi, Kammara, Yerukalas, Yanadis.
6.	Khammam	Koya, Konda Reddis, Sugali, Lambadas
7.	Warangal	Koya, Lambadas, Yerukala, Nayak Pode
8.	Adilabad	Gond, Kolam Pardhan, Thoti, Lambada, Naik Pode, Andh
9	Mahabubnagar	Lambada, Chenchu.

Source: Tribal and Tribal Areas of Andhra Pradesh (Basic Statistics); TCR & TI, Tribal Welfare Department, Government of Andhra Pradesh, Hyderabad-2004.

Table 1.6: Particulars of Scheduled Tribe Population in Andhra Pradesh

Sl. No.	*Year*	*Total General Population*	*Scheduled Tribe Population*	*Per cent to total General Population of All India*
1.	**1961**	35983447	1324368	4.43
2.	**1971**	43502708	1657657	4.36
3.	**1981**	53549673	3176001	6.15
4.	**1991**	66508008	4199481	6.20
5.	**2001**	76210007	5024104	5.96
6.	**2011**	84580777	5918073	6.99

Source: Scheduled Caste and Scheduled Tribes in Andhra Pradesh 1961-2001, Publication of Directorate of Economics and Statistics, Government of Andhra Pradesh, Hyderabad-2001 and Director, Census Operations, Government of India, Hyderabad, 2011.

The above table explains about the total scheduled tribe population increase system with Percentage and Rank of the State of Andhra Pradesh. In 1961, the scheduled tribe population was only 1324368 (4.43 per cent) but it increased up to 5918073 (6.99 per cent) in 2011. Andhra Pradesh State comprises of 23 Districts. These 23 Districts are covered under the three Regions namely: 1. Telangana, 2. Coastal Andhra, and 3. Rayalaseema. The Region-wise scheduled tribe population is given in the following table.

Table 1.7: District-wise Scheduled Tribe Population in Andhra Pradesh

Sl. No.	*Name of the District*	*1961*	*1971*	*1981*	*1991*	*2001*	*2011*
				Telangana Region			
1.	Adilabad	131971	169299	272886	354902	416511	495794
2.	Nizamabad	739	578	90262	120716	165735	192941
3.	Karimnagar	13116	16433	60567	83017	90636	106745
4.	Medak	85	120	68516	95042	134533	168985
5.	Hyderabad	1551	4667	14488	28946	34560	48937
6.	Ranga Reddy	-	-	72656	109394	146057	218757
7.	Mahabubnagar	4750	5600	155240	227405	278702	364269
8.	Nalgonda	471	519	195660	275638	342676	394279
9.	Warangal	32936	43287	292772	385309	457679	530656
10.	Khammam	171284	201670	429959	558958	682617	765565
	Total	**356903**	**442173**	**1653006**	**2239327**	**2749706**	**3286928**
				Coastal Andhra Region			
11.	Srikakulam	192276	212459	105142	134067	151249	166118
12.	Vizianagaram	-	-	153344	190185	214839	235556
13.	Visakhapatnam	213820	299970	354127	46886	557572	618500
14.	East Godavari	100343`	119027	143422	176083	191561	213195
15.	West Godavari	44058	51723	66586	84648	96659	109072
16.	Krishna	37473	50742	66927	91767	107611	132464
17.	Guntur	95457	105478	139749	181588	208157	247089
18.	Prakasam	-	55111	77847	98854	118241	151145
19.	Nellore	131509	130277	177497	214062	242257	285997
	Total	**814936**	**1024787**	**1284641**	**1640140**	**1888146**	**2159136**
				Rayalaseema Region			
20.	Kadapa	22457	26611	37580	47414	61371	75886
21.	Karnool	30640	32407	39914	56455	69635	82831
22.	Ananthapur	48500	64878	82026	111207	127161	154127
23.	Chittoor	50932	66801	78834	104938	128085	159165
	Total	**152529**	**190697**	**238354**	**225569**	**386252**	**472009**
Grand Total		**1324368**	**1657657**	**3176001**	**4199481**	**5024104**	**5918073**

Source: Scheduled Caste and Scheduled Tribes in Andhra Pradesh 1961-2001, Publication of Directorate of Economics and Statistics, Government of Andhra Pradesh, Hyderabad-2001 and Director, Census Operations, Government of India, Hyderabad, 2011.

Table 1.8: Population of Scheduled Tribe in Rural Areas in Andhra Pradesh

Sl. No.	*Year*	*Total General Population*	*Scheduled Tribe Population*	*Per cent to total General Population of All India*
1.	1961	29708939	1267287	4.27
2.	1971	35100181	1572627	4.48
3.	1981	41062097	2978593	7.25
4.	1991	48620882	3880254	7.98
5.	2001	55401067	4646923	8.39
6.	2011	56361702	5232129	9.28

Source: Scheduled Caste and Scheduled Tribes in Andhra Pradesh 1961-2001, Publication of Directorate of Economics and Statistics, Government of Andhra Pradesh, Hyderabad-2001 and Director, Census Operations, Government of India, Hyderabad, 2011.

The above table explains about the total rural scheduled tribe population increase system with percentage, in Andhra Pradesh. In 1961, the scheduled tribe population in rural area was only 1267287 (4.27 per cent) but it is increased up to 5232129 (9.28 per cent) in 2011. The detailed district-wise rural scheduled tribe population in Andhra Pradesh is given in following table.

Development Policy: On Paper and Praxis the Indian Experience

Indian development paradigm, post-independence, has been not different from any other developed or developing country, which continues to haunt the marginalised and vulnerable section of the society even today, especially the indigenous and tribal population. From the First Five Year Plan 'Nehruvian socialism' virtually followed the capitalist path for economic progress using the Mahalanobis model and concentrated on capital goods industry to attain self-sufficiency in a short time. Construction of big dams, with a conviction of "development", for irrigation to increase agricultural production and power for the industry led Nehru to comment that dams were the 'temples of modern India' (in a speech that he grew to regret in his own lifetime). And we in modern India true to our love for temples took Mr Nehru literally and threw ourselves into the spree of dam building with unnatural fervour and became world's third largest dam builder. The development policy which seemed to have been "grow fast and the trickle down will bring distributive justice", backtracked, with limited growth that hardly trickled down.

Table 1.9: District-wise Rural Scheduled Tribe Population in Andhra Pradesh

Sl. No.	*Name of the District*	*1961*	*1971*	*1981*	*1991*	*2001*	*2011*
				Telangana Region			
1	Adilabad	131479	167336	268277	344013	396531	463089
2	Nizamabad	724	447	87462	116439	161610	185297
3	Karimnagar	13109	15698	57745	76885	81530	92353
4	Medak	83	106	67509	92098	130108	156801
5	Hyderabad	642	1026	-	-	-	-
6	Ranga Reddy	-	-	67493	87517	119781	133890
7	Mahabubnagar	4699	5496	153203	223671	273558	345359
8	Nalgonda	432	487	189305	266400	326306	366300
9	Warangal	32539	42841	282077	369655	444409	486034
10	Khammam	169946	197807	413134	527089	641727	709904
	Total	**353653**	**431244**	**1586205**	**2103767**	**2576160**	**2939027**
				Coastal Andhra Region			
11	Srikakulam	191524	210814	103836	131225	148757	160438
12	Vizianagaram	-	-	150235	185759	208633	226130
13	Visakhapatnam	212789	298360	349935	460882	538608	579968
14	East Godavari	98687	116680	139061	168137	181589	198698
15	West Godavari	41306	48463	60230	77474	88863	99659
16	Krishna	31478	43361	52548	70767	88711	93915
17	Guntur	78317	84911	107971	144196	170459	190905
18	Prakasam	-	48448	64865	81324	99116	124386
19	Nellore	115569	119105	149403	177459	211264	240972
	Total	**769670**	**964142**	**1178084**	**1497223**	**1736000**	**1915071**
				Rayalaseema Region			
20	Kadapa	21270	24952	34234	40761	53187	58181
21	Karnool	27811	27982	33654	45453	58240	64735
22	Ananthapur	46933	61927	75057	99131	111457	126362
23	Chittoor	47950	62380	71359	93913	111879	128753
	Total	**143964**	**177241**	**214304**	**279264**	**334763**	**378031**
Grand Total		**1267287**	**1572627**	**2978593**	**3880254**	**4646923**	**5232129**

Source: Scheduled Caste and Scheduled Tribes in Andhra Pradesh 1961-2001, Publication of Directorate of Economics and Statistics, Government of Andhra Pradesh, Hyderabad-2001 and Director, Census Operations, Government of India, Hyderabad, 2011.

The urge for development after independence led to an initial amnesia, claiming its glory in imitating the west, of building big dams and justifying their need to fulfil the power and irrigation demands of the industries and agriculture respectively, for the so called "self sufficiency", riding on the emotional trump card that labelled them as things of national pride and branded the sufferings as "sacrifices in the nation building". But unfortunately the bender continues unabatedly till date.

The state power of "eminent domain" "the power of a state to take private property for public use" to acquire land and/or appropriate natural resources has been deployed ostensibly for public good, with compulsory acquisitions for the projects meant to promote public purposes i.e. 'developmental projects', which invariably necessitates involuntary resettlement of people or in other words the displacement. These persons are called displaced persons (DPs) or the project affected persons or families (PAPs/PAFs), the number whereof is largest among all kinds of displacements. Displacement linked to development, according to Alfe Morten Jerve, could be caused either by:[36]

1. governments decision to acquire land for implementation of public project; or
2. state decision to change the use of land owned or claimed by itself; or
3. changes in the use of the land owned by state agencies; or
4. not complete change of ownership but introduction of new restrictions on current use of land; or
5. Indirect impact of the project on the land use in the impact area like pollution, erosion, etc.

However, displacement is not confined to physical removal of one from his house it can also be a deprivation of productive land, or other income generating assets, the displacement of collectivises causes an economic crisis for all or most of those affected with sudden disarticulation and sometimes also triggers a political crisis as well.[37] It is a complex phenomenon, as Upendra Baxi has put it, which is not a one-time event but a series of happenings affecting human lives in myriad ways.[38]

The notion of development, it seems, has not changed since independence, the policy framework is grounded on the theory of "public interest" or "public purpose", and it is the government or more specifically some bureaucrats exercising the executive power finalise the policy which has ineluctable ramifications on the lives of lakhs of peoples affected by such projects. The subsistence of any such project primarily depends on availability of dispensable land for the purpose and in the second most populous country it is difficult to get large area of land. In such situation the doctrine of "eminent domain" is invoked by the state and for the "greater common good", private and community land is acquired from the people compulsorily to facilitate the projects.

The Constitution under Article 39 (b) and (c) provides for a more broad provision wherein the state is referred to as a community of people, whose ownership and control over material sources are to be so distributed as to subservice common good and not to their detriment. However, the law which has been consistently invoked for land acquisition is a pre-institutional law dated as late as 1894, which was amended in 1984 to allow acquisition not only for the public purpose but for establishing company and private corporations. With 'compensation' as the only remedy for the persons affected by such acquisitions, having celebrated a century of its existence, this law of colonial vintage facilitates the State to acquire land for "any public purpose" or "for a company". The inclusive definition of "public purpose" under the Act refers to acquisition for: planned development of town and country-side State corporations residential purposes of poor and landless carrying out any educational, housing, health or slum clearance schemes of state planned development by the state and its disposal to secure further development and any other scheme of development by the state.

Only three states in India have enacted statutes, post-independence, for resettlement, a step ahead from 'mere compensation', of the project affected people. Maharashtra was the first to enact a law in 1976. After a legal challenge of some of its provisions in courts of law, it was recast in 1986 receiving Presidential assent in 1989.[39] Madhya Pradesh followed suit with a law specially designed to apply for irrigation projects, extendable to other developmental activities at the discretion of the state government.[40] The Karnataka Government passed its law in 1987, but obtained the Presidential assent seven years hence, in 1994.[41] Other states are under severe pressure today from the Courts, financial threats from the lenders, compulsions under international obligations and under a fear of agitation by the NGOs, to come up with rehabilitation and resettlement policy before they finalise any developmental project. The similar policies by Odisha and Andhra Pradesh in the recent times are illustration to the same.

Displacement, unfortunately, is often regarded as one time phenomenon despite being a process rather than an event which starts much before the actual displacement and continues for a long time after the improvement has taken place, as the projects take years and decades before completion and during this period the status of the project affected people remains in limbo. Even the constitutional protection envisaged to the scheduled areas are allowed to disappear by the state in name of, usually unspecified, 'public purpose'. Despite there being legislative protections under the Panchayat Act in favour of self-rule the principle of eminent domain has always preceded all other legal provisions and protective measures. Ironically, in taking such decisions no attention was ever paid to the victims of development, i.e. the ousters or the displaced persons, nor any plan or policy framework followed to rehabilitate and resettle them, except for certain temporary arrangements culled out from the policy prepared by National Working Group on Displacement.[42] There is virtually no uniform Law for rehabilitation and resettlement in India till date.

Amrita Patwardhan in her paper[43] points this fact in a succinct way: "Lack of proper national policy and lacunas in the existing policy documents is a major problem. Apart from that, there are serious problems at the level of implementation as well. In most cases, there is a wide gap between the framed policy on paper and what gets translated in reality. For example, the policy at times has a provision for a choice between cash or land for land compensation. But Project Affected Persons (PAPs) as in case of Narmada Sagar, Maheshwar in Madhya Pradesh are not informed about provisions, thus, forcing the people to take whatever is offered, under the threat of impending submergence. The state policy in Madhya Pradesh has a provision for the affected people to get land in the command area, but, there is not a single case where this clause has been invoked for, rehabilitating people in the command area of the project.

Most state level policies or the National policy in the making, have provisions for land for land compensation, but due to several loopholes, affected people, in many cases are just given arbitrary cash compensation. Despite the provisions in the Madhya Pradesh Act, in two major projects, Hasdev Bango and Bargi, where displacement occurred after the enactment of the Act, people were given some scanty compensation sum, and no land.

Rehabilitation of people displaced by dams like Hirakud, built way back in 1950s is not yet complete. Compensation amounting to Rs 154,146994 was not paid after years. When the compensation was paid to some people, cash was distributed to PAPs in their original village and signature/thumb prints were taken. Some money from this was pocketed by the officials. People remembered this sense of humiliation 30 years after, when they were struggling for survival. In Sardar Sarovar, Gujarat has one of the most progressive rehabilitation packages, but resettling 25 per cent of the families displaced by the reservoir have taken 15 years and there is a wide gap between the tall promises and the ground reality. Once people are shifted from the submergence villages, officials do not bother about their complaints and the ousters are often left to fend for themselves."

The on-paper projected costs of any large project at the inception will multiply manifold by the time it is started and further escalate during the execution and by the time of completion it turns up to something which one would have not imagined while it was initiated, or in other words, not have even been initiated. Added to it is the interest to be paid on the loan incurred, thus, by the time the loan is paid off the total cost of the project at that point of time (the actual cost of the project) becomes unimaginably exorbitant. And this fact and statistics is never brought to the notice of the tax-payers.

Ultimately development has induced people (displaced) to accept enormous sacrifices in the name of national interest, but its stated fruits a "progress, prosperity, modernity and emancipation are yet to reach the displaced." The result: the displaced and the dispossessed, to development projects, question the legitimacy of the developmental process. They reiterate that "planning for the people", "people's participation", "people's needs", "and humanisation of development" are but mere rhetorics.[44]

India is the third largest in dam building in the World and it now has over 3,600 large dams and over 700 more under construction.

India's development policies and strategies have focused attention on indispensability of irrigation as important input for agriculture. Large-Scale Irrigation Projects are important for higher agriculture growth, besides establishment of Industries and Power Projects. India gave tremendous encouragement to the large river valley projects or large multipurpose dams. The dominant ethos was 'big is the best' and the conviction is that large multipurpose projects are the panacea to all the problems of poverty and under development. It is important to note that most of the projects are located in the most backward Scheduled Areas of various tribal communities, as the forest and mountainous tracts, which are the traditional habitats of them endowed with rich minerals, resources, and abandoned flora and fauna. Most of the rivers originated and drain through several tribal regions. The resources, which are available in the tribal areas, are being perceived, by the policy-makers, as the property of the Nation, but not as the basis of the people who live in this region. At this juncture, it is extraordinarily significant to make an appraisal on the Indian tribal situation.

Indian Tribes - An Overview

India has the second largest concentration of tribal population, after that of the African continent. Tribal are generally called as *'Adivasis'* implying *'original Inhabitants'* of the land. There are about 360 tribal groups speaking more than 100 languages and dialects in India. They have been specified as Scheduled Tribes (STs) in accordance with the Presidential orders issued since 1950. The Scheduled tribes' population of the country, according to 2011 Census, was 104,281,034 and constitutes 8.61 per cent to the total Indian population. The areas inhabited by the STs in the Country are termed as 'Scheduled Areas'. These are popularly known as 'Agency Areas' since the Colonial times. These areas are specially defined in Para 6 of the Part 'C' of the Fifth Schedule of the Indian Constitution. Although the genesis of the concept of Scheduled Areas was traced back in the Scheduled Districts Act of 1874, in the Pre-Independence period, the Scheduled Areas were retained to assist the tribal in enjoying their customary rights without exploitation and to develop and protect the tribal and their environments. Accordingly as per the provisions of the Scheduled Areas, Part - A States order of 1950 and the amended Scheduled Areas, Part - B States order of 1950 certain tribal areas in the States of Andhra Pradesh, Madhya Pradesh, Maharashtra, Odisha, Rajasthan, Bihar, Gujarat and Himachal Pradesh were declared as Scheduled Areas.

Socio-economic Dimensions of Tribal Communities

The tribal have been living in forest and mountainous regions, within the close proximity of nature. The economy of the tribal has been primarily hunting-foraging and shifting cultivation. More than 90 per cent of the tribal, to a large extent depend on forests and forests resources for their livelihood. The scheduled tribes have been facing many socio-economic and psychological problems since historical times. The forest laws have curtailed the free movement of tribal in forester ions. The tribal rights on the forest lands have severely affected. Shifting cultivation *(Konda Podu)* has been regulated by restrictions on the use of forests. Use of Minor Forest Produces (MFPs) by tribal has been reduced to a large extent. Exploitation by money lenders and contractors, problems of credit and market for MFPs, poverty, hunger, malnutrition and impoverishment are the important evils, which the tribal have been facing since long time.[44] Land alienation and displacement are the major problems, which have been haunting most of the tribal groups. Most of the tribal groups have virtually reached a state of total collapse and seem to be fighting a grim battle for survival. The occurrence of tribal revolts for land rights indifferent parts of the country is its testimony. The large scale land transfers to non-tribal culminated in armed tribal uprisings in the late nineteenth and early twentieth centuries. British administration in India introduced several legislations to prevent tribal land alienation. In order to ensure that the customary rights of the tribal on land are protected, the Agency Tracts Interest and Land Transfer Act (ATILTA) were promulgated in 1917.[45]

Constitutional and Legal Safeguards for the Welfare of Tribal

In the Post-Independent period, there are various safeguards for the protection and development of STs in accordance with the special provisions mentioned in the Indian Constitution such as: Article 15(4), 16(4), 19(5), 23, 29, 46, 164, 275(1), 330, 332, 334, 335, 338, 339(1), 339(2), 371(A), 371(B), 371(C), Fifth Schedule and Sixth Schedule.[46] In pursuance of the Article 46 of the Indian Constitution, the welfare of the STs is being looked after by the State Government. In order to protect the interest of the STs and to curb exploitation at the hands of others, the Scheduled Fifth of the Indian Constitution, empowers the Governor to modify the State and Central Legislations regarding their applicability to the Scheduled Areas and to frame regulations for good Governance in these areas. Accordingly, Government of Andhra Pradesh has framed 'Andhra Pradesh State Agency Land Transfer Regulation' (APSALTR) of 1959 and the regulation 1 of 1959 protects the tribal interest regarding land issues. In 1963 this regulation was amended by regulation 2 of 1963. It was again amended in the year 1970 by regulations 1 of 1970 and 2 of 1970. In exercise of the powers confirmed by sub-section 1 of section 8 of the 'Andhra Pradesh State Agency Land Transfer Regulation' (APSALTR) 1959, the Governor of Andhra Pradesh made rules called the 'Andhra Pradesh State Agency Land Transfer Regulation Rules' (APSALTRR) in 1969.[47] In addition to the above safeguards, there also existed, the other protective regulations and Acts such as: 'Andhra Pradesh Scheduled Areas Money Lenders Regulation' (APSAMLR) of 1960,'Andhra Pradesh Scheduled Areas Debt Relief Regulation'(APSADRR) of 1960, 'National Forest Policy' (NFP) of1894, 1952 and 1988; 'Panchayat Raj Extension Act to Scheduled Areas' (PESA) of 1996, besides several Government Policies and Government Orders (GOs), and Judgments, pronounced by different Courts from time to time.[46]

Development in Tribal Areas

The development philosophy for the STs is neither one of isolation through protections nor assimilation through enculturation. Rather, it's one of the integration which does not pre-suppose assimilation and is not compatible with heterogeneity of cultures. This basic philosophy of Jawaharlal Nehru, the first Prime Minister of India, was pursued over 57 years. Planned economic development was adopted as India's policy, soon after Independence. Planning for the development of tribal areas was thus ushered in as part of a wider National strategy. To bridge the socio-economic gaps between tribal and non-tribal and also for the all-round development of the tribal groups, several schemes and programmes are being drawn in the Post-Independence period. Both Central and State Governments have been spending crores of rupees, on tribal development, but the impact of the programmes is not as envisaged. The developmental efforts have not succeeded in bringing marked change in the conditions of most of the tribal communities. The benefits of the tribal development are not reaching the poor tribal. In many parts of the country, then on-tribal groups are getting the tribal tag, in the process, depriving tribal, by using benefits of tribal reservations and Constitutional safeguards. No efforts were made in the formulation of schemes in accordance with the needs of the tribal communities, who had their own social and cultural milieu. In recent times because of large scale industrialisation and urbanisation, relative isolation of the tribal areas is broken-down. The tribal, and their lands and other resources are now exposed to the exploitative market forces, mostly due to the State and Multi National Companies (MNCs) sponsored developmental projects such as large scale irrigational projects, dams, reservoirs, mining, sanctuaries, industries and tourism projects and the acquisition of lands by the State in tribal areas is common phenomenon.[47]

Land Acquisition and Public Purpose

The Land Acquisition Act of 1894, introduced by the then British Government, still continues, with some amendments in1967 and 1984 and this Act facilitates the governments to acquire the peoples land, by compulsion for both the public and private purposes.[48] This Act helps the State as a weapon for immediate land acquisition. In most of the cases, the government officials have been paying the compensation to ousters after prolonged time, where as they acquire the lands with one notification and with in no time, but the Land Acquisition Act did not say anything on the type or nature of compensation payable to ousters and time period for payment of compensation.[49] Land acquisition in Scheduled Areas is not possible, as there are number of Protective Land Laws, Legislations, Regulations, Forest Laws, Government Policies, Court Orders and Judgments, and GOs which prohibit the land transfer in Scheduled Areas. Inspite of all these protective and welfare laws made by the government for the welfare of tribal, the governmental agencies have been acquiring the tribal lands in the name of National interest in contravention to all the Constitutional Provisions. It indicates that all the Agency Laws are being manipulated where the legal access to tribal lands and resources is denied.[50]

Large Scale Displacement and National Interest

It is clear that displacement involves injustice to the tribal people and gross violation of their constitutional rights. The tribal people can't be deprived of their right to life merely by paying some money at the cost of their livelihood. In fact, that whole legal frame itself is wrong in which the right to life of the people and their survival as community is being violated. At times the people are being forced to move out of their homes on the strength of payment of compensation. Right to life of some persons cannot be compromised or bartered just for providing more comforts to many people. Many ousters are still awaiting cash compensation promised by the project authorities. Very few ousters have been fortunate enough to get permanent employment in the projects. Reports of several studies sponsored by the World Bank also admit that poor rehabilitation is not a matter of the past. In fact, in 1993 during the presence of the World Bank executed study team in the Singrauli region, a number of houses were bulldozed and ousters were forced to move without adequate arrangements, and this was documented in its main report.[51]

Emergence of R&R Policies

The rehabilitation and resettlement policies are the result of concerns expressed by the social activists, academicians and Non-Governmental Organisations (NGOs). Most of the Pre-1980 projects in India did not have a clear-cut resettlement plans. Resettlement was taken on a case-to-case basis and only a few of the projects offered. resettlement in the form of house sites and infrastructure to the displaced. As a result of this ad-hoc approach, many of the displaced were left out of the process. The Rehabilitation and Resettlement (R&R) Policies for the PAFs at the National and Andhra Pradesh State levels were formulated.[52] The Governments (Central and State) did not frame any rehabilitation and resettlement policies prior to 1988. It shows the lukewarm attitude of the governments towards the plight of PAPs, even before they were up rooted.[53]

R&R Benefits as Per National and State Policies

1. Preference in allotment of land to land or cash compensation.
2. Additional financial assistance equivalent to 500 days of minimum agricultural wages (MAWs) for the loss of

customary or grazing rights/usages, to other R&R benefits to the tribal PAFs.

3. Resettlement is closely located to their habitat in compact block, so that they retain their ethnic, linguistic and cultural identity.
4. The families settled out of the district to get higher R&R benefits to the extent of 25 per cent in monetary terms.
5. The tribal land alienation in violation of the laws and regulations in force on the subject to be treated available only to the original tribal land owner.
6. The tribal families residing in the Project Affected Areas (PAAs) with fishing rights in the reservoir area.
7. Additional land on free of cost for community and religious gatherings.
8. Rehabilitation and Resettlement (R&R) committees should include representatives of PAPs, women, elected representatives, and NGOs member and government machinery.

The R&R Policy of Andhra Pradesh and the Welfare of Displaced tribes

The Andhra Pradesh Rehabilitation and Resettlement Policy of 2005 (APRRP), echoes the policy of National Policy on Rehabilitation and Resettlement of 2004 (NPRR), expecting a few modifications in the provisions. Both the policies suffer from several deficiencies, as they don't reflect any potential insights or basic principles to assess the losses of the ousters property and there are no special welfare measures or arrangements against displacement problem. It is interesting to note that the R&R Policy-makers of the Andhra Pradesh, in its order, para-1 of the abstract reveals the effects of compulsory acquisition of land and displacement on PAFs and the need for rehabilitation with utmost care and concern. But in practice it is quite opposite in implementation of the R&R package, and there is no proper concern, humanitarian approach and foresight as it was proved in the earlier studies on the issue of displacement. The policy is one-sided and does not show any consideration to the needs and aspirations of the displaced people. According to the existing rehabilitation policy in Andhra Pradesh, there is no safeguard against double or triple displacement, which has happened in the past due to poor planning of resettlement process, and project assessment, especially in the dam related submergence areas. This is one of its major lacunae. As a result the displaced tribal and other weaker sections are getting marginalised. Ultimately, this is causing large scale migration to urban centres. As all these people are not skilled they don't find any employment in urban set-up, and they are forced to occupations like rag picking, rickshaw pulling and even bonded labour. This can be illustrated by the experience of the 'Yandai' tribal, who were displaced due to setting up of tiger sanctuaries at Srisailam and Indian Space Research Organisation (ISRO) at Shriharikota. Most of the displaced 'Yanadi' tribal lost their livelihood which is primarily fishing-hunting-and-foraging in the lowland forested river basins. Most of them ended up as bonded labour in the fish and aqua forms of the coastal districts. A few of them are also engaged in the rag picking business in the urban areas of Vijayawada, Guntur and Eluru. World Commission on Dams (WCD) suggests that "an approach based on 'recognition of rights' and 'assessment of risks'...be developed as a tool for future planning and decision-making. Secondly, in line with the point emphasised in the guiding principles that the Primary duty and responsibility for providing humanitarian assistance to internally DPs lies with project authorities" in order to overcome the inadequacies of the R&R policy and its current form of dealing the impoverishment risks, and socio-cultural and politico-economic needs of the DPs. The Commission also opines that 'there is a need to link development with displacement policy, which assumes greater importance in view of the onslaught of national and international capital in the age of so-called liberalisation, globalisation and privatisation to protect the rights of vulnerable communities to be an equal partner in developmental process'.[51]

Importance of the present study

Millions of people since independence have been displaced by various projects in India and Andhra Pradesh in the name of development. Displacement means people forgoing their villages, lands, work, income, culture and the way of life established and accumulated since the time immemorial. It amounts to a total destruction of the existing economy in the process of creating a new one for a new set of people and regions. Consequently, a set of losers and gainers have been created. Losers are those who are displaced and the gainers are those who live in command area of an irrigation projects, industrialists, bureaucrats, contractor-politician combine.

The magnitude of displacement is very high in India and Andhra Pradesh. Michael Cernea, senior advisor, social policy and sociology, World Bank in one of his papers observed that in the absence of proper R&R policy, people have been thrown into landlessness; joblessness; marginalisation; increased morbidity and mortality; food insecurity; loss of access to common property and services and community disarticulation.

The present study deals with the R&R policies followed by different political regimes during post-state formation periods (1956-2014) of Andhra Pradesh. The question before any planner is how to build the destroyed economy of the displaced people of a project.

The aim of the present study is to find out what measures have been taken and what policy has been adopted by the governments for displaced tribal people (DTP). The focus of analysis is on the concern shown towards displaced and their R&R.

Many of the studies on the issues relating to rehabilitation of tribes conducted in India and Andhra Pradesh or elsewhere have emphasised or highlighted the following:

1. Tribal economy with emphasis on occupational structure and change in livelihood means from hunting to food gathering, from forests to agriculture, ownership of land, economic relationship between tribal and non-tribal communities, different patterns of industrialisation in the tribal areas, role of market, social cost of industrialisation, economic role of women, role of moneylenders in tribal life, and economic transformations.
2. Religious beliefs and rituals, magic, witchcraft, religious movements (Like Bhagat, etc.), and the impact of Christian missionaries on tribes.
3. Political organisation with focus on the concept of law and justice, Panchayat leadership, impact of political parties, voting behaviour and political participation.

4. Cultural life, which describes folk music, dances, fairs and festivals, etc.

Further, the studies are basically anthropological. These studies have not focused much on the role of the government, government institutions and tribal welfare in the overall context of changing tribal life. The tribal people living in either plain areas or in forest area have by and large similar problems. The tribal people have been facing lot of problems like poverty, unemployment, social and economic inequalities, problems relating to enrichment, malnutrition, competition and also they are displaced from their own place by the establishment of industries, irrigation projects, and mining projects. Therefore, there is a need to examine the causes to these problems and also the government policies and programmes for the displaced tribal living in the tribal and plain areas. The present study is a modest attempt in that direction.

Objectives of the study

- To study the reasons for displacement of tribal in India and Andhra Pradesh.
- To analyse the R&R policy and programmes for displaced tribes in India and Andhra Pradesh.
- To examine the socio-economic background of the respondents who are displaced by developmental programmes by the central and state governments in Warangal district.
- To study the impact of the compensation given to the displaced tribes during the developmental programmes in Warangal district.
- Finally to provide suggestions for strengthening the implementation R&R policy for displaced tribes regarding to the developmental programmes which are implemented by the central and state governments.

Methodology and Scope of the study

For the purpose of the present study, Warangal District of Telangana Region in the old Andhra Pradesh is selected. The district has five revenue divisions viz., Warangal, Mahabubabad, Mulugu, Narsampet and Jangoan. The district consists of 51 Mandals and 1098 villages.

For the purpose of the study, affected tribal habitations through irrigation projects are selected in the Warangal district. For the purpose of the present study, five Thandas have been taken as samples, viz., Janakamma Banda Thanda located at Moripirala Village of Ryaparthy Mandal, Vidynagar Thanda located at Ryaparthy Village and Mandal, Guguloth Bondalu Thanda and Gyama Thanda which are located at Parvathagiri Village and Mandal finally Dongachelima Thanda located at Narmetta Manda of Warangal district.

While selecting the area, proper weightage is given to the performance of the programme. The study covers a few case studies and opinions of the 171 victims of the irrigation project. The information and opinions of the respondents are collected through questionnaire and also participant observation methods in order to get objective picture of the implementation of the resettlement and rehabilitation programmes. The needed data for the study is collected from the Primary Source and Secondary Source. A questionnaire is prepared and administered to the displaced tribes. The Officials, Non-Officials and Non-government organisations are also consulted in this regard. I had also paid visits to the libraries, Tribal Culture Research and Training Institution; Department of Irrigation, Chief Planning Office, Commissionarate of Tribal Welfare and ITDA, MADA Project Office, National Institute for Rural Development, Hyderabad, and State Planning Board for collecting the Secondary Data.

Chapterisation

The study has been divided into six chapters. The details are explained in the following lines:

First chapter "Introduction" deals with the brief details about the R&R Policy, Scope, Objectives and Methodology of the study.

The Second chapter entitled "Review of the Literature on Displacement and Rehabilitation in India" deals with the various studies related to tribal's issues and R&R Policy particularly related to tribals.

The Third Chapter on "Displacement of scheduled tribes in India and Andhra Pradesh" deals with scenario of the displacement of scheduled tribes in India and Andhra Pradesh through various projects.

The Fourth Chapter entitled as "Resettlement and Rehabilitation Policy in India and Andhra Pradesh" deals with the implementation and impact of the Resettlement and Rehabilitation Policy in India and Andhra Pradesh.

The Fifth Chapter entitled as "R&R Policy: Implementation and its impact on Scheduled Tribes in Warangal District and Response of the Project Affected Tribes" deals in-depth with the implementation and impact of the R&R Policy on Scheduled Tribes in Warangal District and Response of the Project Affected Tribes.

Finally the Sixth Chapter "Conclusion and Suggestions" deals with the analysis of the study including with finding-outs and gives some suggestions to betterment of the R&R Policy and Project Affected Tribal population.

References

1. George F. Gant,The Concept of Development Administration, in Lawrence R. Jones (ed.) Comparative Public Administration (Research in Public Policy Analysis and Management, Volume 15), Emerald Group Publishing Limited, Bingley BD16 1WA, United Kingdom - 2006, pp. 257-285.
2. Chatterjee, S.K., Development Administration with special Reference to India, Surjeet Publications, Delhi - 2005, p.1.
3. Sanjay Sangvai, "Politics of Displacement and the State in the Age of Globalisation" in Rehabilitation Policy and Law in India: A right to Livelihood'- Walter Fernandes, Vijay Paranjapye. Indian Social Institute, Delhi and 'Econet', Pune - 1997. https://jharkhandonline.wordpress.com/2009/01/27/dam-displacement-deprivation
4. Arundhati Roy, "The Greater Common Good", (Frontline, June 4, 1999). p. 7.
5. Ravi Hemadri, et al, "Dams, Displacement, Policy and Law in India", Contributing Paper of the WCD, WCD, Vlaeberg, Cape Town, South Africa. www.dams.org
6. The Constitution of India originally provided the right to property (which includes land) under Articles 19 and 31. Article 19 guaranteed that all citizens have the right to acquire, hold and dispose of property. Article 31 stated that "no person shall be deprived of his property save by authority of law." It also indicated that compensation would be paid to a person whose property has been taken for public purposes (often subject to wide range of meaning). The Forty-Fourth Amendment of 1978 deleted the right to property from the list of fundamental rights with an introduction of a new provision, Article 300-A, which provided that "no person shall be deprived

of his property save by authority of law" (Constitution 44th Amendment, w.e.f. 10.6.1979). The amendment ensured that the right to property is no more a fundamental right but rather a constitutional/legal right/as a statutory right and in the event of breach, the remedy available to an aggrieved person is through the High Court under Article 226 of the Indian Constitution and not the Supreme Court under Article 32 of the Constitution. State must pay compensation at the market value for such land, building or structure acquired (Inserted by Constitution, Seventeenth Amendment) Act, 1964, the same can be found in the earlier rulings when property right was a fundamental right (such as 1954 AIR 170, 1954 SCR 558, which propounded that the word "Compensation" deployed in Article 31(2) implied full compensation, that is the market value of the property at the time of the acquisition. The Legislature must "ensure that what is determined as payable must be compensation, that is, a just equivalent of what the owner has been deprived of".

7. Chittaroopa Palit, "Short-changing the Displaced: National Rehabilitation Policy", Economic and Political Weekly, July 3, 2004 p. 2961.
8. Though, one of the critical requirements of the NWDTA is that the rights of the displaced Adivasis are ensured before work on the dam begins. It states that any individual or community facing submergence owing to proposed construction should be rehabilitated one year before actual submergence. This norm has been consistently violated. Frontline Vol. 81 issue 21, Oct-13-26, 2001.
9. Biswal, G.C., "Tribal Development and Education, some Issues", Vanyajathi, Vol. XXXII, No. 1, January – 1985, p.14.
10. Pravathamma, C, "Scheduled Castes and Tribes: A Socio-Economic Survey", Asish Publishing House, New Delhi - 1984, pp. 4-5.
11. Bhowmick, K.L., "Tribal India, A Profile of Indian Ethnology," The World Press, Calcutta - 1971. p.1.
12. Morris Desmond and Peter Marsh, "Tribes", Pyramid Books, London - 1988. p. 6.
13. Ghurye, G.S., "The Scheduled Tribe in India", Transaction Publishers, New Brunswick (USA) and London (UK) 1980.
14. Lewis, I.M., "Tribal society in International Encyclopedia of Social Sciences", the Macmillan Co, and the Free Press. Vol.16, 1968, p. 147.
15. Naik, T.B, "What is Tribe Conflicting Definitions, in L.P. Vidyathi (Ed)", Applied Anthropology, Allahabad - 1968, pp. 92-93.
16. Vimal Chandra, "Hand Book on Scheduled Castes and Scheduled Tribes", Office of the Commissioner for Scheduled Castes and Scheduled Tribes, Government of India, New Delhi - 1968, pp. 27-28.
17. Fuchus Stephen, "The aboriginal tribes of India", The Macmillan Company, New Delhi – 1973, p. 25.

18. Beleille Andre, "The Definition of Tribe, Caste and Religion" MacMillan, India, New Delhi, p. 7.
19. Suresh Chandra Rajora, "Tribal Society and its Differential Profile", Vanyajati, Vol. XXIII, No. 1, January 1986, pp. 7-10.
20. Gail Om Vedt, "Are Adivasis Sibaltern, Economic and Political Weekly, Vol. XXIII, No. 39, September 24, 1988, p. 2001.
21. Ralph Linton (Ed.), "The Science of Man in World Crisis", Columbia University Press, New York - 1945, pp. 4-17.
22. Nadeem Hasnain, "Bharatiy Girijanulu", Orient Langman, Hyderabad, 1996.
23. Kumar, A., "Tribal Development in India", Sarup & Sons, New Delhi – 2002.
24. Majumdar, D. N., and T. N. Madan, "An Introduction to Social Anthropology, Asia Publishing House, New Delhi - 1960, p. 21.
25. Lewis, I.M., op.cit.
26. Majumdar, D.N., op.cit.
27. Andru Beteille and T.N. Madan, "Encounter and Experience: Personal accounts of Field Work", Vikas Publishing House, New Delhi – 1975.
28. Majumdar, D.N. and T. N. Madan T.N. op.cit. p. 241.
29. Naik, T.B. op.cit.
30. Kumar, A., op.cit.
31. Arthur, S. Wilke, Fran French and Raj P. Mohan, "Tribal India: Unintentional Acculturation", Bulletin of the international Committee on Urgent Anthropological and Ethnological Research, No. 21, 1979.
32. Majumdar, D.N., op.cit., p. 21.
33. Arthur S. Wilke, op.cit., p. 25.
34. Director, Census Operations, Government of India, Hyderabad.
35. Tribal and Tribal areas of Andhra Pradesh (Basic Statistics); TCR&TI, Tribal Welfare Department, Government of Andhra Pradesh, Hyderabad-2004.
36. Alf Morten Jerve "Social Consequences of Development in Human Rights Perspective: Lessons from the World Bank", in Human Rights in Development Global Perspectives and Local Issues, edited by Hugo Stokke and Arne Tostensen, Kluwer Law International, The Hague - 1999, at p. 51.
37. Michael Cernea, "Development's Painful Social Cost Introductory Study" in S. Parasuraman, "The Development dilemma Displacement in India", Macmillan Press, London - 1999, p. 3.
38. Upendra Baxi, "Notes on Constitutional and Legal Aspects of Displacement and Rehabilitation". In Walter Fernandez and Enakshi Ganguly Thakral (Ed.), "Development, Displacement and Rehabilitation", Indian Social Institute, New Delhi, 1989, p.164.

39. Maharashtra Project Affected Persons Rehabilitation Act, 1986.
40. Madhya Pradesh Pariyojna Ke Karan Visthapit Vyakti (Punarsthapan), Adhiniyam, 1985.
41. The Karnataka Resettlement of Project Displaced Persons Act, 1987.
42. This group functioned under the joint convenership of Medha Patkar and Smitu Kothari, Girish Patel, B D Sharma, Vasant Palshikar, Bittu Sahgal were some of the other members who drafted this document which was widely discussed in smaller groups through participatory process of consultation.
43. Amrita Patwardhan, "Dams and Tribal Peoples in India" contributing paper prepared for thematic review, World Commission for Dams, accessed from http://www.dams.org/
44. Malika Basu, "Where lies the Hope?" Development and Discontent. 5-10-96.
45. Misra, K. Kamal, Study on Land Alienation in Scheduled Areas of Andhra Pradesh. NIRD-UNDP Research Project. 2000.
46. Rao, K. Mohan, 'Tribal Development in Andhra Pradesh: Problems, Performance and Prospects', Published by TCR&TI, Dept. of Tribal Welfare, Government of Andhra Pradesh, Hyderabad - 1999.
47. Varma, R.C., "Indian Tribes through Ages", Directorate of Publications Division, Ministry of Information and Broad Casting, Government of India, New Delhi - 1990.
48. Reddy, R. Padala and Reddy S. Padala, "Agency Laws in Andhra Pradesh", S.P. Goria, Asia Law House, Hyderabad - 1995.
49. Swamy Maheswara, Shorter commentaries on the Land Acquisition Act, 1894, (with special Reference to the state of Andhra Pradesh) with allied Acts and Rules, Gogia Law Agency, Hyderabad - 1996.
50. Upadhyay, Sanjay, Ram and Bhavani, "Land Acquisition and Public Purpose", the other media publications, New Delhi - 1998.
51. World Bank, "Early Experiences with Involuntary Resettlement: Impact Evaluation on India-Maharashtra Irrigation II Project, OED, 1993.
52. Notification Number. A.C.Q.13011/4/2004 of the Ministry of Rural development and with the Government Order MS. No. 68 of the Irrigation and Canal Area Development (CAD) Department, issued on 8th April, 2005 respectively.
53. Ram Babu, M., "Ethnomedicinal Practices of the Koyas of Bhadrachalam: A Case Study of Boddugudem Village, Khammam District, Andhra Pradesh", (Unpublished) M. Phil Thesis Submitted to University of Hyderabad -2000.

Chapter 2

Review of Literature

Studying a social group in its relation with the larger society is an ever interesting task of a social science enquiry. The priority areas of social science enquiry for a long time are confined to the study of constitutional institutions and analysis of the social relation existing within the various strata of society. In brief, the tribal studies in post-independence era have found a considerable place in the field of social science research, but the focus on certain fields of research like clan, custom and primitiveness of the tribal society are more visible than any other areas of the subject.[1] The analysis of tribal policies, administrative structure, tribal participation in the planning and implementation of the socio-economic development schemes and their impact on the living conditions on the tribal are limited. Hence the present study assumes importance.

After Independence several studies were undertaken by the administrators, sociologists, political scientists, economists and social workers on the problems of tribes. The government also constituted a number of committees to study some specific and general issues through the Commissioner for Scheduled Castes and Scheduled Tribes. The research institutes are established in various states which brought out volumes of literature on the tribal society of India. The Asiatic Society, the Anthropological Society of Bombay, the Gujarat Research Society; the Ethnographic and Folk-Culture Society, Lucknow; the Cultural Research Institute in West Bengal, Bharatiya Adimajati Sevak Sangh, New Delhi and its branch in Nellore district of Andhra Pradesh State.

A. N. Sinha Institute, Patna; Indian Council for Social Studies Research and the Ministry of Home Affairs of India, have done a great deal of research on the tribal life. Apart from these several individual voluntary organisations, civil liberties associations, parliamentarian and non-parliamentarian political parties have enriched the knowledge on the subject with their occasional reports.

Accumulation of scientific knowledge is a slow and gradual process in which an investigator builds on the works of researcher's findings and policy out-looks serve as a starting point for the future. The links that can establish between and among studies enrich knowledge and offer policy insights.[2] In the context of the Indian tribes, Hudson has traced the complex historical evolution of various tribes of India.[3] Hulton[4] has further analysed their conditions. Stephen Fuches[5] has written a comprehensive account of the aboriginal tribes of the Indian subcontinent. Dalton[6] has provided an account of the tribal societies of north-eastern states. Guha[7] has discussed the racial affinities of the Indian aborigines in different perspectives. The major demographic structure of tribal India has been analysed by Mamoria, C.B.,[8] Sengupta, P.N.,[9] has studied the consumption and nutrition pattern of the aborigines. Vidyarthi, L.P., and B.K. Roy[10] has produced valuable studies on the socio-cultural-economic organisations of the Indian tribes. Ghurye[11] has depicted the historic development of the Indian tribes and made a chronicle of tribal development since independence. Ambastha, N.K.,[12] has studied the educational system vis-à-vis the income and expenditure pattern of the tribes. Bhowmic, K.L., [13] has dealt with the ethnographic structure and other characteristics of important tribes of India. Bose, N.K.,[14] has discussed the socio-cultural features of the Indian tribes. Ashok Ranjan Basu[15] opines that development strategy of tribal communities has to be in tune with the development strategy of the nation. Dube, S.C.,[16] has examined the changing pattern of socio-cultural organisation of the tribes.

Sharma, B.D.,[17] investigated into the impact of socio-cultural practices on the economic development of tribes. Various seminars and workshops on Tribal Development have been organised from time to time indifferent academies and institutes. A few such seminars relevant in this content need be mentioned here. A seminar on Tribal Development problems was organised at HCM State Institute of Public

Administration, Jaipur in May 1975. The Centre for Tribal Development of the Manikya Lal Verma (CTDMLV) Tribal Research and Training Institute in collaboration with the tribal area development department, Udaipur and convened a seminar on tribal development: Past Efforts and New Challenges (December 1987). The observations and findings of the seminars have been compiled in the form of a book entitled Tribal Development: Past Efforts and New Challenges by J.P. Singh and N.N. Vyas. The authors are of the opinion that notwithstanding the substantial benefits accrued to tribal people over plan periods the results have not been commensurate with expectations.[18]

Besides a good number of Articles, Thesis, Books and Reports of various committees/commissions published from time to time to highlight the tribal problems. In the above said context, in this chapter the researcher made a humble attempt to review the existing literature on the concerned in the form of articles, books and dissertations etc.

Varrier Elwin,[19] brought the publication of problem-oriented monographs for the first time. This was the first systematic and analytical about tribal problems.

Radha Krishna Murthy, A.,[20] is confined to a particular geographically contiguous areas with a long, common history and similar economic organisation, the socio-cultural aspects are studied along with the economic aspects and he has delimited the scope of his enquiry to planning and an appraisal of planned development in Andhra Pradesh with a view to bringing the vital aspects of planning into a sharper focus. The sub-title specifies such delimitation in the thesis though the main title might suggest a wider range of tribal problems in its coverage.

Raghavaiah, V.,[21] a pioneer social worker on the tribal development who made several attempts to analyze the tribal life in Andhra Pradesh as well as India, brought out two volumes, and presented a review of the problems of the tribal.

Kulkarni, M.G.,[22] examined the problems of tribal development in Nasik district of Maharashtra.

Muthayya and Mathur[23] studied socio-economic and attitudinal problems of persons who were rendered homeless in the Pattancheru, neighbourhoods of Hyderabad city of Andhra Pradesh. He suggested that the displaced villagers needed some amount of psychological support to mitigate their anxiety about the future, as they have lost their land in the acquisition of land for the location of the Bharat Heavy Electricals Limited (BHEL).

Ramaiah, P.,[24] studied a particular geographically contiguous area with a long common history and a similar economic organisation inhabited by a single dominant tribe i.e., the Koyas. Secondly, the tribal life in a blending of myth and reality. He cuts across many fields-cultural, ecology and physiographic. He chooses an aspect of tribal life i.e., the economic aspect, though he has always kept the other aspects also in his mind throughout. His study is confined to the tribals enumerated in 1971 census. Further he studied the tribal economy of Koyas of Warangal district in Telangana Region from 102 tribal villages. He examined the main tribal problems, namely credit, marketing, land problems and other economic conditions of the tribal area. This is supposed to provide the basis to evolve a developmental plan for the tribal areas.

In his another study Ramaiah, P.,[25] examines the issues concerning the tribal development in detail. He opined that the tribal people are prepared to make an entry into the new era, and the development should be in a phased manner. As he observes, the Indian economists also have realised that development should be a phased one so as to soften the shocks consequent upon economic development. He also felt that the development of tribal cannot be isolated from that of the general economic development of the community as a whole.

Janardhan Rao, B.,[26] concentrated to cover the impact of land transfer regulations in a scheduled village. The major objective of his work is to portray the factors that have a crucial bearing on the process of land alienation in scheduled tribal areas (STAs). More specifically he attempted to understand the impact and implementation of land transfer regulations as an instrument of economic advancement and welfare of the tribal communities in the limited context of the selected villages.

Janardhan Rao[27] in his another study concentrated on the aspects related to the causes and consequences of land alienation and the impact of land transfer regulations in these areas. The major objective of the study was to portray the factors that had a crucial bearing on the process of land alienation in STAs. In addition to this, it was attempted to understand the impact and implementation of the land transfer regulations as an instrument to counter the fast-becoming deprivation process of the tribal communities in these areas. Further, it paid attention in examining the efficiency of the measures of "support–structure" which had initiated several of the developmental programmes such as the irrigation, credit network and other efforts in the allied fields of the development of tribal areas. Finally, the study intended to probe the gravity and reasons for land evictions in the tribal areas which had been the sole reason for underdevelopment and pauperisation of these committees.

In another study Janardhan Rao[28] explained in each Five Year Plan period, *Adivasis* have progressively witnessed further displacement. Lakhs of people were displaced by various development initiations. They were forced to become migrant labourers or urban slum dwellers in the metropolitan cities and subjected to traumatic psychological and socio-cultural consequences. And, many people have become beggars, vagrants, and prostitutes. In all such situations, the net result had been the rapid "Positional Decline" of the *Adivasi Communities*.

Suryanarayana, M., and Gangadharam, V., [29] the authors examine mainly the impact of development programmes on the traditionally food gathering tribal communities in India in detail.

Somasekhar, A.,[30] studied economic conditions of tribals with specific reference to Koyas in Bhadrachalam taluk of Khammam district. He emphasised on economic conditions of tribal, the social and cultural factors are not neglected. He dealt with the tribal economy such as agriculture, forests, exploitation besides the profile of Godavary Valley in which the majority of Koyas inhabit and ekes out their livelihood.

Ajit K. Singh,[31] argues that the development is a dynamic concept which is an all pervading human activity which discovers the latent potentials and mobilises them to achieve the social goals.

Rajagopal,[32] analysed the major problems of agriculture labour in Bastar district. These problems were (1) low productivity in agriculture;

(2) disguised unemployment and improper utilisation of manpower; (3) landless labour force and lack of industrialisation of agriculture and (4) low standard of living.

Vidyut Joshi's Study in Submerging Villages[33] says 19 villages-in Gujarat will submerge by the Sardar Sarovar Project. In the large number of the people displaced by development projects in India ate tribal. The problems of rehabilitation of ousters has been; till-recently, viewed by the government as an administrative flaw, aberrance in the ultimate goal of development. It seeks to describe the overall patterns of village types, social groups, economic conditions, leadership and attitudes of the tribal towards rehabilitation.

Narsing Rao,[34] investigate into the economic conditions of tribal, their assets, occupations, income and consumption etc., and their exploitation by non-tribal. He examined the various tribal development programmes being implemented by the government. He explained the impact of the development programmes on asset formation, employment, income, consumption level, indebtedness and exploitation by non-tribal.

Ranga Reddy, M.,[35] compels holding a distinct perspective on development of tribal primary education which is a continuing process running beyond the walls of formal education in classrooms. It was a comprehensive study of complex fields related to tribal education such as historic, ethnic, hereditary environmental, socio-cultural-economic tradition and base etc. It has constructed a realistic picture of the privilege situation of education among tribes in Visakhapatnam and Mahabubnagar.

A detailed survey report on the conditions of the ousters of Srisailam made by Lokayan[36] a path breaking revelations on the overall aspects of rehabilitation process, and had shown the real character of the welfare governance. Continuous litigation encouraged by the middlemen in handling the compensation process to the victims is elaborately dealt in the study. Creative interpretation of the responses from the judiciary and government departments are recorded and debated in greater details.

To understand this positional decline, it is necessary to examine the very development transition taking place pertaining to the spheres of land, forest and water resources which were once largely enjoyed by the tribal. The process of development, therefore, is obvious that it had pushed the forest dwellers to the receiving end and eroded their original autonomy status. A collective effort is done by a group of Scholar activitists of Lokayan[37] on the issue of displacement and rehabilitation. The essence of all these essays unanimously argued for an Act on displacement and fully covered rehabilitation process rather than package. The common thinking present in all these drafts was the balancing of the national priorities and the extension of the justified package to the victims of the displacement.

Agnihotri, S.K.,[38] in his article, the author observes that the STs are distinct racial and cultural entities. As such, a newcomer to tribal areas is not to be bewildered by the difference in the nature of people there. The efficiency and success of a public official largely depends on the manner in which he interacts with the people. As far as these areas are concerned, however brilliant an officer may be he will be a failure unless he behaves in a sober and tactful manner with the affected people.

The study on Narmada Project undertaken by Claude Alvares and Ramesh Billorey[39] provide much information about environmental aspects and they explained Cost-Benefit Analysis of the Project in detail. The study explored the whole official and non-official reports and data among the Narmada Valley Projects.

The wide range of work of the World Bank prepared by Michael, M., Cernea[40] on displacement, gives various theoretical dimensions of the problem. Displacement is considered as part of the progress. Only now they are beginning to consider the rehabilitation of ousters. Their situation is considered as human rights issue. Cernea also addresses the policy issues and operational implications of development projects that cause involuntary resettlement. In this study, he explains involuntary resettlement has been and still is, approached as a salvage and welfare operation, rather than as a part of development objectives. The knowledge generated by social science research on resettlement is relevant and useful for and economic problems of relocation.

Kanchan Roy,[41] discussed the tribal problems leading to tribal disintegration from the mainstream of our national culture. He also points out that there are more important components especially related to the tribal economy and the ongoing development activities or National Plan for Tribal Upliftment, which have not been considered adequately.

A Report of the Working Group on Development and Welfare of Scheduled Tribes, appointed during the Eighth Five Year Plan (1990-1995) on the Rehabilitation of Tribal, based on a comprehensive study of 110 projects concludes that, of the 16.94 lakh people displaced by these projects, almost 50 per cent (8.14 lakhs) were tribal.[42]

Study on Sri Ramsagar Project (popularly known as Pochampadu, by Muthyam Reddy,[43] is an important work on the theme of displacement and rehabilitation process effected in the major irrigation projects in Telangana region of Andhra Pradesh. The study discussed the aspects of changes in land ownership, encroachment of the lands, administration of compensation system and other socio-cultural aspects of decline and increase of the status both in the pre- and post-displacement periods. The performance of the related government departments of Revenue, Forest and special Collectorate of Land Acquisition was admittedly non-coordinative and thrown an exhausting experience to the oustees devoid of the appropriate justice and welfare gains from the public policy.

Soma Satyanarayana,[44] concentrated on the impact of commercial bank finance at the micro level in a village dominated by Lambada tribal in Devaruppula Mandal of Warangal District in Telangana region of Andhra Pradesh.

Vaswani, Kalpana, Dhagamwar, Vasudha and Thukral in their book on Land Acquisition Act and You [45] an explanatory work prepared by MARG for the use of various groups and social activists who are fighting against unplanned displacement, denotes an interesting account of the whole legal basis of the land legislations meant for displaced victims. This book contains a step by step explanation of the various sections of the Land Acquisition Act, 1894, which land is acquired and the authorities who need to be approached.

Shantha Kumari, K.,[46] attempted to understand the changing socio-economic background of tribal women. She found the impact of welfare legislations, programmes over the status of tribal women. She examined the relevance of the development strategy and its orientation of the welfare programmes towards the resources utilisation in the context of tribal women and society. She worked out the relationship between the loss of command over resources and its impact over the varying degrees of tribal women status. She found different levels and spheres of tribal women participation in the twin areas of agriculture and forest. And she records the alternative aspirations and preferences of tribal women expressed towards the alternative formulation of developmental strategy.

Marianna, Ch.,[47] examined the changes in the agrarian pattern in the selected tribal areas of the Khammam district of Andhra Pradesh. The transition from 1978 to 1988 on agrarian patterns had been analysed by comparing the changes between two points of above years. The findings that emerged from this work are based on 87 sample tribal households selected randomly from seven tribal villages. He has undertaken this work as a part-time research scholar and as such he could not attempt a much larger study.

Alexander, K.C., Jahangir, M.P., and Prasad, R.R.,[48] emphasised the preservation of forest as an important indicator of preservation of nature and environment preservation of animals like tiger as an indicator of preservation of the forest and its ecology. The authors explained the relation between Tiger Reserves, Ecology and Tribal. This study based on a house to house survey, dealt with the policies and principles of rehabilitation of tribal families who were displaced by the Similipal Tiger Reserve in Odisha.

A study undertaken by the Walter Fernandas and Enakshi Ganguli Thukral,[49] views that the displacement of millions, many of whom end up as bonded and migrant labourers exploited both in the rural and urban areas. The outcome of the displacement is the perennial neglect of the victims by the government and the performance of the authorised officials dealing with the development and rehabilitation proved to be insufficient.

Despite the severity of the problem of displacement, an adequate data base is still lacking. Commenting-on this, Walter Fernanda's felt that,[50] not much more can be said on the question of displacement because of the absence of a reliable data base and even of good estimates of the numbers involved. A few case studies that exist indicate the official statistics underestimate the extent of displacement. Despite the scarcity of the crucial data on the displacement, recently significant attempts were made to fill the gap. By conservative estimates of Walter Fernandas and other social researchers, 185 lakh persons were displaced by development projects since 1950, more than 74 lakhs of them were tribal.

Most significant of these works is the one that has been undertaken by Walter Fernandes. His studies-on Development, Displacement and Rehabilitation on all" over India context stand as a significant contribution. They gave wide coverage of the aspects of displacement and rehabilitation processes and provide authentic evidence even as a case-wise over the eleven Development Schemes and their implications on the Tribes of Odisha.[51]

Another intensive study brought out by Walter Fernandes [52] focuses on the theme that, forty years later, the tribal who have contributed immensely to national development, have to a great extent became its victims and are searching for a voice in the country.

The significant contribution of Haimendorf, C.V.F.,[53] on *Tribes of India* and his earlier studies on various tribal communities presented a detailed account of the transformation of tribal India. His studies on Andhra Pradesh Tribes such as *Gonds, Koyas, Hill Reddies* and *Chenchus* provide an in-depth understanding over the decade's of dispossession of their land, habitat and living territory. Specific mode of agrarian changes resulted due to the migration of non-tribal population. According to him, the tribes were denied their land rights. He further added that the agrarian form of dispossession of tribal communities is one such systematic displacement that gradually disempowered the tribal permanently from their habitat.

Marianna, Ch.,[54] examined the changes in the agrian pattern in the selected tribal areas of the Khammam district of Andhra Pradesh. The transition from 1978 to 1988 on agrarian patterns had been analysed by comparing the changes between two points of above years. The findings that emerged from this work are based on 87 sample tribal households selected randomly from seven tribal villages. He had undertaken this work as a part-time research scholar and as such he could not attempt a much larger study.

Shantha Kumari, K.,[55] attempted to understand the changing socio-economic background of tribal women. She found the impact of welfare legislations, programmes over the status of tribal women. She examined the relevance of the development strategy and its orientation of the welfare programmes towards the resources utilisation in the context of tribal women and society. She worked out the relationship between the loss of command over resources and its impact over the varying degrees of tribal women status. She found different levels and spheres of tribal women participation in the twin areas of agriculture and forest. And she records the alternative aspirations and preferences of tribal women expressed towards the alternative formulation of developmental strategy.

Philip Viegas[56] conducted a study on Land Alienation among the tribes of Odisha and bordering Andhra Pradesh. He summarised the study findings by stating alienation of tribal lands is a form of enslavement. The very process of enslavement paves way for overall displacement by jeopardizing the very identity of the tribal as human beings.

Mahapatra, L.K.,[57] in his work raised a few basic questions related to the very nature of the development process stepped into the vast rural and tribal areas. He observed that "this displacement is not merely spatial, it invariably involves or brings about the uprooting and dismemberment of social, moral and economic webs of life built over generations. What is more, though it is for what is considered national development, there is a difference between the class that benefits from the project and those who pay the price. In most cases, a very large number, even the majority, of those displaced, are tribal and persons from the Scheduled Castes (SCs)". Thus, the study focused not only on the aspects of displacement but also explained the very nature of implications to the existence to the vulnerable social groups.

Amir Hasan,[58] evaluated the various strategies of tribal development since independence. He critically examined the various faces and facts of tribal development with special reference to Uttar Pradesh. He has tried to distinguish the development measures taken for development of the tribal people from those for development of tribal areas.

An evaluation study on resettlement and rehabilitation plan under Sriramsagar Lower Manair Dam project[59] was undertaken by the Centre for Economic and Social Studies (CESS), Hyderabad. The study specifically covered the aspects of efficacy of income generating schemes and rendering the infrastructural facilities under Integrated Rural Development Programme (IRDP) package. The study viewed that these welfare programmes offered to the poor are not known to the very project affected people. Incompatibility of the nature of the programmes with the very needs of the beneficiaries is logically explained in the study.

The Debate on displacement process is discussed with a balanced view by Bharat Dogra.[60] He felt that there is a worldwide concern for social and environmental aspects of large dams co-existing with giant, multi-stage projects which fail to incorporate and reflect these concerns in a satisfactory way. The exact information on real intensity of the displacement problems is not even evolved, he commented.

Jai Prakash Jha,[61] examined the food habits of tribal households. The tribal were forced to depend much upon agriculture and mainly on produce like vegetables, rice and some coarse grains such as maize, millet etc. The study revealed tremendous changes in the food habits of tribal.

Mridula Singh and Ranjan Kumar Samantray[62] explained the fate of the Nagarjuna Sagar Dam ousters and their present position and its expected and reaching potential of the Irrigation and Electricity. The study strongly claim that the ousters whose conditions after a half century remain unaltered and on the other hand it had further worsened.

Bhowmic, P.K.,[63] examined the life style of selected tribal groups with a view to establish the reasons for acceptance or rejection of various schemes by them. He pointed out that the ecology and environment have molded the culture of the people and this, in course of time, developed into a particular attitude, which acts as the key factor in acceptance or rejection of a development programme.

Bhowmik, P.K.,[64] in another work brought the outcome of research work in the field of sustainable development and bio-diversity conservation has been carried out among the selected tribal communities in the three different ecological setting (viz., Hill Zone, Chotanagpur Platue Zone and Coastal Zone) in the state of West Bengal. The major issues like gradual depletion of global resources over the last century in one hand and conservation of the available resources for future human interests on the other hand was addressed in this work.

Most outstanding contribution on displacement studies is the one conducted by Bradford Morse.[65] Morse review on Sardar Sarovar Project reveal, the critical and positive side of a huge irrigation work. Conflicting claims of the loss and benefit in terms of productive resources distribution and recreation of the habitat and human resources, preparedness of the government for greater core, etc., have been scholastically dealt. The work on the other hand suggested an alternative vision of relocation and rehabilitation which in turn acted as the guidelines for formulation of the future public policies on displacement. Debate on the relevance of large dams has given serious impetus to the issue of enacting policy legislation on the displacement. Considerable extent of the time lapsed even for considering for having broad frame on the Rehabilitation Policy. Time and again the issue was debated and finally in the late 1990; the Government of India has put up a concerted effort to outline the Rehabilitation Policy.

Harshad Tribedi[66] emphasised that in spite of different kinds of inputs for development of agriculture, animal husbandry, industry, forestry, education etc., the most important input is that of human resource development, that will ultimately endure and enhance all achievements of tribal development. This being the crux of the problem, the author strongly advocates the development of tribal learning resource centres of various types suited to local conditions.

Mrinal Miri,[67] presented papers in a seminar on the *Tribal Situation in India*. The papers have been classified under four heads:

1. Culture custom, identity,
2. Demography, health, development,
3. Politics and movements and,
4. Language: Each paper, under the caption, discusses elaborately on the issues like tribal lifestyle, their relation with forests and non-tribal, ethnic identity, health and tribal development etc.

Thippani Krishna Murthy,[68] examined the under currents of the forest policy followed during the British India in specific relation to its impact on the tribal communities. He explained the gravity and implications of the deforestation over the native tribes in Andhra Pradesh for the last forty years. He examined the aspect of the implementation of forest development programmes such as social forestry programmes and their utility to the tribal communities in the selected villages. And also, he examined the changing nature of the forest policy being adopted by the state; it's overall impact in general and in relation to tribal community in particular and assesses the implications of the new forest development programmes like social forestry programmes in the micro context.

Deogaonkar, S.G.,[69] tried to trace the development of the administrative measures for tribal development, right from the beginning up to the time of the Eighth Five Year Plan. Different approaches to tribal development, the organisational set-up adopted and changes incorporated after intervals have also been described. An evolutionary discussion of all those measures has also been interrelated as and where possible. The concept of development has been discussed and its nexus with tribal culture is also outlined. Issues related to personnel policy for tribal development administration also find a place in the discussion and brief ethnographic notes on a few tribes of representative nature have also been given.

Gupta, L.P.,[70] has made a modest endeavour to look into the effectiveness of educational programmes, projects and schemes introduced by the government, and the processes involved thereof in the development of tribal people and society, Darjeeling district in the state of West Bengal was selected for this study.

Singh, C.P.,[71] descriptively and analytically studied Tribal Development Administration (TDA) in Santal Parganas of West Bengal and presented a detailed account of different aspects like evaluation, organisation, training, roles supervision, co-ordination and control and popular participation of the ITDA.

A noteworthy study was undertaken by John Tyson[72] on Jurala Project R&R process and their impact on the project affected people. The most pertinent observation of the study was that "The multiplicity of agencies involved in this work clearly raises problems of co-ordination and monitoring. There are moreover, number of difficulties that arise from the 'modus operandi' of R&R". The study observed that the multiplicity of structures, duplication of the work, non-coordination of the programmes aimed at the rehabilitation of the affected seemed to be less functional and sometimes remain absent. Thus, the outcome of the review of these studies in brief uniformly indicates the increasing misery of the tribal population threatened by the eviction, dispossession and displacement both at the national and state levels.

Behera, M.C.,[73] is an explorative study of the socio-economic life of the *Khampti* tribe in a changing system after implementation of plan programmes. Since, in a tribal economy, economic forces are not pronounced and are intermingled with socio-cultural considerations, the study has been made in a total perspective of the tribal life.

Hymavathi, Y.,[74] the tribal *Lambada* women of Andhra Pradesh are victimised and placed in Lambada community, and there in development. She attempted to see that how one of the tribes of *Lambada* women have responded to some situations at micro level. She chose a few *Lambada* settlements in Nalgonda District of Telangana area of Andhra Pradesh, examined the traditional culture both in production process and in their social economic life style for instance dress making and wearing, herding, collecting the forest products and liquor making.

Medha Patkar[75] a renowned social activist, fighting in favour of the ousted tribal of Narmada Dam Project gave a specific argumentative basis for the whole process of development and displacement. She viewed that the present form of development is essentially 'displacement in a broader sense and destitutionalisation of large masses and hence cannot protect their life. It aims at exploiting human beings and nature to satisfy the consumerist and unbridled demands of a privileged section of the society.

Raman Rao, V.,[76] analysed the performance of Andhra Pradesh Scheduled Castes, Scheduled Tribes and Backward Castes Cooperative Finance Corporations in terms of implementation of economic support programmes and their impact.

Ramesh Munigela,[77] concentrated on socio-economic conditions of one of the eight tribal groups recognised as primitive Tribal Groups, which is known as *Kolam* tribal group. He worked on the socio-economic conditions of *Kolams* living in Andhra Pradesh.

Decline in the socio-economic position of the tribal in Bihar is well studied by Upadhayay, V.S.,[78] in his work on Development Resettlement of people under Subernarekha Project. Problems related to resettlement, compensation and the efficacy of the administrative machinery in dealing with the post-eviction period were explained logically. Upadhayay, V.S.,[79] in his another study evaluated the history of development of tribal and discussed alternative models in the field of tribal development such as intensive model, comprehensive model, group-specific model and Parasitic and Negligence model. Keeping in view the traditional values of tribal people, a multi-dimensional approach on development with basic concepts of ecology, environment, human resources and pollution is discussed by him on the basis of the analysis of the policies for the last 50 years.

India, since its independence launched various development projects under the Five Year Plans. These projects displaced about five lakh persons each year primarily as a direct consequence of land acquisition for various projects. These figures do not include displacement by non-plan projects, changes in land use, acquisition for urban growth, and loss of livelihood caused by environmental degradation and population explosion. The cumulative social implication of these processes has been well explained in the 28th Report of the Commissioner of Scheduled Castes, and Scheduled Tribes of India. It notes that even though tribal people are roughly 7.5 per cent of the population, over 40 per cent of those displaced till 1990 came from these communities underscoring the fact that tribal is disproportionately affected by developmental displacement.[80]

Sharma, B.D.,[81] stresses quality of opportunity is the key-note of the new education policy. A number of measures have been envisaged to bring the educational system in consonance with the social and cultural needs of the tribal people and also to overcome the physical handicaps of the tribal areas. Thus, priority has to be accorded to those areas for opening of schools and residential ashram schools on a large scale. The tribal programme of assistance to children through all the stages of education have to be provided beside special coaching facilities to enable them to attain competitive standards with students from other communities. Special note has also to be taken concerning the problem of language as many a tribal community has its own dialect different from the regional language. The author proposes to prepare the members of tribal communities themselves for assuming the responsibilities of education and work as teachers in the tribal area.

In another study Sharma, B.D.,[82] presented some glimpses of tribal response to the forcible opening up of their small world with the new economic policy or "Globalisation" as its last version. The study brings into sharp focus the basic issue of violation of the constitution, implicit in the New Economic Policy (NEP) particularly in the tribal setting.

Suresh Lal, B.,[83] concentrated on the different aspects of migration of *Banjara* Tribals to find out the impact of migration on them in terms of working conditions, wages and earnings and their living conditions.

Laxmaiah, P.,[84] examined the socio-economic conditions of *Chenchu* households. He estimated the commodity-wise expenditure and per capita expenditure in respect of different income groups and examined the significance of variations that exist across the income groups. He analysed the degree of variations in commodity expenditures and total per capita expenditures among the tribal households belonging to different income groups. He examined the nature of relationship between the levels of income/total expenditure and consumption expenditure on different items for different income groups. He estimated the elasticity of consumption expenditure with respect to total expenditure for different commodities so as to examine the degree of responsiveness of consumption expenditure to the changes in income for different income groups of *Chenchu* households and he examined total household consumption expenditure.

In a very in-depth analysis, Smitu Kothari[85] has developed a convincing argument that minimising displacement or improving resettlement will only be marginal, palliative and temporary if they are not contextualised in a wider socio-political context. Current pattern of economic development, neglect of constitutional mandates which are helpful to the weaker sections, non-democratisation of the resource use are the three contentions of the argument that speaks about the displaced as victims of development. Kothari finally argues strongly for national legislation on displacement.

Bhandari, J.S., and Subhadra Channa[86] informed about the tribal people who lived a life of freedom and self respect till the lands of their ancestors and the abode of their spirits were invaded both physically and ideologically by the forces of colonisation and industrialisation and the formation of the post world war nation states. These states, whether colonial or otherwise had to develop certain policies to handle the people whom, most often on their own, refused to have anything to do with the state power imposed on them.

Mamillpally Vijay Kumar[87] examined the socio-economic background of the *Chenchus* of Mahabubnagar District. He assessed the extent of utilisation of Integrated Tribal Development Agency (ITDA) programmes, namely, irrigation, agriculture, animal husbandry, horticulture/social forestry and overall ITDA programmes by the *Chenchu* families of the Mahabubnagar District. He assessed the degree of political participation of the *Chenchus*. He examined the economic status improved after the utilisation of the ITDA programmes. He found out the association between personal background variables and extent of utilisation of ITDA programmes in Mahabubnagar District. He found out the association between the degree of political participation and the extent of utilisation of ITDA programmes. He assessed the relationship between extent of ITDA programmes utilisation and economic status of the *Chenchu* respondents.

Sreenivasa Reddy, B.,[88] made some attempts for studying the tribal displacement in Andhra Pradesh, particularly on three major Telangana tribes such as *Gonds, Koyas* and *Chenchus* predominantly living in the Districts of Adilabad, Khammam and Mahabubnagar of Andhra Pradesh. He investigated the problems of displaced tribal and non-tribal and their rehabilitation with reference to the projects such as Heavy Water Plant at Manuguru of Khammam District, Satnala Medium Irrigation Project and Rajiv Gandhi Wild Life Sanctuary (Tiger Reserve) in Adilabad and Mahabubnagar Districts respectively.

Lachaiah, N.,[89] examined demographic characteristics of scheduled tribes and the socio-economic development of Scheduled Tribes of the state. He studied the educational development and the occupational mobility of scheduled tribes. It studied the differential development within the scheduled tribes and to draw conclusions and suggested measures for rapid socio-economic development of scheduled tribes of the Andhra Pradesh.

Ravinder, G.,[90] made efforts to understand the contending perspective of tribal integration policy of Indian state particularly adopted towards the assimilation of the tribal communities. He examined the modes and implications of the establishment of development institutions such as ITDA, and other constitutionally introduced development process initiated by the state in the tribal context. He analysed the patterns of tribal and non-tribal responses on the mode of development that had taken place. He assessed the impact of the public policies of development in the tribal areas and the implications of the institutional approach in tribal society.

Chakrabarthy[91] analysed the data set to bring out a comparative picture of levels of welfare of SCs and STs in rural areas of India and he focused on the education, health status and healthcare facilities, income and its distribution, incidence and intensity of poverty.

Veeranna, G.,[92] examined tribal political leadership where inductive logic is employed to draw certain generalisations for Andhra Pradesh State as a whole or extending the logic to the nation as a whole and if such generalisation have specific validity and the limited nature of the investigation and the situation was different from one area to another area and one community to another community. Although the political leadership is a complex one, encompassing innumerable variables, the investigation had chosen to deal with only a few, which he considered to be the significant for the study.

Bhupinder Singh[93] gives the historical account of the Jharkhand movement which has its origin in eighteenth century. He examines the challenges and opportunities new state may face include provision of pro-people administration, harnessing regional resources for the enrichment of quality of life, development of human resources, uphold tribal values and promotion of ecology in the Jharkhand environment.

Mohanth, P.K.,[94] concentrated on forests, shifting cultivation, bonded labour, rehabilitation of displaced families, land alienation, excise policy etc., to be related to the Scheduled Tribes.

Shyam Nand Singh[95] examined the working and impact of different policies in the context of preferential employment policy to mitigate social inequalities adopted by the Government of India and various state governments for the deprived social section – scheduled tribes.

Sankaran, S.R.,[96] evaluated various provisions in the constitution of India specifically pertaining to safeguards for the depressed classes. The welfare is rooted in the constitution based on the values of equality, human dignity, social justice, laws and policies emanating from the constitutional mandate. However, these measures are found to be inadequate though a vast ground was traversed by way of planned development in spite of the heterogeneous nature of Indian society. The paper advocated for concerted efforts of the state and various agencies towards the continued quest for equality and social justice.

Srivastava, B.N.,[97] advocated that the policies should be more focused towards bridging the prevailing disparities viz., education, poverty and other minimum requirements such as roads, electricity, housing, drinking water, health nutrition, sanitation etc.

Ashutosh Thakur[98] focused on the developmental strategies of tribal communities emphasising on the need for viable development programmes to accomplish their wide-range developmental needs.

Chokkaiah, K.,[99] examined the changing nature of the tribal society in the light of the development impact in general and its impact on single Koya tribal community in particularly. He assessed the sequential implications of the developmental activities over the tribal society.

Jain, P.C.,[100] made a classic study on the tribal economy. Globalisation, privatisation etc., are the words, which hurts the feelings of tribal the most. This statement is supported by the author's remarks that there is the danger of exploitation of natural resources prevailing in tribal forest if globalisation is made applicable, irrespective of general as well as agency areas. There is a lurking danger of dislocation of tribal and separation of tribal with the forest and disintegration may occur if the globalisation of tribal economy happens to be implemented. Thus, the author opposes the globalisation of tribal economy.

Prasanna, K., Samal Yespal, S., Topal and Pushpa Pant[101] focused on the development initiatives and their impact on the tribe, depicts that the initiatives, largely, failed to take into account the actual needs of the tribal people who are at the lowest level of socio-economic development and hence, did not achieve the anticipated goals. They identified the problems of the community, locate lacunae in planning and suggest a framework for its sustainable development and they covers the entire tribe including all the families and population in central Himalayan region of India.

Ramulu Vennamalla[102] traced out the causative factors which led the tribal to the present status in the society. He critically evaluated the administration of existing vocational educational programmes for tribal development in Andhra Pradesh. He examined the tribal perceptions on the implementation of vocational education programmes, and suggested measures to overcome the emerging problems for the better implementation of the vocational educational programmes.

Ratha, S.N.,[103] reviewed the tribal development efforts in the state of Odisha and found that the achievements are negligible and uneven. He opined that the tribal development strategy should not be treated as a mere administrative jargon, but it should be related to the organisational values of the tribal community, environment and the community resources.

Sandeep Joshi,[104] highlighted the splendid work done by the Ramakrishna Mission under its Abujhmarh Rural Development Project in Bastar District of Madhya Pradesh, in the fields of education health and malnutrition, economic development, agricultural development and watershed mission etc.

Sastry, V.N.K.V.K.,[105] attempts to enumerate the experiences and explore the prospects in participatory tribal development in Andhra Pradesh.

Venkata Rao, P.,[106] made a comprehensive study on the tribal development with respect to tribal position before and after India's independence. Further a discussion on constitutional safeguards for tribal, protective legislative measures, and planning strategies also figures. The author critically evaluated the structural and organisational factors, the different approaches with respect to participatory planning. An attempt is made to describe the participatory schemes. Further, the vital educative subjects like the role of tribal women in development process, economic reforms, education scenario, the relationship of tribal with forest and development are discussed elaborately.

Dwaruika Nath Padhy[107] did an in-depth study on the role of cooperatives for the development of Tribals in Koraput District of Odisha. This book presents the role of co-operatives in general and a specific of history, trend of growth of co-operatives and tribal development programmes impact on co-operatives with reference to socio-economic development of tribal. Besides, it also highlights the national policies, problems and suggests measures for the existence and viability of co-operative institutions, designed specifically for the welfare of the common man in general and for upliftment of tribes and weaker sections of the society in particular.

Mohanthy, P.K.,[108] conducted a comprehensive survey of the development of primitive tribal groups in India with main thrust on *Lodhas* of West Bengal and Odisha, *Chenchus* of Andhra Pradesh and *Totos* of West Bengal, and detailed in a well-written article regarding several welfare programmes in these regions.

Deepak Kumar Behera and George Pfeffer [109] primarily concentrated on the aspects like structural process, development issues, transition and change.

Ghadoliya, M.K,,[110] examined the infrastructure development programmes in tribal sub-plan area of Udaipur district of Rajasthan.

Mahalati, S., and Gulnar Kapade, M.V.,[111] in their article analysed the various sources of loans and repayment of loans by the ITDP beneficiaries of Dhar district in Madhya Pradesh. The paper is divided into four parts. The first part traces the working structure of ITDP. The main objective and methodology of analysis are discussed in the second part. The third part presents the product analysis of the primary data and the fourth and the last part discusses the findings and offers suggestions based on the findings.

Manis Kumar Singh,[112] deals with the development among the tribal in India in general. The related problems of the people faced and the policies concerning the tribal welfare are also explained.

Musalaiah, Jadi[113] covered the developmental programmes which have been implemented by the government in the sub-plan area of ITDA, Bhadhrachalam. Main discussion and focus is on the schemes like agriculture, education and medical and health. The programmes relating to horticulture, animal husbandry, power, women and child welfare, communication, fisheries, small scale industries, and construction of roads were also discussed.

Musalaish Jadi[114] in his another study examined the historical evolution of tribal development policy in India with a political perspective that involves planning and strategies, adopted in various eras. A blueprint for the administration of tribal areas was first evolved in the British rule which went on to acquire a form of policy in Independent India.

Prasad, L.M.,[115] observed that with the adoption of new strategies for the economic and educational development of SCs and STs during the Sixth Plan, it has now become more important to involve voluntary organisations fully in this gigantic task of tribal development. Voluntary organisations are now coming forward to take up various developmental programmes for the STs. According to the author the decision-making about the type of programmes should be entrusted to such voluntary organisations, so that there may be a clear-cut demarcation of areas of operation between the programmes undertaken by the State Governments and those entrusted to the voluntary organisations to avoid duplication.

Prasad, L.M.,[116] stresses the point that the ethics has greater role to play in tribal administration than in any other administration. This is because of the fact that tribal constitutes a different social group in view of their socio-cultural characteristics and geographical setting. Economically the STs form the lowest strata of the society. A major portion of the STs population is still living below the poverty line. These developmental objectives demand an ethical administration in the tribal areas.

Jagannatha Pati[117] examined the role of media in tribal development in India with particular reference to Jharkhand. He evaluated the social relevance of broadcasting service as viewed by the tribal listeners; it highlighted the opinion of tribal people towards All India Radio (AIR) programming as an educational information entertainment sub-system. He has explored the areas for democratic decentralisation of media and the role of broadcasting media and now it was effectively used for influencing tribal and rural mass in the Southern plateau region of Jharkhand state were about 50 per cent of inhabitants are tribal.

Meenakshi Hooja[118] analysed the changes in approaches, strategies and schemes for tribal development in India over the five year plan periods. The special attention was paid on the problems and achievements of tribal development programmes and administrative arrangements in India's central tribal belt comprising the states of Odisha, Andhra Pradesh, Bihar, Jharkhand, Madhya Pradesh, Chhattisgarh, Gujarat, Maharashtra and Rajasthan that contains nearly three-fourths of the country's tribal population.

Sarit Kumar Chandhuri[119] has made an attempt to evaluate various tribal development schemes implemented for the primitive tribes of West Bengal. It explored multiple constraints for which success remained partial in spite of refinement of tribal development policies in successive five years plans during the post-independence period. Finally it provides some context and specific suggestions which may pave the way for the formulation of realistic action plan for tribal brethren. It is an attempt to identify the nature of constraints in tribal development particularly with reference to primitive tribes of the West Bengal and it suggested a few corrective measures and policy guidelines for future action plan.

Kamal Kishore Sahay[120] made the study based on the structural view of Dhawaipani Village of Gumla District of Jharkhand. He viewed in the perspective of wider process of social change in the life of *Gond* Tribe.

Rajan Kumar Sahoo[121] confined only to *Saura* Tribe. It dealt mainly with economic aspect of the tribes of the non-scheduled areas of Kodala and Polasara blocks from the non-scheduled area of Ganjam district in

Odisha. Keeping in view of the greater concentration of *Sauras*, eight panchayats of both blocks are selected.

Suvendera Jehamani[122] examined the rationale, relevance and efficacy of various development programmes IRDP, NREP, RLEGP, ITDP, DPEP, PDS, and ICDS and adapt towards eradication of poverty with special reference to Kalahandi district of Odisha state.

Vasudeva Rao, B.S.,[123] has done a collection of studies based on field experiences of tribal nature. It presents situation of development programmes and their strengths and weaknesses for further planning and implementation.

Yakaswamy, P.,[124] concentrated to understand the historical and socio-economic problems of the tribal and focuses on the state and central government programmes for the development of tribal. His main thrust of the work is whether the Girijana Cooperative Corporation (GCC) is catering to the need of the tribal and how far the GCCachieved its aims and objectives of the programme and to examine the role of corporation in fulfilling the monetary requirements of the tribal. For this work he chooses the Warangal District of Andhra Pradesh.

Romesh Singh, M.,[125] examined the problems of tribal development in Manipur and explores unrest problems associated with the tribal development process in the state for a larger audience.

Parameswarudu, P., and Salla Ramesh Babu[126] explained the National Rural Employment Guarantee Scheme (NREGS) in the Tribal Areas of Khammam district of Andhra Pradesh, particularly in Bhadrachalam Division and its effects on wage-employment.

Srinivas, L.,[127] explained the work participation rate of tribes in Andhra Pradesh, category of workers in agriculture. He gave special attention to ITDA agricultural programmes and IFAD programmes in Andhra Pradesh.

Subba Rao, N.,[128] has covered the tribes of Andhra Pradesh, nature and characteristics of tribal people, development efforts by government interventions by government and other agencies in Gondipakala village and Araku Vally agency region in Visakhapatnam district, with special reference to Coffee Plantation Programme.

Niranjun Pani and Jitendra Sahoo[129] tried to explore the tribes' problems and to potray the measures for their development. Further a special focus is given on Korput district of Odisha as a micro area study.

The review also confirmed that the tribal sufferings have been intense due to the displacement effect continued from decades and in some places they suffered with second and third time displacement. The effect of the displacement would be further worst if the resettlement strategies yield only partial results. Thus, it is necessary to link the problem of displacement with the rehabilitation strategies. According to Planning Commission Study[130] assessment, nearly ten lakh tribal families got eviction threat due to the various kinds of displacement-It is also of the view that the evaluative studies on the implementation of rehabilitation programmes remain scarce and limited. Hence, the data on these dimensions of harrowing human experience, i.e., displacement remain limited. The non-sensitivity of the governments to build-up the relevant information on such crucial problem also makes the administrative system less functional and respective.

Consequently, increasing protests and militancy among people against the developmental initiations are seen around. Struggles from Narmada Valley to Coastal Kerala, from south Bihar to Thane are part of such occurrences.[131] They are asserting the need to democratise the pattern of development as well as to seek alternatives to them.

However, the situation has changed today as people have become conscious of their problems. When the development plans demonstrated, their non-concern towards displaced persons and against western-interests of not taking consideration of alternatives, also cost-benefit measures, a number of persons from various backgrounds and disciplines, like Academics, Social Scientists, Environmentalists, Anthropologists, Human Right Activists, and Social concerned agencies have shown concern for the human suffering caused by large scale displacement. Individuals and interested social groups started assessing the suffering of the ousters. Several research and voluntary organisations organise seminars and are putting their efforts to make people conscious of the problems of the displacement and rehabilitation and the need for their speedy resettlement.

Tribes in their own internal sphere of thinking feel that this patterns of development which threaten their cultural and social fabric and which seek their "sacrifices" for a 'public good' that is both disputable, and dubious, are fundamentally flaws. Harsud rally on 26th September, 1989 against Narmada Valley Project and a struggle against Baliapal Test Range (Odisha) is giving a message, "We are not against development in the true sense of the term, but only against the so-called development in the name of which vested interests are destroying the country's natural resource base and dislocating the lives of the tribal and rural people".[132] The later had to be shelved in face of the resistance by the local people and nation-wide protest.

There have been a number of suggestions towards formulating appropriate rehabilitation policies. International Agencies like World Bank also have been insisting and mounting pressure on governments to formulate and implement a rehabilitation policy. Because of these pressures, there has been a virtual flurry of policies and even though the "Policy on Tribal displaced by development projects" has been in the process of drafting for the past five years, it is only now that a range of different policies have emerged. Some like the National Thermal Power Company (NTPC) and Coal India Policy (CIP); documents have been prepared with a view to serve as a guiding document across the range of their operations and the operations of their subsidiaries. It is significantly disturbing that, none of the policies have been made available for public debate. Clearly, legislative framework, not ad-hoc patch work, nor more executive generosity, is needed to fashion viable programmes of 'Rehabilitation'.[133] It is in this context the present attempt is undertaken for studying the tribal displacement in Andhra Pradesh, particularly focusing on the major Telangana Tribes predominantly living in the district of Warangal. The tribal communities along with other groups have been subjected to the process of displacement in the recent past as an effect of the few projects undertaken in these areas.

Against this background, the present study is an attempt to investigate the problems of displaced tribal and their rehabilitation with reference to the projects selected for the study such as Gandi Ramaram Reservoir, Parvathagiri Reservoir and Maylaram Reservoir in Warangal district.

Summing Up

This chapter has dealt with the review of the existing literature on the tribal displacement, R&R policy in Andhra Pradesh in particular. All the major contributions of the scholars in the field of tribal development Administration and R&R policy in Andhra Pradesh in particular have been reviewed in this chapter with a view to gain a comprehensive understating on the existing literature related to the topic of the present study.

The review has covered both articles published in all the major journals, books and dissertations related to tribal development administration and tribal displacement, R&R policy in Telangana and also in Andhra Pradesh which are published by eminent scholars and teachers of tribal development administration in India and abroad. It also included some of the doctoral thesis of tribal development administration. The studies pointed out that the poverty, unemployment, illiteracy, lack of political awareness, lack of knowledge, skills and money to invest on productive activities, in-proper utilisation of man power, low standard of working, low productivity of agricultural sector, lack of credit and marketing, less priority to tribal development in national plans, land alienation, bonded labour, social inequalities, malnutrition, deprivation of natural resources, over population etc, are the major problems of the tribal. However, the studies also highlighted that opening of residential ashram schools, involvement of NGOs in the implementation of the developmental programmes, effective implementation of land transfer regulations, irrigation facilities, credit network, enhancing of healthcare facilities and wealth status, rehabilitation of displaced families, providing infrastructural facility, like roads, electricity, housing, watersheds and vocational education programmes enforcement of constitutional rights, establishment of co-operative institutions, preparation of realistic action plans, ensuring democratic decentralisation etc., would improve the socio-economic conditions of the tribal.

The review of literature reveals that the studies focused on tribal living in the scheduled areas and confined to certain states. Hence, there is a need for a specific study on the R&R in Andhra Pradesh in particular with in Andhra Pradesh with special reference to tribal Area at micro level. More and more micro-level studies would bring out the strengths and weaknesses of the policy and programmes. The present study, as mentioned earlier, is essentially empirical in nature.

References

1. Kumar, A., "Tribal Development in India", Sarup & Sons Publications, New Delhi – 2002.
2. Pawan K. Karma, "Cooperative management, Practices, Problems and Prospects" Deep and Deep Publications, New Delhi-1987.
3. Hudson, T. C., "The Primitive Culture of India. The Royal Asiatic Society", London-1922.
4. Hulton, J. H., "Primitive Tribes, in O Malley, L.S.S. (Ed.) Modern India and the west", Oxford University Press, London-1968.
5. Stephen Fuchs, "The Aboriginal Tribes of India", The MacMillan, India, Delhi-1973.
6. Dalton, E. T., "Descriptive Ethnology of Bengal", Government of Bengal, Calcutta-1872.
7. Guha, B. S., "The Aboriginal Races of India", Science and culture, Vol. 4, No.12 1939. "Indian Aborigines and Their Administration", Journal of Asiatic Society, Vol.17, No.1, 1951, pp. 19-44.
8. Mamoria, C.B., "Tribal Demography in India", Kitab Mahal, Allahabad-1957; "Tribes in India their Classification", the Modern Review, Vol.150, No. 4, 1957, pp. 278-283.
9. Sengupta, P.N., "The Aborigines, Their Nutrition and Welfare" Bulletin of the Bihar Tribal Research Institute, Vol.1, No.1, 1959, pp. 56-66.
10. (a) Vidyarthy L.P. (ed), "Anthropology and Tribal Welfare in India", Council of Social and Cultural Research, Bihar, 1959.
    (b) Vidyarthy, L.P., "Rise of Anthropology in India" (two Volumes), Concept Publishing Co., Delhi-1978.
    (c) Vidyarthy, L.P., and B. K. Roy, "The Tribal Culture of India", Concept Publishing Company, Delhi-1976.
11. Ghurye, G.S., "The Scheduled Tribes", Popular Prakashan, 3rd revised edition, Bombay - 1963.
12. Ambastha, N.K., "A Critical study of the Tribal Education", S. Chand, Delhi-1969.
13. Bhowmick, K.L., "Tribal India, A Profile in Indian Ethnology", The Word Press, Calcutta-1971.
14. (a) Bose, N.K., "Tribal Life in India", National Book Trust, New Delhi - 1971;
    (b) Bose, N.K., "Some Indian Tribes", National Book Trust, New Delhi - 1972.

15. Ashok Ranjan Basu, "Tribal Development Programmes and Administration of India", National Book Organisation, the Mail, Shimla - 1985.

16. Dube, S.C., "Tribal Heritage of India (in IV volumes)", Vikash Publishing House, New Delhi - 1977.

17. Sharma, B.D., "Tribal Development-Concept and the Frame", Prachi Publications, New Delhi-1978.

18. Bhowmick, P.K., "Reports on Scheduled Tribes, An Appraisal, in L.P. Vidyarthi (Ed.,), "Tribal Development and its Administration", Concept Publishing Company, New Delhi - 1986, p. 49.

19. Varrier Elwin, "Leaves from the Jungle: Life in a Gond Village, OUP Bombay - 1958.

20. Radha Krishna Murth, A., "Tribal Economy in the Andhra Agency (An Appraisal of Planned Development)", Department of Indian Institution of Economics, Osmania University, Hyderabad – 1967.

21. Raghavaiah, V., "Tribal Revolts, Nellore: Andhra Rashtra Adimajathi Sevak Sangh, 1971.

22. Kulakarni, M.G., "Problems of Tribal Development- A Case Study" Parimal Prakashna, Aurangabad – 1974.

23. Muthayya, B.C. and Mathur, J.S., Existing Socio-Economic condition and attitudes to the present life situations of the residents of Ramachandrapuram New Settlement, NIRD, Hyderabad -1974.

24. Ramaia, P., "Tribal Economy in Telangana – with special Reference to the Warangal district (A Case Study)", Ph.D., Thesis; Department of Economics, Kakatiya University, Warangal - 1980.

25. Ramaia, P., "Issues in Tribal Development", Caugh Publications, Allahabad - 1988.

26. Janardhan Rao, B., "Land Alienation in Tribal Areas - A Micro Study", M. Phil., Dissertation, Department of Public Administration, Kakatiya University, Warangal - 1981.

27. Janardhan Rao, B., "Land Alienation in tribal Areas – A Study", Kakatiya School of Public Administration, Warangal-1987.

28. Janardhan, Rao B., and Sreenivasa Reddy B., Indian Tribes – from Impoverishment to Starvation - A Note on Development Logic, A Paper submitted to a Seminar on "Starvation and Society", New Delhi, 17th December, 1994.

29. Suryanarayana, M., and Gangadharam, V., Chenchus and Development Programmes, in Chaudhary, B. (Ed.), "Tribal Development in India: Problems and Prospects", Inter India Publication, New Delhi – 1982, pp. 247-251.

30. Somasekha, A., "Economic Conditions of Tribal – A Case study of Koyas of Godavari Valley", Ph.D. Thesis, Department of Economics, Osmania University, Hyderabad – 1983.

31. Ajit K. Singh, "Tribal Development in India", Classical Publications, New Delhi-1984.
32. Rajagopal, "Agricultural Labour in Tribal Areas", Kurukshetra, Vol. 34, No.4, January 1986, pp. 17-18, 24.
33. Joshi, Vidyut, Submerging Villages - Problems and Prospects, Ajanta Publications -Delhi, 1987.
34. Narsing Rao, "Impact of Tribal Development Programmes – A Case Study of Adilabad District", M.Phil., dissertation, Department of Economic, Osmania University, Hyderabad – 1987.
35. Ranga Reddy, M., "Development of Education among Tribes in Andhra Pradesh Namely Visakhapatnam and Mahabubnagar", Ph.D. Thesis, Department of Education, Osmania University Hyderabad – 1987.
36. Lokayan, Special Report on Srisailam Dam Oustees, Telugu Version, Hyderabad Book Trust, Hyderabad, May, 1985.
37. Lokayan Bulletin, Special Issue on Displacement, and Rehabilitation, Vol.11, No.5, March-April, 1995.
38. Agnihotri, S.K., "Administration in a Tribal Area: Behavioural Aspects", IJPA, Vol. 34, Jan-March, New Delhi - 1988, pp. 112-118.
39. Alvares, Claude and Billory, Ramesh, Damming the Narmada - India's Greaters Planned Environmental Disaster, Third World Network/Appen, Malaysia - 1988.
40. Cernea, Michael, M., "Involuntary Resettlement in Development Projects-Policy Guidelines in World Bank Financed Projects," Washington D.C. - 1988.
41. Kanchan Roy, Educational and Health Problems in Tribal Development: A Study on National Integration, Concept Publications, New Delhi – 1989.
42. Report of the Working Group on "Development and Welfare of Scheduled Tribes during Eight Five Year Plan, 1990-95", Ministry of Welfare, Government of India, New Delhi - 1989.
43. Reddy, Muthyam and Narsimha Reddy, "Development, Displacement and Rehabilitation – The Andhra Pradesh Experience", paper presented at the 8th Andhra Pradesh Economic Annual Conference, Hyderabad - 1990.
44. Soma Satyanarayana, "Banking for the Development of Weaker Sections – A Micro Level Study of Lambada Tribal in Warangal District", M.Phil Dissertation, Department of Economics, Kakatiya University, Warangal-1990.
45. Vaswani, Kalpana, Dhagamwar, Vasudha and Thukral, Enakshi Ganguli, The Land Acquisition Act and You, MARG, New Delhi - 1990.
46. Shantha Kumari, K., "Tribal Women and Development – A Study of Welfare Administration", M.Phil Dissertation, Department of Public Administration and HRM, Kakatiya University, Warangal –1991.

47. Marianna, Ch, "Changing Agrarian Patterns of Tribal Communities – A Study". M.Phil dissertation, Department of Economics. Kakatiya University, Warangal-1991.

48. Alexander, K.C., Jahangir, M.P., and Prasad, R.R., "Tribal Rehabilitation and Development", Rawat Publication, New Delhi-1991.

49. Fernandes, Walter and Thukral, Emikshiganguly (Ed.), "Development, Displacement and Rehabilitation - Issues for a National Debate", Indian Social Institute, New Delhi - 1989.

50. Fernandes. Walter, "Power and Powerlessness: Development Projects and Displacement of Tribal". Social Action, July-September, New Delhi -1991.

51. Fernandes, Walter, et.al., "Development, Displacement and Rehabilitation in the Tribal Areas of Odisha", Indian Social Institute. New Delhi - 1992.

52. Fernandes, Walter (Ed.,), "National Development kind Tribal Deprivation", Indian Social Institute, New Delhi - 1992.

53. Hamendorf, C.V.F., "Tribes of India", Oxford University Press, New Delhi - 1991.

54. Marianna, Ch., "Changing Agrarian Pattern of Tribal Communities – A Study", M.Phil Dissertation, Department of Economics, Kakatiya University, Warangal - 1991.

55. Shantha Kumari, K., "Tribal Women and Development – A Study of Welfare Administration", M.Phil Dissertation. Department of Public Administration and HRM, Kakatiya University, Warangal - 1991.

56. Viegas. Philip, "Encroached and Enslaved - Alienation of Tribal Lands and its dynamics". Indian Social Institute, New Delhi - 1991.

57. Mahapatra, L.K., Development for Whom? Depriving the Dispossessed Tribal, Social Action, Vol. 41, No. 3. July-Sep. 1991, pp. 270-287.

58. Amir Hasan, "Tribal Development in India – An Appraisal". Print House, Lucknow- 1992.

59. Chalam. K.S.R.V.S, *et. al.*, Report of the Concurrent Evaluation of Resettlement and Rehabilitation Plan under Sriram Sagar (LMD) Project, Centre for Economic and Social Studies (CESS). Hyderabad - 1992.

60. Dogra, Bharat, "The Debate on Large Dams". Paschim Vihar, New Delhi - 1992.

61. Jai Prakash Jha, "Food Distribution in Tribal Area: A Case Study", Yojana, May 15, Vol. 36, No. 5. New Delhi -1992, pp. 7-12.

62. Singh, Mridula and Samantray, Ranjan Kumar, "Whatever happened to Muddavat Chenna? The Tale of Nargarjuna Sagar" in Enakshi Ganguli Thukral (Ed.,) "Big Dams Displaced People - Rivers of Sorrow, Rivers of Change". Sage Publications, New Delhi - 1992.

63. Bhowmic, P.K., "Dynamics of Tribal Development". Inter India Publication, New Delhi - 1993.

64. Bhowmic, P.K., "Tribal and Sustainable Development", Kalpaz Publications, New Delhi – 2005.

65. Morse Bradford, and Berger Thomas, "Sardar Sarover – The Report of the Independent Review", Resource Futures International, (on the Narmada Dam), Chapter 17, June 18, Ottawa, Canada - 1992.

66. Harshad Tribedi, "Planning and Tribal Development", Routledge - 1993.

67. Mrinal Miri, "Continuity and Change in Society", Indian Institute of Advanced Study, Shimla – 1993.

68. Thippani Krishna Murthy, "Social Forestry and Tribal Development – A Study of Alternative Policies of Forest Regeneration", Ph.D Thesis, Department of Public Administration and HRM, Kakatiya University, Warangal - 1993.

69. Deogaonkar, S.G., "Tribal Administration and Development with Ethnographic profiles of Selected Tribes", Concept Publishing Company, New Delhi -1994.

70. Gupta, L.P., "Administration for educational development of Tribes – A Study of Female Students in Darjeeling", Classical Publishing Company, New Delhi -1994.

71. Singh, C.P., "Tribal Development Administration: A Case Study", Mittal Publications, New Delhi – 1994.

72. Tyson, John, Review of Resettlement and Rehabilitation implementation arrangements in Mahabubnagar District and the Jurala Project Area, Centre for Economic and Social Studies, (CESS), Hyderabad - 1994.

73. Behera, M.C., "Planning and Socio-Economic Development of the tribal", Commonwealth Publishers, New Delhi – 1994.

74. Hymavathi, Y., "Role of Tribal Women in Development- A Micro Level Study in Nalgonda district", "M.Phil Dissertation, Department of Economics, Kakatiya University, Warangal - 1994.

75. Patkar, Medha, Towards a National Allience of Right to life, National Working Group on Displacement, Rashtriya Mukthyalaya, Gandhi Bhavan, Gujarat - 1994.

76. Raman Rao, V., "Impact of Economic Support Programmes of Scheduled Castes, Scheduled Tribes and Backward Class Cooperative Finance Corporations in Andhra Pradesh", Ph.D. Thesis, Department of Economics, Osmania University, Hyderabad – 1994.

77. Ramesh Munigela, "Socio-Economic Conditions of Primitive Tribal Groups – A Study with Special Reference to Kolams", M.Phil dissertation, Department of Economics, Kakatiya University, Warangal-1994.

78. Upadhyay, V.S., "Developmental Resettlement of People affected by the Subernarekha Multipurpose Project", Indian Institute of Technology, New Delhi - 1994.

79. Upadhyay. V.S, "Alternative models for Tribal Development", Journal of Rural Development, Vol. 19(4) NIRD, Hyderabad-2000.

80. Commissioner for Scheduled Castes and Scheduled Tribes, 28th Report of the Commissioner for Scheduled Castes and Scheduled Tribes, New Delhi - 1995.

81. Sharma, B.D., "New Education Policy and the Tribal People", IJPA, Vol. 33, No. 3, July-Sept, New Delhi – 1986.

82. Sharma, B.D., "Globalisation, the Tribal Encounters", Har Anand Publication, New Delhi - 1995.

83. Suresh Lal, B., "Rural-Urban Migration of Tribal Labour: A Case Study of Tribal Rickshaw Pullers in Warangal District", M.Phil Dissertation, Department of Economics, Kakatiya University, Warangal-1995.

84. Laxmaiah, P., "Consumption Patterns of Tribal Households – A Case Study of Chenchus in Mahabubnagar District of Andhra Pradesh", Ph.D. Thesis, Department of Economics, Osmania University, Hyderabad – 1996.

85. Kothari, Smitu, "Whose Nation is It: The Displaced as Victims of Development," Economic and Political Weekly, Vol. XXXI, No. 24 June 15, 1996, pp. 1476-1483.

86. Bhandari, J.S., and Subhadra Channa, "Tribes and Government Policies", Cosmo Publications, New Delhi -1997.

87. Mamillapally, Vijay Kumar, "Tribal development Programmes Utilisation Patterns among Chenchus under ITDA in Mahabubnagar District, Andhra Pradesh: An Evaluation Study", Ph.D. Thesis, Department of Sociology, Osmania University, Hyderabad – 1997.

88. Sreenivasa Reddy, B., "Displacement and Rehabilitation of Telangana Tribes – A Study of Welfare Governance", M.Phil Dissertation, Department of Public Administration and HRM, Kakatiya University, Warangal – 1997.

89. Lachaiah, N., "Tribal Development in Andhra Pradesh – A study in Social Geography", M.Phil Dissertation, Department of Geography, Osmania University, Hyderabad – 1998.

90. Ravinder, G., "Development Institutions and Tribal Transformations – A Study", Ph.D Thesis, Department of Political Science, Kakatiya University, Warangal – 1998.

91. Chakrabarty, G., "Scheduled Castes and Scheduled Tribes in Rural Andhra Pradesh, their Education, Health Status and Income", Journal of Rural Development, Vol. 18, No.2, NIRD, Hyderabad-1999.

92. Veeranna, G., "Tribal Political Leadership in Andhra Pradesh – A Study", Ph.D Thesis, Department of Political Science, Kakatiya University, Warangal -1999.

93. Bhupinder Singh, "Need to uphold Tribal Values in the new Jharkhand State", Journal of Rural Development, Vol. 19, No. 4, NIRD, Hyderabad-2000.

94. Mohanthy, P.K, "Development of Scheduled Castes and Scheduled Tribes in independent India: Leads and Lags", Journal of Rural Development, Vol. 19, No.4, NIRD, Hyderabad-2000.

95. Shayam Nand Singh, "Impact of Reservation Policies for Tribal in India", Journal of Rural Development, Vol. 19, No.4, NIRD, Hyderabad-2000.

96. Sankaran, S.R." Welfare of Scheduled Cates and Scheduled Tribes in Independent India- An overview of State Policies and Programmes", Journal of Rural Development, Vol. 19, No.4, 2000, NIRD, Hyderabad – 2000, pp. 507-534.

97. Srivastava, B.N, "Working of the Constitutional Safeguards and Protective Measures for the Scheduled Castes and Scheduled Tribes," Journal of Rural Development, Vol. 19, No. 4, NIRD, Hyderabad-2000.

98. Ashutosh Thakur, "Tribal Development and its paradoxes", Authors Press, Delhi – 2001.

99. Chokkaiah, K., "Tribes and Development Institutions A Case Study", M.Phil Dissertation, Department of Public Administration and HRM, Kakatiya University, Warangal – 2001.

100. Jain, P.C., "Globalisation and Tribal Economy" Rawat Publication, Jaipur - 2001

101. Prasanna, K. Samal, Yespal, S., Topal and Pushpa Pant, "Retrospective and Prospective Analysis of Development of Rajis:a Primitive Mountain tribe in Indian Central Himalaya", Journal of Rural Development, Vol. 20, No.1, NIRD, Hyderabad – 2001.

102. Ramulu Vennamalla, "Administration of Vocational Educational Programmes for Tribal Development in Andhra Pradesh", Ph.D. Thesis, Department of Public Administration, Osmania University, Hyderabad-2001.

103. Ratha, S.N, "Welfare of the Scheduled Tribes and Their Development: the Odisha Case", Journal of Rural Development, Vol. 20, No.1, NIRD, Hyderabad – 2001.

104. Sandeep Joshi, "Role of Voluntary Organisations in Tribal Development – A Case Study of Abujhmarh Rural Development Project in Madhya Pradesh, Journal of Rural Development, Vol. 20, No.1, NIRD, Hyderabad – 2001.

105. Sastry, V.N.K.V.K., "Participatory Tribal Development in Andhra Pradesh - Experiences and prospects", Journal of Rural Development, Vol. 20, No.1, NIRD, Hyderabad – 2001.

106. Venkata Rao, P., "Tribal Development Policy and Practice", Sarup & Sons, New Delhi – 2001.

107. Dwarika Nath Padhy, "Role of Co-Operatives for Tribal development", Mohit Publications, New Delhi – 2002.

108. Mohanty, P.K., "Development of Primitive Tribal Groups in India", Kalpaz Publications, Delhi – 2002.

109. Deepak Kumar Behera and George Pfeffer, "Contemporary Society, Tribal Studies", Concept Publishing Company, New Delhi -2002.

110. Ghadoliya, M.K., "Infrastructure Development Program in Tribal Sub-Plan area in Rajastan". Quoted in Musalaiah Jadi, "Tribal Development Policy: Implementation and Impact – A Study of Bhadrachalam ITDA in Andhra Pradesh", Ph.D Thesis, Department of Political Science, Osmania University, Hyderabad -2003.

111. Mahalati, S., and Gulnar Kapade, M.V., "Repayment of Loand by Integrated Tribal Development Projects (ITDA) Beneficiaries", Quoted in Musalaiah Jadi, "Tribal Development Policy: Implementation and Impact – A Study of Bhadrachalam ITDA in Andhra Pradesh", Ph.D Thesis, Department of Political Science, Osmania University, Hyderabad -2003.

112. Manish Kumar Singh, "Tribal Development problems and Prospects" 1991 Quoted in Musalaiah Jadi, "Tribal Development Policy: Implementation and Impact – A Study of Bhadrachalam ITDA in Andhra Pradesh", Ph.D Thesis, Department of Political Science, Osmania University, Hyderabad -2003.

113. Musalaiah Jadi, "Tribal Development Policy" Implementation and Impact – A Study of Bhadhrachalam ITDA in Andhra Pradesh", Ph.D. Thesis, Department of Political Science, Osmania University, Hyderabad – 2003

114. Musalaiah, Jadi, "Evolution of Tribal Development Policy in India", South Asian Journal of Socio-Political Studies (SAJOSPS), Vol. 8 No. 2, Jan-June-2008.

115. Prasad, L.M., "Voluntary Agencies for Development Scheduled Castes and Scheduled Tribes- Their Role and Functions". IJPA, Vol. 33, No. 3, New Delhi -1987, pp. 588-612.

116. Prasad, L.M., "Ethics in Tribal Administration". Quoted in Musalaiah Jadi, "Tribal Development Policy: Implementation and Impact – A Study of Bhadrachalam ITDA in Andhra Pradesh", Ph.D Thesis, Department of Political Science, Osmania University, Hyderabad -2003.

117. Jagannath Pati, "Media and Tribal Development", Concept Publishing Company, New Delhi – 2004.

118. Meenakshi Hooja, "Policies and Strategies for Tribal Development – Focus on the central tribal belt", Rawat Publications, New Delhi – 2004.

119. Sarit Kumar Chaudhuri, "Constraints of Tribal Development", Mittal Publications, New Delhi – 2004.

120. Kamal Kishore Sahay, "Development of Gond Tribes in Modern Perspective (A Sociological Study)", Classical Publishing Company, New Delhi – 2005.

121. Rajan Kumar Sahoo, "Tribal Development in India", Mohit Publications, New Delhi – 2005.

122. Suvendra Jehamani, "Poverty and under Development in Tribal Areas – A Geographical Analysis", Concept Publishing Company, New Delhi – 2005.

123. Vasudeva Rao, B.S., "Tribal Developmental studies", the Associated Publishers, Ambala Cantt – 2005.

124. Yakaswamy, P., "Organisation and Working of Girijan Cooperative Corporation – A Case Study", M.Phil Dissertation, Department of Public Administration and HRM, Kakatiya University, Warangal – 2005.

125. Romesh Singh, M., "Tribal Development in 21st Century an Experience from Manipur", Mittal Publications, New Delhi, 2006.

126. Parameswarudu, P., and Salla Ramesh Babu, "Economic Development Schemes of Tribes", Seminar on Tribal Development in Andhra Pradesh, Issues and Challenges, Andhra Pradesh Economic Association with collaboration of Government Degree and Post Graduate College, Bhadhrachalam, on 9th September 2007.

127. Srinivas, L., "Agriculture and Tribal Development in Andhra Pradesh", Seminar on Tribal Development in Andhra Pradesh, Issues and Challenges, Andhra Pradesh Economic Association with collaboration of Government Degree and Post Graduate College, Bhadhrachalam, on 9th September 2007.

128. Subba Rao, N., "Tribal Development in Andhra Pradesh: Need for effective Interventions by Government and other Agency", Seminar on Tribal Development in Andhra Pradesh, Issues and Challenges, Andhra Pradesh Economic Association with collaboration of Government Degree and Post Graduate College, Bhadhrachalam, on 9th September 2007.

129. Niranjan Pani and Jitendra Sahoo, "Tribal Development", Mahamaya Publishing House, New Delhi - 2008.

130. Planning Commission, The Third Five Year Plan, Government of India, New Delhi - 1961.

131. Kothari, Smitu, op.cit.

132. Alvares, Claude and Billoiy, Ramesh, op.cit.

133. Kothari, Smithu, "Developmental Displacement and Official Policies –A Critical Review", Lokayan Bulletin, Special Issue, March-April, Delhi - 1995.

Chapter 3

Development and Displacement of Scheduled Tribes in India

The popular paradigm of development has ruled the whole post-War discourse irrespective of the cultural, social and political ideologies of the nations, each one aspired to run past this race of development, unfortunately, six decades later, we are as near to the goal as to a mirage. In the process every effort and every sacrifice is justified unless the horizon of development stops receding. Not only this, today the goal itself is showing cracks, is crumbling and stands like a ruin in the intellectual landscape. The delusion and disappointment around the much hyped notions of development, in the long run, only echoed: it did not work. The conditions which catapulted the idea have vanished; the hopes and desires are exhausted, rendering it obsolete and outdated. However, the miscellany of the idea still dominates the social, economic and political discourses equally in official declarations and the grassroots.[1] In this chapter an attempt is made to question this very structure of the dominant paradigm, "development".

The established perception of development has been nothing more than a myth, a misconceived enterprise or a fantasy devoid of any reasonable conclusions, what is required is to come out of these imaginary credos and take on the real challenges faced by humanity, because adherence to an outmoded approach, (based on the concept that whatever is big, capital-intensive, modern and industrial is best) can lead to incalculable and irreparable loss to humanity. The notion of increased production and creation of growth, against a background of national (Government) interest and security, with intention to develop the society as a whole focus primarily on those having land, collateral and resources to invest, and all this at the cost of disadvantaged and poor in the society. The resources are extracted by the elites of the society and those who are "resource poor" have no involvement in this process and the so called "development" have not impinged much on their lives than being harmful and taking away the little they had, and in the process reducing them to "objects" of development.[2] They are lamented as "what one might call 'people in the way of progress' having to move to make way for, and suffer for, the kind of infrastructural development that is, for many people, the hallmark of progress. It is seen as unfortunate, but nevertheless as expedient, 'for the sake of nation', that some should suffer".[3]

Historically, the idea of "development" has been mostly materialistic and objective and with all the responsible instruments combined together to bring about development the mankind is still groping in the dark for the ideal set up for the same. The mankind, unable to withstand the onslaught of the fast-paced, factory-loving industrial civilisation which exploited and tried to enslave nature and men alike, in the emerging paradigm shift, favour, well meaning individuals and communities, patriotic and global identities and relations, helping to live in harmony with nature and to live without impoverishing or endangering future generations, what has come to be known as sustainable development. This is the beginning of the larger debate of whether the dominant perception is put to rest? Has the new turn percolated to popular perception? Does peoples participation (as in case of Narmada Bachao Andolan) has brought any change in the dominant paradigm?

The present chapter tries to understand that whether the paradigm shift has actually exposed the inability of the established notions of development to answer the larger economic, social, political and ethical questions? Or there is need of a holistic approach to the whole discourse of development; moreover, examines why the policy ideals could never be actualised in letter and spirit, rather created a gulf between policy on paper and in practice, besides alienating the poor from the developmental process? Moreover, the role of democracy as a political system has been neglected and missed the attention of the social scientists, anthropologist and the activists alike in this whole debate. To what extent do democratic processes, decentralisation of power and Local Self Governance, reach to the vulnerable and marginalised section of the society becomes imperative to dwell irrespective of the political ideologies. The answer to which could help in countering the blind run to "materialistic development", (wherein, virtually, every development project has dispelled people from their living for the advantage of only some compartments (usually the resourceful) of the society) and to understand the phenomenon in its totality.

The present chapter does not confine and nor is limited to the raging impact of an awful project like Sardar Sarovar Dam (it none the less is one) or the despair and despondency caused by the displacement or the failure to address the issues of resettlement, rehabilitation and reparation of the displaced. The irony is that there are numerous clones of Sardar Sarovar, (nearly 4500 big and small) besides the multifaceted and multidimensional predicaments of development.

As any evasion of a problem would lead, problems that development has created have also multiplied faces and dimensions over time. Today the problem is not confined to construction of dams or industries per se; rather different genres altogether are in vogue. To illustrate a few, the distributive policies, increase in heights of dams, careless mining induced by industrialisation, unplanned urban settlements vis-à-vis natural disasters, mega infrastructural projects like the national road quadrangle and the river interlinking, besides, globalisation and privatisation as contemporary manifestations of mainstream development are put under the scanner in this chapter.

Development, or a version of it, is creating disadvantaged people. Even as it creates wealth for a few, it leaves the others with an irreparable sense of loss and impoverishment. And when these people make an attempt at resistance, they inevitably come into conflict with the law. Already marginalised, they are further faced with the daunting task of facing up to state power, reinforced by 'wealth out to create more of it' and lastly by a politically articulate community comprising mostly of an educated, urbanite middle class impregnated with the rhetoric; whereof 'development', synonymous with 'progress' and 'modernisation' is the panacea for all the ills of the third world.

This chapter made an attempt to view the development debate from the angle of real people, the ones, who actually bear its 'real costs' till long after the matter has settled for the rest and also touch upon its legal, social and environmental ramifications. For most part, the problem has been studied through the eyeglass of a few big projects and the violence wrought in their wake. The chapter also briefly looks at the larger canvas, of which the abovementioned is but a small part, namely the processes of development in their entirety.

The feasibility of the seminally western paradigm of development that has inexorably affected the entire third world, has been question marked since the last couple of decades. But the contagion, it seems, has deep-roots, and in spite of its very fundamentals under attack and the west having realised its inherent negativity and having put in place proscriptions of development, the developing world is almost fatalistically falling into the very same trap. About a decade ago, the world community came up with alternatives to the prevalent model, suggesting designs that shifted the emphasis away from the 'economic' dimension of development. The alternative visions; 'sustainable' and 'social development' effectively challenged (still to do that in praxis) the supremacy of the economic growth model. Ironically the developed west was more than welcoming of the idea, whereas the third world, though instrumental in its very first propositions, is still bereft of any examples of its effective application. One of the many reasons could be a cynical, yet reasonable apprehension on the part of the developing world that the rich apparently relieved of the threat from the poor have now very conveniently realised the extent of environmental depredation and very much aware of the consequent threat to their own well being would be tempted to resolve it at the poor's expense. [4]

The Notion of Development: An Epistemological Clash

Development refers to economic, socio-political processes and cultural processes of change in human societies. Development from the foregoing conclusion would then amount to a realisation of human potential. And furthermore the juxtaposition of human rights with development implies that it is something that can be identified, measured and implemented. Antony N. Allot invented the 'General Felicity Index (GFI)', according to which the measure of development is directly proportional to the measure of felicity of the individual. One measures 'not just the increase in the number of factories or expansion of services, but whether life is happier and more fruitful and enjoyable for the individual. In doing so one has to balance one factor against another."[5]

Underdevelopment on the other hand is a series of complex interacting phenomena, resulting in flagrant inequalities of wealth and poverty, stagnation, a relative backwardness when compared with other countries, production facilities which fail to progress to the required standards, economic, cultural, political and technological dependence.[6] Further questions: Does development always mean the same thing to all parties? And most important and fundamental, the question of whether or not the consequences of the processes set off by the dominant paradigm could be acceptable as 'progression' towards the aforementioned object for its subjects. The questions are many, the answers not too forthcoming; but one aspect is more or less resolved: the need for a change in the dominant paradigm. And modalities for the same are underway; yet there remain serious and longstanding conflicts posited by the old paradigm, if I may wishfully call it so. These crises, it is now firmly believed, spawned, not out of a misguided application; but their causes lie rooted in the political, economic and as a corollary, the epistemological underpinnings of the dominant paradigm.

The dominant paradigm of 'development', a direct continuation of the 500 years of colonial history, is predicated on a belief in the superiority of the West, of western knowledge, and western technology and of western civilisation as a whole.[6] After the Second World War and the decolonisation process, the direct financial responsibility of maintaining colonial administrations was replaced by minuscule aid programmes, managed by new administrative organisations. Both economic and political interests were at stake, which is why development aid was deployed as a means in the struggle for world hegemony by the western powers. This important aspect of the power struggle between the 'first' and 'second' world; one that generated 'violence' in the 'third' world was largely hidden from the view of western citizens who lent their support to post-war development projects through their taxes and gifts. Ironically, the so called 'cold war' became the basis for the maintenance of peace and welfare on that side of the earth, while the competition for development clients in the 'third world' led to a series of 'hot wars' here. This struggle for world hegemony was euphemistically referred to as development cooperation.[6]

The above mentioned proposition could also be used for an exposition of the conceptualisations supplied by the two major paradigms that have dominated the field; namely the 'dependency theory' and the 'modernisation theory'. The first theory argues that the sources of underdevelopment are to be found in the history and structure of the global capitalist system. This theory premises underdevelopment as a product of historical forces and a direct result of the interaction between the hitherto underdeveloped social formations and the forces of western imperialism.[7] The other theory holds that development is an inevitable evolutionary process of increasing societal differentiation that would ultimately produce economic, social and political institutions like those in the west. The outcome, it is claimed would be the creation of a free market system, liberal democratic political institutions, and the 'rule of law'. It is mostly believed that the two theories articulate dichotomous paradigms in the field.

But the outcome predicted by the 'modernisation theory' is only halfway through and with the realisation of its eventual consequences; it seems that the world view is moving towards an alternate vision. Furthermore, if one was to accept the proposition that development rhetoric was used as a mere tool in the heady competition for global hegemony, the 'dependence theory' would in fact substantiate the hitherto acceptance and application of the 'modernisation theory'.

Development rhetoric divides the post-war period into decades, wherein the fifties and sixties constitute the period of the economic and political recovery. Large amounts of capital were injected into third world countries to strengthen their infrastructural sectors so as to facilitate the development of their (multinational) trade and industry. This period was marked by an emphasis in the linear, evolutionary model of modernisation in theory as well as in praxis.[8] By the late sixties and early seventies the optimism of the western 'modernisation theory' of development began to fade in the light of experience gained in the third world. One thing became very clear the development theories based on the western model of economic growth were profoundly inadequate.[9]

The experience in the developing countries showed a polarisation between the poor and self enriching top layer. And therefore focus shifted to the 'poor people' of the third world.[10] But the real consequences of the ostensible shift in policy remained the same as before. Like before, the oligarchies that had captured organs of state continued to enrich and empower themselves as a class relative to the wider society, to whom "development plans" one after the other were offered at a national and subsequently at the global level, as a hope for a 'chimera' like prosperity. The result: the economic benefits of such supposed development have not even trickled down to the vast majorities in the countries that are euphemistically referred to as 'developing'. But the most fundamental loss has been the obstruction of the evolution of the indigenous alternatives for societal self-expression and authentic progress.[11] The dominant model was inherently myopic; its emphasis was on industrialisation, science and technology, ruthless exploitation of natural resources and letting loose of market forces, completely ignoring the cultural and social sensibilities of its subjects. The social aspects of the development debate were highlighted in the early eighties and their importance was underscored at the World Summit on Social Development held in March 1995 at Copenhagen. From the documents arising out of the Summit, it can be inferred that social development by then, had acquired a new and expansive meaning. It was apparently more comprehensive than mere economic development; it subsumed the latter; but it specifically aimed at the attainment of much wider social objectives. Social development in the UN quarters broadly refers to improvements in human well being, brought about by a modification in societal conditions. Development thinking during this period had come to accept people or human centredness as its fulcrum. Social transformation (not to be equated with social differentiation) conducive to eradication of poverty, promotion of productive employment and acceleration of social integration was the key to social development. Policies were to be aimed at reducing and eliminating polarisation of societies, social exclusion, unemployment and poverty and to provide opportunities or the disadvantaged groups to improve their living conditions.[12]

Another very important issue that has almost always been relegated to the background in this whole development discourse since the beginning is its impact on culture and vice versa. The search for a homogenous process of development has been accompanied by a deepening erosion of cultural identities. The western paradigms have adversely affected the cultural distinctiveness of the developing countries and the 'modernised' version of development has succeeded in establishing the hegemony of essentially occidental cultural constructs;[13] which in a cynical vein, is simply a covert and more sophisticated form of imperialism than the prior model; the object of them though still stands; that it is the destiny of the West to civilise and convert the backward peoples of the earth to the truths vouchsafed to the West alone.[14] The issue of obdurate traditions and cultural constructs that resist change are sometimes cited as reasons for the failure of development strategies premised on economic growth. It must however be remembered that not everything in tradition is negative and therefore it would be imprudent to reject tradition as a whole in order to facilitate an alien culture that promotes gross materialism and personal consumption at the cost of social justice.[15] Which by no means is an assertion of the "everything's great about our culture" syndrome but an acceptance of the fact that culture per se has critical functions that development does not offer adequate replacement for, and therefore it cannot be dispensed with to promote growth. In fact, any worthwhile growth would by necessary implication have to take into account relevant cultural factors and coexist with them.

In connection with social development two allied concepts have found mention in the current debate; that of 'human development' and 'sustainable development'. The concept of human development implies people-centred development; a development where people are empowered to make their own choices. It emphasises the relevance of local knowledge and values as guidelines and tools for making these choices thereby equipping people with the requisite knowledge and resources to take charge of their own destinies. Sustainable development on the other hand is its extrapolation into a broader idea as is very aptly and ideally elucidated by the UNDP report, "Sustainable development is development that not only regenerates economic growth but distributes its benefits equitably; that regenerates the environment rather than destroy it; that empowers people rather than marginalising them. It gives priority to the poor, enlarging their choices and opportunities and, providing their participation in decisions affecting them. It is development that is pro-poor, pro-nature, pro-jobs and pro-women and pro-children."[16] A major step in the direction of human development was the articulation and adoption of the Millennium Development Goals (MDGs) by the UN General Assembly in 2000, at a special meeting attended by the 147 heads of state or government.[17]

In theory, the MDGs are the most prominent initiative on the global development agenda and have a great deal in common with human rights commitments. But neither the human rights nor development communities has embraced this linkage with enthusiasm or conviction. In brief, the eight MDGs aim to:

1. Eradicate extreme poverty and hunger;
2. Achieve universal primary education;
3. Promote gender equality and empower women;
4. Reduce child mortality;
5. Improve maternal health;
6. Combat HIV/Aids and other diseases such as malaria;
7. Ensure environmental sustainability; and
8. Develop a global partnership for development.

These goals have sought to record priorities across the development spectrum. If human rights are not seen to be part of that agenda, the rhetoric of the past couple of decades about the integration or mainstreaming of human rights into development efforts will have come to naught.[18]

Attempts to link the human rights approach to development issues, at least within the UN context go back as far as the mid-seventies to the report of Manoucher Ganji on economic, social and cultural rights. The next step was the proclamation of the UN Commission on Human Rights in 1977 of the existence of a right to development. Initially there were hopes that this concept would provide a context in which efforts could be made to investigate the complex links between the two sets of concerns. But the subsequent quarter of century of debates has not produced any tangible results in the quest to link human rights and development. What we have is innumerable speeches, major diplomatic battles over the wording of resolutions and the creation of a UN expert committee followed by a UN governmental working group, followed by an independent expert, followed by a new UN working group. One thing is clear that something is definitely not working.

Within the UN system the spirit of rights based approaches is encapsulated in the "Common Understanding on the Human Rights Based Approach to Development Cooperation," adopted in 2003 at a meeting involving some ten UN agencies and a wide range of other development agencies, which gave an imprimatur of sorts to such analyses. The three main elements of the "Common Understanding" were:[19]

1. All programmes of development cooperation, policies and technical assistance should further realisation of human rights as laid down in the Universal Declaration and other human rights instruments.
2. Human rights standards contained in, and principles derived from, the universal declaration and other international instruments guide all development cooperation and programming in all sectors and in all phases of the programming process.
3. Development cooperation contributes to the development of the capacities of "duty bearers" to meet their obligations and/or of "right holders" to claim their rights.

These formulations do little more than restate the fundamental dilemma and do not actually offer a lot of guidance on a resolution. They are mostly expressed at a level of abstraction (which though not uncharacteristic of the human rights discourse would come across as abstract) untargeted and untested to the development economists. Despite all their sophistication they offer little in respect of applicability in concrete situations and appear to simply gloss over real life complexities which inevitably require hard decision making and trade-offs.[20]

The politics of human rights seems to have inhibited the development of enforcement mechanisms at the international level, although there have been egregious achievements in formulating norms and standards over five decades.

Development projects often involve the introduction of direct control by a developer over the land previously occupied by another group. Natural resource extraction, urban renewal or development programmes, industrial parks, and infrastructure projects (such as highways, bridges, irrigation canals, and dams) all require land, often in large quantity. One common consequence of such projects is the upheaval and displacement of communities. While the literature on development-induced displacement and resettlement is clear in its focus on physical development projects that require land expropriation, these are not the only types of projects that can result in displacement. Conservation programmes, such as wildlife re-introduction schemes and the creation of game parks and bio-diversity zones, also often oust communities. Issues surrounding conservation-induced displacement are dealt with in another thematic research guide. Other types of policies can also induce migration. For example, a distributive policy decision that shifts jobs between two regions might cause some people to move in search of new employment. However, the literature on development-induced displacement and resettlement does not consider these types of policies. The focus is clearly on physical forms of development that require displacement by decree.

In much of the development-induced displacement and resettlement literature, scholars and activists consider development displaces to be those persons who are forced to move as a result of losing their homes to development projects. However, wider considerations of "project-impacted persons" have been advocated. Scudder (1996) suggests that our conception of project-impacted persons should include not only those directly displaced by loss of home, but also the host population that takes in displaces; all others who are neither directly displaced, nor hosts, yet who live in the vicinity of the project; and project immigrants. The latter group includes those tasked with planning, designing, and implementing the project, as well as those who later move to the region to take advantage of project-related opportunities these, Scudder notes, are often beneficiaries of the project, whereas the two former groups are often adversely affected by projects. Similarly, the World Commission on Dams (WCD) report refers not only to physical displacement, but also to livelihood displacement, which deprives people of their means of production and displaces them from their socio-cultural milieu. Mobile groups have been prone to this type of displacement as state and private-sector land demands have sometimes overlapped with the land claimed by these groups for grazing, hunting, migration, and other activities.[21]

Types of Development Projects Causing Displacement

As mentioned in the introduction, the types of development projects causing displacement range across a wide spectrum. For the purposes of this research guide, these types of projects have been divided into three categories: dams, urban renewal and development, and natural resource extraction. Table 3.1, composed of data from the World Bank Environment Departments (WBEDs) report, gives a breakdown by cause of displacement of the distribution of people displaced by World Bank projects active in 1993. While these figures are likely indicative of broader trends, it is worth remembering that displacement in Bank-assisted projects accounts for only a fraction of the estimated global total about three per cent of global dam displacement and one per cent of global displacement from urban and transportation projects.

Table 3.1: Distribution of Displaces by cause of Displacement in World Bank Projects active in 1993 with Resettlement

Sl. No.	*Cause*	*Projects*	*Per cent*	*People*	*Per cent*
1.	Dams, irrigation, canals	46	31.5	1,304,000	66.4
2.	Urban infrastructure, water supply, sewerage, transportation	66	45.2	443,000	22.6
3.	Thermal (including mining)	15	10.3	94,000	4.8
4.	Other	19	13.0	122,000	6.2
Total		**146**	**100**	**1,963,000**	**100**

Source: World Bank Environment Departments Report, 1996.

Dams

Of the types of development projects that bring about physical displacement, dams and their related infrastructure, including power stations and irrigation canals, stand out as the largest contributor to displace. This is partially a product of the enormous scale of many dam projects China's Danjiangkou Dam displaced 383,000 people, while its ongoing Three Gorges Dam project will displace 1.2 million. The high overall level of dam displacement is also a product of the speed with which dams have been built since 1950. The International Commission on Large Dams (ICOLD) reports that the world had 5,000 large dams in 1950 and over 45,000 by the late 1990s.

The WBEDs has calculated that roughly 40 per cent of development-induced displacement every year over four million people is a result of dam projects. Over the range of projects assisted by the World Bank, 63 per cent of involuntary displacement and resettlement occurs in dam projects. Overall estimates of dam displacement over the latter half of the twentieth century range between 30 and 80 million people. As with the figures for overall development-induced displacement, these estimates often do not cover the full extent of displacement outside dam and reservoir sites.

The literature on large dams and their economic, environmental, and social impacts is vast. Mc Cully's book (2001) and the WCD report (2000) provide comprehensive overviews of the impacts of large dam projects, including direct displacement and resettlement, but also other impacts that could lead to indirect displacement. These include: the inundation of valuable farmland and animal habitat; the capturing of sediment by dams, leading to erosion and soil degradation downstream; the endangerment of freshwater habitats, leading to the extinction or threatening of reverence and wetland life forms; reservoir-induced seismicity; the spread of diseases by insects that thrive in stagnant reservoir water; and environmental destruction and human death as a result of dam failure or collapse. The report by Bartolome *et al.* (2000), prepared to inform the WCD report-writing process, offers a comprehensive discussion of recent practices concerning the displacement, resettlement, rehabilitation, and development of people adversely affected by dam projects. It also suggests a number of ways to improve accountability and facilitate negotiation in future resettlement schemes.

Case studies of dam projects dominate the literature on development-induced displacement. While only a few are listed here, many more are listed in other sections of this research guide. The volume edited by Picciotto, Van Wicklin, and Rice (2001) includes six case studies of dam displacement and resettlement, including that in the Upper Krishna Project in India, the Shuikou and Yantan dam projects in China, the Pak Mun Dam Project in Thailand, the Kedung Ombo Dam Project in Indonesia, the Itaparica Dam in Brazil, and the Nangbeto Dam in Togo. The WCD website provides online access to countless case studies of dam projects throughout the world, many of which have involved displacement and resettlement. International Rivers Network (IRN), and its regular publication World Rivers Review (WRR), are good sources of news on dam and water infrastructure projects and their impacts on people and the environment.[22]

Global Overview

No precise data exists on the number of persons affected by development-induced displacement throughout the world. Unlike for refugees and internally displaced persons (IDPs), there are no institutions or publications dedicated to tracking overall development-induced displacement and resettlement, either at the global or national levels. For an indication of magnitude, most scholars, policy-makers, and activists rely on the WBEDs estimate that roughly 10 million people are displaced each year due to dam construction, urban development, and transportation and infrastructure programmes. This number is shockingly high, but it still fails to account for large numbers of the displaced. As pointed out in the introduction, displacement tallies almost always refer only to persons physically ousted from legally acquired land in order to make way for the planned project, ignoring those living in the vicinity of or downstream from, projects, whose livelihoods and socio-cultural milieu might be adversely affected by the project. A count that considers this wider conception of development induced displacement would be much higher than the WBED's estimate. Furthermore, the global count of displaces would increase with a consideration of displacement stemming from development projects other than those included in the WBED's count, such as natural resource extraction projects.

While no statistics is available on the geographical distribution of development displaces, trends can be gleaned from the WBED's report on the World Bank's experience with involuntary resettlement. Table 3.2, composed of data from the WBED report, gives a regional breakdown of World Bank projects (active in 1993) that had resettlement components. It is worth keeping in mind that displacement in Bank-assisted projects accounts for only a small fraction of the estimated global total about three per cent of global dam displacement and one per cent of global displacement from urban and transportation projects.[23]

Table 3.2: World Bank Projects active in 1993 with Resettlement, including number of People Displaced

Sl. No.	*Region*	*Projects*	*Per cent*	*People*	*Per cent*
1.	Africa	34	23.3	113,000	5.8
2.	South Asia	29	19.9	1,024,000	52.1
3.	East Asia	58	39.7	588,000	30.0
4.	Europe/Central Asia	5	3.4	27,000	1.4
5.	Middle East/North Africa	7	4.8	32,000	1.6
6.	Latin America	13	8.9	180,000	9.1
	Total	146	100	1,963,000	100

Source: World Bank Environment Departments Report, 1996.

Displacement in India and Avatars of Development

Mega Dams

Massive dams are much more than simply machines to generate electricity and store water. They are concrete, rock and earth expressions of the dominant ideology of the technological age; icons of economic development and scientific progress to match nuclear bombs and motor cars. The builders of Hoover (a colossal dam on the river Colorado in the USA) were advised by an architect to strip the dam of planned ornamentation in order to accentuate the visual power of its colossal concrete face. Theodore Steinberg a historian at the University of Michigan says that Hoover Dam 'was supposed to signify greatness, power and domination. It was planned that way.[24]

The industry defines a 'major dam' on the basis of its height (at least 150 m), volume (at least 15 million cubic metres six times the Great Pyramid of Cheops), reservoir storage (at least 25 cubic kilometres enough water to flood the country of Luxemburg to depth of one metre) or electrical generation capacity (at least 1000 mega watts sufficient to power a European city of a million inhabitants). In 1950, 10 behemoths met this criterion; by 1995 the number had soared to 305. The leading builder of major dams is the US, followed by the ex- USSR, Canada, Brazil and Japan. Most of the world's major river basins are now girdled with dams; many great rivers are now little staircases of reservoirs.[25]

Worldwide, reservoirs have a combined capacity of some 6000 cubic kilometres, equivalent to over three times the volume of water in all the rivers in the world. The weight of the reservoirs is so great that it can trigger earthquakes scores of samples of so called reservoir induced seismicity have been recorded. Geophysicists even estimate that the redistribution of the weight of the earth's crust due to reservoirs may have a very slight but measurable impact on the speed at which the earth rotates the tilt of its axis and the shape of its gravitational field.[26] The floodplains soils which reservoirs inundate provide the world's most fertile farmlands; their marshes and forests the most diverse wildlife habitats. A dam tears at all the interconnected webs of river valley life. The most extreme illustration of the downstream impacts of water diversion would be the Aral Sea (once the largest freshwater body outside of the USA) in Central Asia. The sea has shrunk into less than half of its previous area and separated into three hyper saline lakes. Dams are the main reason why one-fifth of the world's freshwater fish have become endangered or extinct. Amphibians, molluscs, insects, water fowls and other reverence and wetland life forms are similarly affected.

The human consequences of the 'damming' of the world have been as dramatic as its ecological ones. Although the dam builders have not bothered to keep count, the number of people flooded off their lands is most certainly in millions if not in billions. And these would be conservative estimates; according to a detailed study of 54 large dams done by the Indian Institute of Public Administration (IIPA), the average Indian dam displaces about 44,182 people. Admittedly 54 out of 3300 (India has built these many big dams since independence) is not a good enough sample but since it's all we've got, let's do some rough arithmetic. To err on the side of caution lets reduce the number of people displaced per dam to 10,000. It works out to 33 million displaced by large dams' alone.[27] This is the estimate with regards to India alone; one wonders about the global magnitude of human displacement that damming would be responsible for.

Large Dams in India

Table 3.3: Large Dams in India

Sl. No.	*Period*	*No. of Large Dams*		
		>15 m high	*10 – 15m high*	*Total*
1	Up to 1990	28	14	42
2	1901 – 1950	118	133	251
3	1951 – 1970	418	277	695
4	1971 – 1989	1187	1069	2256
5	1990 and beyond	56	60	116
6	Details not available	74	162	236
7	Under Construction	461	234	695
Total		**2342**	**1949**	**4291**

Source: Central Water Commission 1994. Out of these 4291 dams 3159 are located in three states only i.e. 1529 in Maharashtra, 537 in Gujarat and 1093 in Madhya Pradesh.

Available evidence suggests that a very few of these people ever recovered from the ordeal, either economically or psychologically. Many more have suffered the loss of irrigation provided by seasonal floods, loss of fisheries and wood, game and other benefits of now sub-merged forests. Just as valley bottoms flooded by the dams are most favourable to human settlement in the present, so they were in the past, and thus reservoirs have inundated countless important archaeological and cultural sites.

Dams can be lethal too; because they break. More than 13,500 people have been swept to their deaths by the roughly 200 dams outside China which have collapsed or have been overtopped during the twentieth century. A calamitous series of dam bursts in the Chinese province of Henan left approximately 230,000 dead in August 1975.[28]

Table 3.4: Independent estimate of total Persons Displaced by Dams during 1950 – 1990 (in Lakhs)

Category	*Number (in Lakhs)*	*Per cent*
Total number of persons displaced	164	100
Total number resettled	41	25
Backlog	123	75
Total number of tribal persons displaced	63.21	38
Total tribal persons resettled	15.81	25
Backlog	**47.40**	**75**

* This percentage is out of total tribal persons displaced.
Source: Central Water Commission 1994.

Dams: *What they are and what they do?*

Dams have two main functions. The first is to store water; the second is to raise the level of the water upstream to enable water to be diverted into a canal or to increase 'hydraulic head' the difference in height between the surface of the water in the reservoir and the river downstream. The creation of storage and head allows dams to generate electricity; to supply water for agriculture, industries and households; to control flooding; and to assist in river navigation by providing regular flows and drowning rapids.[29]

A growing number of academic and activist researchers, however, have been building up an impressive corpus of data showing the extensive damage that dams and their associated irrigation schemes cause to watersheds, cultures and national economies. Furthermore, the evidence seems to show that dams have not fulfilled the promises made for them. Dams cost many times more than claimed, diverting investments from more beneficial uses. Reservoirs tend to fill up with silt long before predicted; they supply much less electricity than expected. Irrigation schemes are badly managed, destroy soils, bankrupt small farmers and turn lands used to feed local people over to the production of crops for exports. Dams assist the powerful to enclose the lands of the politically weak. By misleading people into believing that they can control floods, dams encourage settlement on floodplains, turning damaging floods into devastating ones.[30]

In the name of development, national elites, through the institutions of the state and market, and often in collaboration with foreign capital, have appropriated natural resources land, water, minerals and forests for conversion into commodities. The circulation goods which this has brought forth, has taken place primarily among the elite. The elite have therefore; through such pseudo developmental activities impoverished the earth of its natural resources.

The earth's impoverishment has meant that communities who depend upon the natural base for sustenance have been deprived of their resources. This alienation cannot be described in terms of loss of material livelihood only; it is most profoundly the loss of culture autonomy, knowledge and power.[31] Thus, no amount of compensation or rehabilitation can make good the same. People have been pushed off their lands, forests and riverbanks and their water taken away by the state for the supposed good of the state. The only people that benefit are the aforementioned elite.

Furthermore the credibility of big dam projects is undermined by the fact that genuine needs of the people can be met in other ways. Water can be provided for draught prone areas, much more quickly and cheaply and equitably with the use of small scale schemes, some using traditional techniques, some using new methods and some using a combination of both. Increasing the efficiency, supply and use of water can hugely expand the availability of water without the need for new dams. Similarly, all countries have a massive potential to reduce their energy use through conservation and efficiency to generate 'megawatts" rather than megawatts. The costs of renewable generating sources (wind and solar power) are now falling rapidly and are already cheaper than hydropower for many areas and uses.[32]

Sometimes people cite small dams as alternatives to large dams without realising that this is a very tricky proposition; on account of lack of a logical and fixed criterion for making the aforementioned distinction. Usually the distinction is made with regards to height, which is not a very reliable guide to the impact of a dam. A 15 metre barrage on a densely populated floodplain could have much more devastating impact than a 100 metre dam in a deep valley. An example could be India's Farakka Barrage (less than 15 metres in height), which has had a devastating impact on the ecology and economy of downstream

Bangladesh. There are a number of different factors that have a bearing upon the impact of a dam and therefore it seems almost impossible that a standard could be laid down for the same. Thus, the alternative of small dams is fraught with intrinsic flaws and therefore advocates of river restoration are now going beyond mitigation to campaigning for dams to be pulled down and letting rivers flow unhindered again.[33]

Resistance to Dams: *The Narmada Bachao Aandolan*

In India, among the many struggles against national 'development', one has received increasing scholarly attention, in the last fifteen years for the resistance in the form of social movements. The ongoing struggle of the *adivasis* in the Narmada valley in central India seems to be a real example of the resistance of indigenous cultural communities to development. In India, the struggle over nature has an inherent class dimension because nature provides the resources which are the bases of production. Unlike elsewhere, In India, conflicts over nature tend to follow the battle lines between those who produce and those who own the means of production. The Narmada Bachao Andolan as the movement is called; is a resistance by the *adivasis* against the dam that the Indian government proposes to build on the river Narmada, harnessing its waters for irrigation. The reservoir of the proposed dam will submerge an area of forested hills, displacing the *adivasis* who subsist upon this environment. While the dam was both, a part and a symbol of development, the movement against the dam seems to embody the cultural resistance and alternative development. This alternative extended to the very model of political action in which the *adivasis* engaged decentralisation, grassroots mobilisation, which by itself, challenged the authority of the state to act on behalf of the people.[34]

The movement brought to the fore fundamental questions, such as: Are big dams really in the public interest? And it answered them also; if yes, then we would be required to expound 'public interest' differently, for public interest would then surely run contrary to the interest of the environment and the interest of the poor. It changed the long held common perception that dams were good for everyone in the long run and therefore the short-term suffering of the displaced was justified in the interest of the country. The issues concerning resettlement and rehabilitation of displaced persons in the Indian context were brought into the public domain mainly on account of this movement.

The movement also led to an awakening, which shattered the myth of dam 'goodness' which was propagated with such complete conviction since independence, that it led Prime Minister Nehru to once comment that dams were the 'temples of modern India' (in a speech that he grew to regret in his own lifetime). And we in modern India true to our love for temples took Nehru literally and threw ourselves into the task of dam building with unnatural fervour. As a result of these exertions, India now boasts of being the world's third largest dam builder. According to the Central Water Commission (CWC), we have three thousand six hundred dams that qualify as big dams, three thousand three hundred of them built after independence. One thousand more are under construction. And yet one-fifth of our population lacks drinking water while another two-thirds is deprived of basic sanitation.[35] It was through the Narmada Bachao Andolans efforts that people began to see the latent cons of the big dams more clearly and this in turn led to a widening of the movement's support base with people from different walks of life coming together to show their solidarity against such pseudo-developmental projects. Another very important aspect that was highlighted by the Narmada Bachao Andolan was the plight of the displaced persons. For the first time since so many projects, people and more importantly the government was forced to take serious note of the sheer magnitude of the problem.

While a scheme and machinery for rehabilitation of the displaced ones as a result of partition did exist transitorily, it must be asserted here that neither during British rule nor in that of independent India till date, can one find a comprehensive national policy or law to relieve the trauma of displacement, especially of the involuntary kind.[36] All that exists today in terms of law and policy is the Land Acquisition Act, 1894 that lays down that the government is not bound to provide a displaced person anything but cash compensation. And this too if the person can show a legal title to the land, which unfortunately most tribes (highest percentage of people displaced are tribes) don't have and therefore are ineligible to claim compensation. Issues like these were for the first time taken up and brought out in the public domain, and as a result, legislations are now in place in Maharashtra, Madhya Pradesh and Karnataka. Also a few other states have evolved a cluster of policy guidelines or have administrative guidelines or have orders issued from time to time, that concern displacement and rehabilitation. The aforementioned legislations though a step in the right direction are full of inconsistencies and loopholes, but then again there's consolation in the fact of a beginning at least.

Apart from this there is another twist that the Andolan can take credit for the pressure mounted by the Narmada Bachao Andolan led the World Bank to institute an independent inquiry in 1991 a move unprecedented in the Bank's behavioural history. The move fooled nobody, yet it was a victory of sorts for the protesting villagers. The committee known as the Morse Committee submitted its report in June 1992 after an intense ten month study. The report concluded that "the distribution of the costs and benefits of the dam seem to accentuate socio-economic inequities."[37]

To quote further from the report, "Important assumptions upon which the projects are based are now questionable or are known to be unfounded. Environmental and social trade-offs have been made, and continue to be made, without a full understanding of the consequences. As a result benefits tend to be overstated, while social and environmental costs are frequently understated. Assertions have substituted for analysis, "We think that the Sardar Sarovar Projects as they stand are flawed, that resettlement and rehabilitation of all those displaced by the projects is not possible under the prevailing circumstances, and the environmental impacts of the projects have not been properly considered or adequately addressed. The history of environment aspects of Sardar Sarovar is a history of non-compliance. There is no comprehensive impact statement. The nature and magnitude of the environmental problems and solutions remain elusive. It is clear that the engineering and economic imperatives have driven the projects to the exclusion of human and environmental concerns. Social and environmental tradeoffs have been made that seem insupportable today."[38]

The report in its recommendations also highlighted the issue of 'encroachers' (*adivasis* who have no formal title to the lands they have been cultivating) rights which was till then a fact very conveniently overlooked by the Indian government. It also, at the very beginning of its recommendations, pointed out that the failure to consult the potentially affected people has resulted in opposition to the projects. On the whole the recommendations expressed complete dissatisfaction with the resettlement and rehabilitation policies that existed and went to the extent of declaring the same almost impossible under the prevailing circumstances.

With respect to the environmental recommendations this is what the committee had to say, "There has been no comprehensive environmental assessment of the canal and water delivery system in the command area. The information we have gathered leads us to believe that there will be serious problems with water logging and salinity. We also found that many of the assumptions used in project design and for the development of mitigating measures are suspect."[39] The above cited environmental hazards interestingly are one of the major reasons that have led to de-commissioning of big dam projects in the developed world. With regards to the projects as a whole this is what the committee had to say, "It would be prudent if the necessary studies were done and the data made available for informed decision-making before further construction takes place. Implementation requires that the bank take a step back. Otherwise, the possibility of making sound decisions will be further compromised." "Little can be achieved while construction still continues."[40]

What the Morse Report reveals in temperate terms vindicates the stand of the Narmada Bachao Andolan (contrary to expectations) and further, indicts the Indian government and the World Bank for what could be called a developmental crime, which in its consequences equals the magnitude of devastation caused by major natural catastrophes and wars.[41] In spite of all this the Bank was still not prepared to give up. It continued to fund the project. Two months after the Independent Review, the Bank through one of its bogus committees suggested a patchwork remedy to salvage the projects. The Indian government was only too happy to oblige.

It didn't however stop at that, for in the year 2000, the Supreme Court of India with regards the petition of the Narmada Bachao Andolan against the government decreed that large dams do not cause environmental damage but in fact bring about improvement in the conditions of the ousted and are essential for the economic prosperity of the country. Their reason for the above decision seemed to be the fact that the country has built so many such dams in the past and the adverse consequences as claimed by the Narmada Bachao Andolan have not followed in those cases; therefore the fears of the Narmada Bachao Andolan seem unfounded. The court obviously refuses to see beyond what is obvious lest the diabolical machinations of its political bosses are made manifest. The recent judgment of the Supreme Court based on the Sunglu Committee Report is also debatable.

The crisis is not confined to Narmada, the Tihri Dam Project is completed, even after lots of hue and cry and submerging one of the oldest township of social, cultural and archaeological importance, and now is finally ready to be commissioned in it full capacity. After an exhaustive evaluation of the project, the Environment Appraisal Committee clearly recommended against continuing with the Tihri Dam Project. Bharat Dogra then reasoned "If our engineers are clearly told to go by the maxim 'development without destruction,' i.e., projects which minimise ecological risks, they will no doubt prepare such projects. It is time for policy-makers to give them a clear direction so that controversial projects like Tihri Dam Project can be avoided."[42]

The hegemony of the Development Theology had been such in this country that nobody cared to look for the nearly 75000 people who had virtually vanished that fateful night when the Rihand dam was filled without any notice, in 1961. Even those who settled at the brim of the dam were subject of multiple displacements. The same was the fate of oustees of Nagarjunsagar dam who were ousted forcibly by the police in face of impending submergence. The oustees of Koyana, Bhakra dams, Ukai, Mahi-Kadana in Gujarat, Pong in Himachal Pradesh are in no better condition than of a destitute.[43]

The Hirakud dam, when it was being built between 1948 and 1957, affected 285 villages of which 249 were in Odisha. To quote Jena, "due to displacement, the livelihood of 22,141 families consisting of 1,10,000 people was disrupted. Around 4,744 families, all belonging to the Scheduled Castes and Scheduled Tribes, were displaced forcibly with the help of the police. Only 2,185 families were resettled in 17 rehabilitation camps..." Intergenerational impoverishment has been the inevitable effect. The Niamgiri Hills in Odisha is another example where five million hectare of forest has been used for industrial purpose displacing three million people, and the rehabilitation where of is still not completed.[44]

Vulnerable groups and displacement

The displacement caused by the large projects are class biased and the ethnic "otherness" is evident on the face of it, however, besides the impact it has on the tribal population it also affects the status and life of women, children and elderly persons. The heart-trending story of Nanhe, a displaced from Sardar Sarovar Project, is just an illustration. The Scheduled Tribes constituted about 8.1 per cent of the total population of the country according to 1991 census but they also constituted 55.16 per cent of total displaced people which indicates victimisation of the tribes. Many of the tribes have been displaced for creation of national parks. Over 40 per cent of those displaced from 1950 to 1990 were from tribal communities. Since 1990 the figure has risen to 50 per cent. Planners and administrators invariably capitalize on and manipulate the relatively weaker socio-economic and political position of most of the people facing displacement. Their numbers are underestimated, they are treated indifferently and only minimal cash compensation, if at all, is paid. They are rarely granted security of tenure on alternative developed land sites. All too often after a painful and traumatic period of establishing a new lifestyle, they are informed they must move again to make way for yet another project. Despite the scale of the displacement and the efforts of some governmental and independent groups, resettlement efforts continue to be shoddy and grossly inadequate.[45] The following table gives an idea of the tribal displacement done only by Dams.

Arundhati Roy points out this fact in her work as "A huge percentage of the displaced are tribal people (57.6 per cent in the case of the Sardar Sarovar Dam). Include dalits and the figure becomes obscene. According to the Commissioner for Scheduled Castes and Tribes, it's about 60 per cent. If you consider that tribal people account for only eight per cent, and dalits 15 per cent, of India's population, it opens up a whole other dimension to the story. The ethnic 'otherness' of their victims takes some of the pressure off the Nation Builders. It's like having an expense account. Someone else pays the bills. India's poorest people are subsidising the lifestyles of her richest."[46]

Table 3.5: Dams and the Displacement of Tribal People

Sl. No.	*Name of the Project*	*State*	*Population facing displacement*	*Tribal People as percentage of displaced*
1.	Karjan	Gujarat	11,600	100
2.	Sardar Sarover	Gujarat	200,000	57.6
3.	Mabeshwar	Madhya Pradesh	20,000	60
4.	Bodhghat	Madhya Pradesh	12,700	73.91
5.	Leha	Bihar	30,800	80
6.	Chandel	Bihar	37,600	87.92
7.	Korl Karo	Bihar	66,000	88
8.	Mahi Bajaj Sagar	Rajasthan	38,400	76.28
9.	Polavaram	Andhra Pradesh	150,000	52.90
10.	Maithon and Panchet	Bihar	93,874	56.46
11.	Upper Indravati	Orissa	18,500	89.20
12.	Pong	Himachal Pradesh	80,000	56.25
13.	Tultuli	Maharashtra	38,100	76.28
14.	Inchampalli	Andhra Pradesh, Maharashtra	13,600	51.61
15.	Daman Ganga	Gujarat	8,700	48.70
16.	Bhakra	Uthar Pradesh	36,000	34.76
17.	Masan Reservoir	Bihar	3,700	31.00
18.	Ukar Reservoir	Gujarat	52,000	18.92

Source: Ravi Hemadri *et. al,* "Dams, Displacement, Policy and Law in India", contributing paper for thematic review 1.3: www.dams.org.

The fact again was brought to the notice of the Supreme Court, which in its 1997 Samatha judgment has banned transfer of land and mining lease and license to the non-tribal in 5th Schedule Area. The judgment has declared as void and impermissible all transfer of land belonging to the state of Andhra Pradesh at any time in the past or present in "Scheduled Areas" to non-tribes and all mining leases or prospecting licenses when so ever granted by the concerned State Government in such areas to non-tribes. The judgment was quite explicit in favour of tribal and declared that the government is a non-tribal person and all land leased to the private company in scheduled area are null and void. However, it did not seem explicit enough for the Odisha Government which decided, against the judgment, not to put a

Table 3.6: Conservative estimate of Persons and Tribes Displaced by Development Projects from 1950-90

Sl. No	*Projects*	*All DPs (in lakhs)*	*Per cent of DPs*	*DPs resettled (in lakhs)*	*Per cent of resettled DPs*	*Back Log (lakhs)*	*Back Log Per cent*	*Tribes Displaced (lakhs)*	*Per cent of all DPs*	*Tribes DPs and resettled (lakhs)*	*Per cent of Tribal DPs*	*Back log of tribal DPs*	*Per cent of Back Log*
1.	Dam	164.0	77.0	41.00	25.0	123.00	75.0	63.21	38.5	15.81	25.00	47.40	75.0
2.	Mines	25.5	12.0	6.30	24.7	19.20	75.3	13.30	52.20	3.30	25.00	10.00	75.0
3.	Industries	12.5	5.9	3.75	30.0	8.75	70.0	3.13	25.0	0.80	25.0	2.33	75.0
4.	Wildlife	6.0	2.8	1.25	20.8	4.75	79.2	4.5	75.0	1.00	22.0	3.50	78.0
5.	Others	5.0	2.3	1.50	30.0	3.50	70.0	1.25	25.0	0.25	20.2	1.00	80.0
Total		**213.0**	**100**	**53.80**	**25.0**	**159.20**	**75.0**	**85.39**	**40.9**	**21.16**	**25.0**	**64.23**	**79.0**

Source: Fernandes, 1994, pp. 22-32.

blanket ban on granting mining lease in the Scheduled areas. Due to such approach of the government, natural resources and livelihood of tribes are in great danger, which had virtually pushed the tribal to the abject of poverty and hunger.[47] The following table gives a conservative estimate of persons and tribes displaced by development projects from 1950-90.

A significant number of tribal people, who are generally dependent on the natural and common resources, are displaced, and their ethos and lifestyle is dismantled and denigrated for the sake of developmental projects. Apart from the loss of land, living and lifestyle (of generations) displacement causes other traumatic, psychological and socio-cultural consequences, making their life further more miserable and impoverished.[48] In the name of development, tribes are displaced from their traditional habitats and livelihoods with little or no rehabilitation, and are rendered destitute, bewildered and pauperised by the development process. They are pushed into a vortex of increasing uselessness, unemployment, debt bondage and hunger due to loss of access to traditional sources of livelihood viz., land, forests, rivers, pastures, cattle etc.

In these large development projects, tribes lose their land and also the new economic opportunities in commerce and petty industry to project authorities and outsiders alike, even wage employment for them is rare. In Chotanagpur area, though the tribes constitute more than 50 per cent of the total population, there are not more than five per cent of them in the industrial working force. In some of the large firms like Tata Iron and Steel Company Limited (TISCO), Jamshedpur and Bharat Coking Coal Limited, Dhanbad, the tribes employed are less than five per cent. Development for the nation has meant displacement, pauperisation, or, at its very best, peonage for the tribes.[49]

In addition to what displacement has brought, in particular, for the tribes it has unleashed very similar or even worse consequences for women, children and elderly men in general. Studies have effectively documented how women and children are disproportionately burdened by displacement. The payment of compensation in cash directly disembowels women, who are impaired traditionally in influencing any decision on how the money is to be spent.

Also, any loss of access to traditional sources of livelihood land, forest, sea, river, pasture, cattle or saltpan land marginalises women on the labour market. It is only when land and other sources are replaced that women at least partially regain their economic status. Women not only suffered in terms of health and nutrition, they also lost the capacity to provide a secure future for their children. By resorting to seasonal migration they have unwittingly denied their children access to school, healthcare, child welfare, and other welfare services. Further, considering widow, deserted and unmarried adult daughters as dependents ceases their right to claim separate or independent rehabilitation package with no land allotment in their names. The Uttar Pradesh policy is even more gender biased. If a couple holds property separately, they will be considered one unit and will receive one package. In this situation, a woman will have to forego her right to the package as it will be given to the head of the family: the man. Besides, the profound vulnerability of the landless agricultural workers, there are people like the destitute, beggars, the uncared for aged, women victims of violence and abandonment, the disabled, leprosy patients, the mentally ill, and children deprived of adult care, who are anyway condemned to the margins of society and are likely to be the first to fall by the wayside.[50]

Larger social, economic and environmental threats

Involuntary and forced displacement induced by development projects, besides the above discussed problems, pose certain larger social, economic and above all environmental threats which have perpetual or irreversible impact on the project affected people in particular and their habitat in general. Displacement forces people to leave their usual habitation to which they are used to, in doing so they leave behind, besides their personal belongings, the common utility assets, the social bondage and security, an essential part of their life. Not only the land-owners are evacuated but the land less agricultural labourers, carpenters, blacksmith, cobbler, barber, tailor and so on those depended on these land and the village society lose their livelihood too. The common properties like grazing land, ponds, wells, sacred grooves, worship places, playgrounds, and fuel sources are lost in the village; on the other hand in urban context people lose their place of work like hawking/vending, self employment etc.

The worst form of social impoverishment is caused due to loss of networks which are built up over generations; people who are used to traditional way of living are exposed to entirely new and alien living conditions and environment that is hostile to them. They are forced to think and live individually, unlike the usual common living and dependency, wherein only the well-off sections of the community survive.

People start to confront and fight within family for compensation money, the callous settlement of different ethnic and caste groups develop inter community hostility. Many are rendered jobless and even if jobs are offered they find it beneath their dignity of once being landowners to work as labourers. The affected peoples have no political voice, and as they are resettled in new fragmented conditions and there is lack of uniformity, the living conditions at different places of resettlement are different, and the common interest is vanished leaving the marginalised ones further to the periphery.

Not alone the social conditions of the project affected persons is deteriorated, it is same with the host community where these persons are resettled. "The inflows of displaced increases pressure on resources and scarce social services, as well as competition for employment. Prices of commodities tend to rise and health risks in the host area increase. Cultural clashes are quite likely, and social tensions tend to endure long. Secondary adverse effects on the environment hurt both the hosts and the displaced."[51]

Conventionally, people had to worry for the displacement caused due to Big Dams alone, which would affect the population of a region where the dam is being constructed or limited to the submergence area. However, contemporarily the cause of displacement has multiplied in numbers and dimensions with varied and enormous impact not only on the physical population of the nation but also affecting the social and economic fabric with serious threats to environment and the ecological balance. The fast-track industrialisation has turned our cities inhabitable, forests barren and man to machine, a country which was predominantly a sustained traditional economy has been transmogrified into modern growth-led economy devoid of human considerations. Those who cherished the new economic policy failed to wield the same in application, the long hidden agenda inherent in the policy, best identified with the western culture, took over in the fact of privatisation of essential commodities in a state once firmly based on the principles of socialism.

The modern agents of development has made inroads to an extent that even the natural resources are not left from the encroachments of foreign hands, wherein, the indigenous, the rightful owners, have to pay for the things once considered to be natural and common. Privatisation of drinking water supply with vesting river rights onto a private entity, the Seonath River in Chhattisgarh, the ground water exploitation and contamination by Cola giants in (Plachimada in Palakkad) Kerala, on the cards privatisation of water supply for Tirunanthapuram and Vizag to be facilitated (displacing millions) by construction of Polavarm Multipurpose Dam, besides the already privatised electricity and water supply in number of metropolitan cities including Delhi and Mumbai are some of the many instances of this draconian run. The web of Industrialisation, Privatisation, Globalisation, Liberalisation, and the excuse of Development, it seems, has become irreversibly complex. And this complexity has been integrated and seeped deep into the economic *et al* policies of the state.

Development projects, nevertheless, symbolising economic growth, an important component of development, cannot be a goal in itself, nor can go indefinitely. A project howsoever technically perfect will not bear the desired results if we keep the "substance" out of it. Development means the development of the "people". Why care for the people? And, as E.F. Schumacher wrote, "Because people are the primary and ultimate source of any wealth whatsoever. If they are left out, if they are pushed around by self-experts and high-handed planners, then nothing can ever yield fruit."[52]

Moreover, no development can be accepted at the cost of environment which essentially means human survival, rather 'the survival of the humanity'. Unsystematic and piecemeal approach to development has cost us dearly in the form of depletion of the environment and loss of ecological balance. The large scale deforestation due to mining and establishment of industries has resulted in climate change and inconsistent weathers. Big Dams submerge huge area of forest cover causing irreversible loss to varieties of flora and fauna besides the land area. The pollution (air, water, soil and noise) caused by the industries accentuate the miseries of the present as well as the generations to come, added to this pollution by industries and urban centres is the garbage and toxic waste that is generated over time. No wonder that the environmental impact assessment of most of the big and mega projects reveal that such hyped and appreciated mega ventures are nothing but surviving at human and environmental costs. It is high time we realise the need of transforming our developmental policies to answer the larger human and environmental requirements until it becomes too late.

Economic cost alone can never be the only consideration in a project that is going to affect the lives of lakhs of people, the ecology and the environment, not just in the short term but for centuries. Almost all the developmental projects today are woven into economic fabric with the thread of liberalisation, privatisation and globalisation (LPG), and up for sale in a market driven economy, thus ruling out the commoners from being among the beneficiaries of such a development. On the contrary, the development is achieved at the cost of the commoners by causing their displacement.

If we consider displacement as the factor responsible for causing impoverishment, then the maximum of the impoverishment is caused due to industrialisation-induced displacement, next only to the displacement caused by Dams. Since it creates a vicious circle of displacement, beginning with acquisition of land for the establishment of industry and culminating in mass slums, the existence of slum in every industrial city is a sufficient testimony to this fact. However, the extended threat in the modern context is that all the activities are run and controlled by private entities, leading to concentration of the natural and economic resources and wealth, belonging to the people, in limited hands, to an extent of excluding immediate institutional remedies from the state. In LPG the state has found a disguise to escape its social and welfare responsibilities. It is only when the state finds the situation out of control coupled with peoples' movement, it aversely takes some steps for resettlement and rehabilitation only to subside and undermine the mass movements.

After Enron, Maheshwar Hydro-Electric Project and UNOCAL it seems fair to conclude that the globalisation has been depriving the people from their livelihood, as happened in the influx of over 200 mega-trawlers of the MNCs in the Indian coasts, harming the interests of the lakhs of small fish-workers. The NEP and the package of LPG, and particularly the globalisation, have further deepened the problem of the displacement in India. The tribes, peasants, dalits, women, workers, and their organisations have a difficult task of resisting the interests of these new capitalist forces which are supported by the State, the majority of media, urban-industrial and commercial middle class and the experts. The struggle against the displacement has thus become the struggle against the larger politics of globalisation.

And in the course the civil society is challenged to deal with varied forms of inconsistencies from within and out of the society; the answer may not be found in one-sided approach to the problems. What is required to reach any harmonious solution ensuring better management production and distribution of the resources with sustainable development as its end result is a holistic view and consideration in totality of the needs, necessities and wants of different sections of the society, with state as the major stakeholder in the whole process; forming a fine balance between the 'right to development' and the 'right against displacement'.

Development Disasters and people's participation

It is imperative to note here that any kind of disaster, natural or man-made Natural disasters may be broken down into three sub-categories sudden impact, slow onset, and epidemic diseases while human-made disasters include two sub-categories industrial/ technological disasters and complex emergencies[53] is equally responsible for the impoverishment of peoples coming under its impact; and to address the negative impacts of the natural as well as the human-induced disasters, a comprehensive and concerted steps at all levels of policy-making, planning, execution, and enforcement should be undertaken, keeping in mind the long-term perspectives of human and environmental survivals, besides the search for sustainable livelihoods (see chart below) in an era of economic globalisation and supposedly pro-poor national policies.

Forced Displacement, Sustainable Livelihoods and Impoverishment Risks a Revised Framework for Analysis

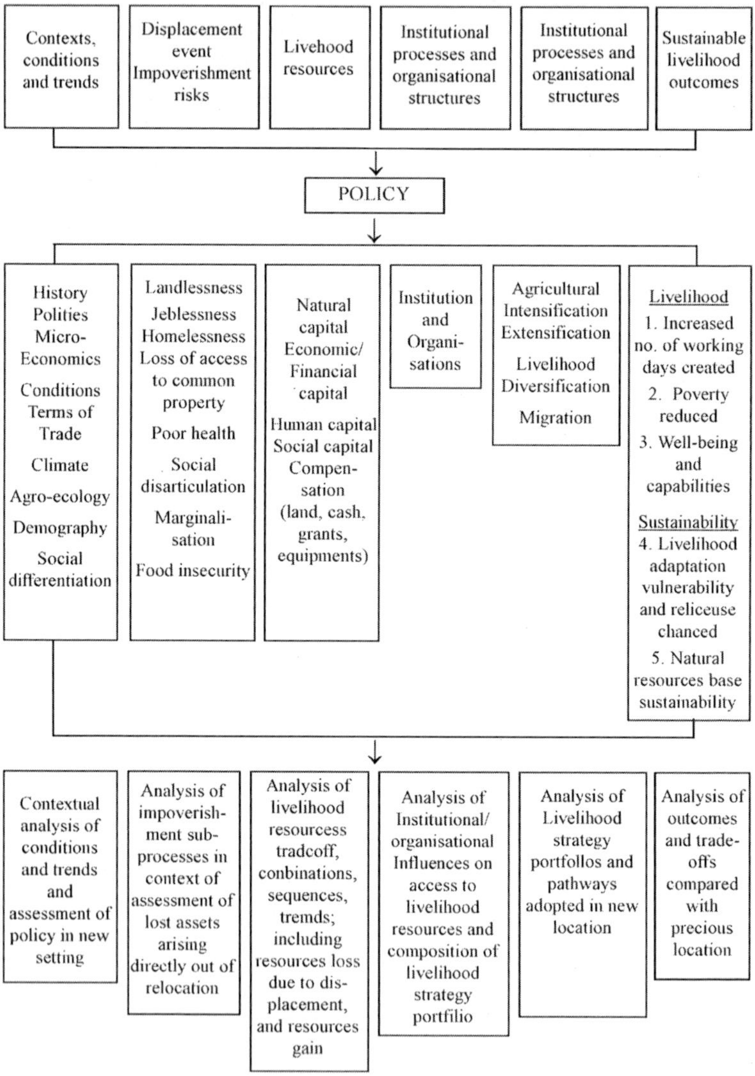

Source: Christopher McDowell, "Involuntary resettlement, Impoverishment Risks, and Sustainable Livelihoods", The Australasian Journal of Disaster and Trauma Studies, Volume: 2002-2.

Any piecemeal approach would entail drastic consequences in the long-term. Thus, 'sustainable development', a global principle of environment protection and development becomes all the more significant. In this regard, Cernea's impoverishment risk and reconstruction model offers a valuable tool for the assessment of the many risks inherent in development-induced displacement. State's obligation to provide humanitarian assistance and promote observance of human rights, in case of development-induced displacement, requires a balance of the state's right of "eminent domain" against a human being's right to home and property. In this light, development can be the proper expression of a state's responsibility to ensure the protection and welfare of its citizens. Where development leads to arbitrary displacement, injustice and impoverishment, the responsibility still falls primarily on the state to take corrective action.[54]

The states' indifference, apathy and at times inability to deal in a proper manner with the disaster situations (both natural and manmade) has forced the society as a whole to think and come up with alternative arrangements to deal with the crisis. The peoples' support and participation for the reconstruction of Bhuj in the aftermath of Gujarat earthquakes or the Post-Tsunami relief and rehabilitation endeavours of the NGOs is commendable. The role that civil society plays to counter the impoverishment risks is highlighted in the fact of public movements and institutionalisation of the public expertise. It is pleasing to note that a number of significant people's movements have been instrumental in stopping deforestation and depletion of wildlife.

Chipko Andolan March of 1973 in Gopeswar in Charob District Representative of sports goods factory based at Allahabad to cut down 10 ash trees near a village Mandal. When told not to do so they persisted the villagers hit upon the idea of hugging the marked trees thus forcing them to return empty handed. The movement, led by Sundarlal Bahuguna and Chardi Prasad Bhatt grew into a big people's movement. San Silent Valley Movement initiated by KSSP against the proposed hydro electric project of the government in the rich tropical evergreen forest of the Western Ghats in Kerala. With collaboration with others the movement grew within and outside of Kerala forcing the government to postpone the project.[55] The role of civil society and public movements was imperative, rather forced for the constitution of the WCD, in an independent assessment of the Commission it was observed that, "Based on the growing evidence of dams" negative impacts, protests and mobilisations have multiplied the world over. These protests have matured into sustained social movements that have effectively slowed down or stalled further work on proposed or ongoing dams. Among the more notable examples are the Bakun Dam in Malaysia, the Maan, Tehri, and Maheshwar Dams in India, and the Lesotho Highland Stage II Dam in Lesotho. In the case of proposed dams, such as the Arun III in Nepal, national mobilisation and intensive global campaigns have led to the cancellation of these projects. On the Koel-Karo and the Suvarnarekha Rivers in India, projects have been shelved after ground had been broken and significant infrastructure work had been completed. Even in the industrialised world whether in the United States, Europe, or Japan public opposition and the growing evidence of the adverse economic and ecological impacts have led to a rethinking of large dams as an option for irrigation and energy.[56]

Additionally, social movements and their supporters have criticised the role of multilateral funding agencies such as the World Bank in the legitimating and construction of large dams."[57] Narmada Bachao Andolan has been a front runner in this regard. "Such movements, be they the resistance to displacement in the Narmada Valley or the struggle against the mining activities in Jaduguda or against the setting up of production units that are bound to affect the environment adversely in many parts of the country, are, however, finding it difficult to take on the mighty establishment. The forces of *status quo*, after all, are not restricted to one political party or their combine but are spread across civil society."[58]

Development, to have a real positive impact on the society must conform to the principles of sustainable development, i.e. not only the immediate concerns but the long-term social and environmental considerations should guide the policy decisions, and those affected should be allowed to participate in such decision making so as to promote and uphold participatory democracy. However, one must be cautious to understand the actual interests involved and not the vested interests. In this respect the role of NGOs and other voluntary organisations has to be consciously evaluated. Not all of them serve public cause; the long list of blacklisted NGOs tells the other side of the story. The Council for Advancement of People's Action and Rural Technology (CAPART), a Government of India organisation that supports the projects and activities of NGOs, recently blacklisted 400 such organisations. The Central Social Welfare Board (CSWB), which funds NGOs on behalf of the Department of Women and Child Development, has a long blacklist of 3,000 NGOs. As Dhillon (1997) observes, the concept of voluntary work appears to have changed with NGOs becoming a source of income and employment generation for people sitting in plush, air-conditioned offices in the capital or other major cities, hopping from country to country for conferences around the globe, and doing 'advocacy work' a fancy term for churning out reports that put you to sleep by the time you reach page three.

This further raises the question of effectiveness of the NGOs to address the real issues concerning displacement i.e., the resettlement, rehabilitation and compensation, as most of the time the organisations take a rigid stand against the projects itself and thus shy away from any management and reconstruction works after the project is initiated; since their whole resource and energy the name and ego are at stake to oppose the project per se, such resettlement and rehabilitation works are done and undertaken by inexperienced small local NGOs or voluntary groups with ultimate control and supervision of the state. The very object and purpose of the NGO is frustrated, rather it is being used as a farce by some such groups (particularly where the NGOs concerned are unapologetic about their source of funds) in such a manner that even sections that mean well turn out to be articulate apologists of the mainstream development followed by the state. These NGOs, which serve as distribution centres for the funds from the international institutions and donor agencies from the West and also as a major employer of elite, stand aloof of the social movements.

Therefore, not all but most of the times, 'Negotiation' of the issues aggravates the crisis. On the other hand, 'people's movement' or the 'democratisation' of the issues is more yielding and effective in addressing the issues and is more thriving in mobilisation of the peoples' support and participation for the social cause. Narmada Bachao, Chipko, San Silent Valley, Koel Karo Jan Sangathan all success stories form part of the People's movements and not NGO affiliations.

Moreover, though the World Bank was eventually forced to withdraw from the Narmada valley projects, the work carried on nevertheless, and the dam that is now (realistically was always) a foregone conclusion, is not without conceding the fact that Narmada Bachao Andolan has managed to bring into the public domain, issues which were hitherto never critically analysed and were resignedly accepted as collateral damage. The entire viability of mega dams was brought into question and was subjected to unprecedented scrutiny in the media.

Consequences of forced displacement

Consequences of forced displacement in India varied depending upon the social economic and cultural factors of the displaced persons. It has affected the social system resulting in the disorganisation of the community, collapse of kinship groups, family system and informal social net work. Even with rehabilitation, displacement remained for the affected, a traumatic experience with serious psychological, physical and socio-cultural consequences. Plagued by the 'grieving for a lost home syndrome' the oustees found to have gone through the anxiety concerning the unknown future and the feeling of helplessness at one's inability to protect one's home and the community from disruption. Forced abandonment of symbolic objects and places such as ancestral shrines and graves, mountains, water courses and trails have severed the oustees psychological linkages with past and snapped the roots of their cultural identity. Illness and morbidity rates have been very high during the transition period that has even continued for a number of years following relocation. The cessation of a range of economic, social and religious activities which were tied to the oustees old habitat has broken the community into factions with loss of leadership in traditional authority and management systems.

The pattern of R&R has always been deficient and studies reveal that fewer than 25 per cent of the persons displaced by development projects were rehabilitated properly. Post-independent India continued with the British system of cash compensation to the oustees without taking into account the socio-cultural consequences of displacement upto the eighties in respect of projects in irrigation power and road construction. This had the inevitable demerit of making the displaced economically vulnerable, as cash was often used on immediate social obligations rather than on creation of long-term productive assets.

In majority of the projects, the displaced persons were compelled to change their occupational pattern and on the face of official apathy, they have found their own coping mechanisms, invariably of a destructive nature both to themselves and the environment. This pattern has always been found to be present in almost all irrigation projects. Case studies in respect of a few of multipurpose irrigation projects throw light on the pathetic levels of depredation that the displaced have been subjected to.[59]

Hirakud Dam: After the construction began, complexity began to creep into the system of the traditional occupation beyond the comprehension of illiterate tribes and villagers with the result that they became increasingly vulnerable to exploitation. Most of the oustees were reduced to a state of landlessness. The rehabilitation involved clearing up vast areas of rich forests, reclaiming land for cultivation. But the extremely limited resources of the region put restrictions on the availability of alternative occupation. This continued trail of hardship and suffering has been so deeply etched in the minds of the oustees that a recent announcement of the construction of the 320 MW hydel project with three giants size barrages across river Mahanadi near Hirakud Dam has met with strong resentment and protests.[60]

Ukai Dam: The R&R of the population displaced reveal an almost complete lack of approach and inadequate response of the government. In the absence of a well planned policy the implementation were callous and half-hearted. The ignorance about the human and environmental consequences of involuntary resettlement on the part of the policy-makers, planners and bureaucrats has been conspicuously present.[61]

Pong Dam: The post-rehabilitation scenario has been marked by sporadic protests because of absence of an alternative plan for resettlement. To put it in the words of one of the oustees of the project: "What have we got? Children of many ousted families have only learnt to graze cattle. The latter generation will be even worse off. If government goes on building dams like this, then the poor and backward people will die."[62]

A study by Lokayan on Srisailem Multi-purpose Project reveals that there has been a tremendous change in the life style and occupation of the oustees percentage of large/medium and small farmers decreased with many of the owner-cultivators becoming agricultural labourers.[63] In Bethdi Hydro Electric Project in Karnataka, large number of families once dependent upon forests which they did not own, were left to them to find alternative employment. In many cases the oustees have became bonded labourers and daily wage earners under timber contractors and smugglers.[64]

The tussles over the future of the Sardar Sarovar Project continue to remain in the public eye, the protest movement being spearheaded by the Narmada Bachao Andolan gaining in strength. Madhya Pradesh Government's demand to lower the height of the dam in order to cut on submergence and renewed discussions on the power component of the multi-purpose project and its economic soundness has added to the apprehensions of ecological disaster of a massive type. Besides, the ecological costs of the displacement have been enormous. The disturbance in the bio-diversity entailed by displacement and consequent eco-imbalance has impacted heavily on the traditional life pattern. The indigenous groups are being completely swamped by the immigrants and their resource base and means of livelihood eroded by depletion of natural resources. The environmentally harmonious 'eco-system people' are being faced with a situation of potential conflict over a limited resource base on the arrival on ecological refugees from alien eco-systems displaced due to destruction of their means of sustenance. Both sets are further threatened by the uncontrolled resources manipulation of the bio-sphere people. The eco-system people in their natural habitat have always had a tradition of prudent resources use and evolved indigenous methods to adapt to the spatial and tempered variations in the environment. Advent of modern commerce along with the demands of development projects has taken away the control over their resource base due to over exploitation and depletion. Basket weavers were forced out of their eco-system when bamboo- the source of their livelihood - disappeared with the advent of commercialisation. The nomadic shepherds were left in the lurch when traditional grazing grounds were either been brought under the plough or converted to plantations. Years of planned growth with unplanned management of natural resources and the eco system has seen to it that today the country's resource base is primarily devoted to meet the ever growing needs of the bio-sphere people having access to the resource of the bio-sphere through market mechanism.

The destruction of the environment has posed serious threat to marginal cultures and occupations of nomads tribes is fisher folk, the worst affected being women forced as they are in foraging around for fuel fodder and water that became rarer. It is almost as if all development is ignorant is women's need at best, and anti-women at worst, literally designed to increase their work burden. With deforestation, penetration of cash economy and male-migration, the women, in all rural cultures especially in poor landless marginal and small farm families have literally reached the end of their carrying capacities. No wonder, therefore, that the so called illiterate women, the prime movers of the Chipko movement, are first to grasp with intuitive ease, the elemental truth that natural resources are as precious as life. Nature's children- the tribes, forestry for them being as important a pursuit as agriculture, have suffered a great deal on account of massive erosion of forest resources at the behest of industry, irrigation and urbanisation.

Displacement, thus, is an off-shot of the present pattern of development-sophisticated and technology based and capital intensive geared, mainly to the profit of the corporate owner. It is a pattern, where technical aspects of the projects are worked out meticulously, the nature of displacement and of rehabilitation of financial requirements thereof are often underestimated. Discontent of the oustees is the inevitable outcome what with no participation or share in the benefits of the projects that displaces them. Hardship and resentment have often been the source of disruption, for as the oustees have to re-establish themselves with resources they are likely to complain and protest with ever greater frequency.[65]

The most vociferous amongst the protests against environmentally destructive policies of the government have been the Narmada Bachao Andolan, opposing the construction of multi-purpose project on Narmada River. Which began as a campaign for better rehabilitation for over a lakh of oustees spread across Gujurat, Maharashtra and Madhya Pradesh, has crystallised into a movement against large dams across the country and cantered on questioning the direction of a development policy which does not weigh the benefits and costs of projects for the people affected. In respect of Tehri Dam in Gharwals the Tehri Bandh Virodhi Samiti protested against the safety of the project after a massive earthquake measuring 6.1 on the richer scale shook the entire region. The Koel Karo Dam in Bihar lying in the tribal heartland of Jharkhand area witnessed the refusal of tribal oustees led by Jharkhand Mukti Morcha to move from the area marked for submergence. There has been resistance to several thermal and nuclear power projects such Dahnau near Bombay, Kakrapara and Kaiga. Even though in almost all cases the protesters have lost, the protests themselves have drawn the attention to the destructive aspects of development which permits the location of a polluting power plant in an ecologically fragile area.

All protests, however, are not environment oriented strictly. People may be resisting displacement from their land on which they have survived so far and not necessarily conscious of the negative aspect of the project. But the resistance itself has made them appreciate their environment which they have earlier taken for granted. The official attitude has always been that India can't afford the luxury of environmental protection underscoring the need to develop forests, build roads, and provide schools, hospitals, electricity and transportation for people including the tribes. The standard response of the government therefore, has been containment and localisation of discontent, offering only to ensure that obstacles to development are speedily and cheaply removed. Expediency rather than moral, constitutional and humanitarian considerations count. The displaced, despite sporadic protests are typically reduced to helplessness. While the need for irrigation and power projects, roads and railways have never been disputed by the protesters, what gets emphasised is the fact that such projects must incorporate environmental and social concerns in the process of the planning and designing.

The need, therefore, is to undertake resettlement and rehabilitation and operations for the displaced population with a view to help restore their life style without affecting social, economic and cultural characteristics. It is imperative to adopt an integrated approach to resettlement and rehabilitation encompassing employment in primary, secondary and tertiary sectors, health, education, housing, transport and communication, environmental protection and creation of institutions which would sustain the development of the area and rehabilitated households. Rehabilitating displaced tribal households would entail guidance on selection of rewarding occupations. It will also be essential to insulate them from cultural shock arising out of displacement from native land.

In a significant development, World Bank has formally advocated a 'land for land' resettlement plan rather than cash compensation for the displaced. This is based on a World Bank report which analysed the psychology of the rural resettlement process in respect of involuntary displacement and found cases of monetary compensation largely fruitless. It found that the economies of many village groups were often disturbed as people were not accustomed to handling large amounts of cash. The liberal cash compensation were not utilised for productive investment as it was typically inadequate.[66]

The government which owns, controls and develops India's forests, dams, power stations, roads, mines and large part of its of industry instead of being the protector has now emerged as the most dreaded destroyer of the country's environment. It has been found to be insensitive to the impact of environmental degradation on lives of women tribes, nomads, fisher folk and others who depend on the environment for survival. The Department of Irrigation continues to construct irrigation headwork and distribution channels without taking fully into account the damage to the soil through water logging. There appears to be no attempts to ensure that irrigation projects are sanctioned only with adequate technical and financial provision for prevention of damage to soil and environment.

Summing Up

Right to development as a human right was declared in 1986,[67] however, was acknowledged in the Second UN World Conference on Human Rights in 1993 in Vienna integrating the economic, social and cultural rights with the civil and political rights; it articulated an amalgamation of the two sets of human rights as an essential core condition for the 'right to opportunities for development' to take effect.[68] Nonetheless, development remains a mere hollow emotional assertion in the absence of Participatory Democracy; where one has no say in determination of policies and decisions that affect him, rather the system in place is marred with fundamental follies in the very policy formulation; where despite the growth in the economy, opportunities do not expand; where the benefits belong to the rich and burden and costs for millions of those on the periphery; where the growth of economy in no way endures to see participation or empowerment; where loss of cultural identity as collateral damage is a non-issue. In such a scenario 'development' amounts to be self defeating, serving to further accentuate and perpetuate social and economic inequities and thereby rendering meaningless its own avowed 'tells'.

The empirical perspective on the worldwide and most definitely in the Indian context reveals a bias in the development discourse; one which has posited the individual and the investor at its helm and on account of which development as we know it, is inherently ill-suited to promote human and social development, as was and is being envisaged. Thus, we face a paradox wherein endeavours to promote the one human right (Development) gives rise to the violation (displacement) of another.

"Development-induced displacement is the forcing of communities and individuals out of their homes, often also their homelands, for the ostensible purpose of social and human development, but which is actually nothing more than "economic growth" and the benefits accruing from such almost never if ever percolate down to the ones that bear its costs. It is a subset of forced migration."[69] From, historically, being associated with the construction of dams for hydroelectric power and irrigation purposes it now also appears in many other forms, some of which have been discussed above; and almost of all which invariably result in some sort of displacement. So much so that displacement and development have almost become synonymous. It is time the disparity between the theory and praxis of development was considered in the light of its flawed metaphysical underpinnings rather than facilely blaming only ineffectual implementation. And what has compounded the problem is that such flawed notion was uncritically accepted as a template and applied across different spatial and temporal milieus disingenuously disregarding the accompanying socio-political and cultural sensibilities. If people are the means and end of all development there's no refuting that can be think then it logically follows that all development policy should be inclusive of culture and tradition, keeping in mind that it's avowed object is the 'preferred futures' of people. How then can one justify the (cultural) disorientation that most development applications result in?

To steer pass this impasse, we need to rethink rather un-think the established perceptions and ask ourselves a certain set of new questions, shifting the focus from after-project impacts to pre-emptive pre-project scrutiny interrogating the inevitability of the thesis of development; the relevant question being: is displacement always inevitable? If yes, can the quantum be reduced to the critical minimum and how? What legal, administrative, cultural measures may be taken to minimise the social, cultural and environmental costs? In the process we need to look for better alternatives, as an optimal response to predictable impoverishment risks, which could eliminate altogether the need to displace people, or could at least reduce the number of displaces'. In other words, the first goal should be to find alternatives that cause minimal displacement, in those instances where displacement is inevitable, it is imperative that the full costs of rehabilitation be internalised into the project cost.

Most of the problems connected with displacement, resettlement and rehabilitation can be traced to the "Unbalanced growth strategy". Development, which has entailed many large-scale forced evictions of vulnerable populations, without the countervailing presence of policies to assist them to rebuild their lives, has only accentuated the negative aspects of displacement, such as lack of information, failure to prepare in advance a comprehensive plan for rehabilitation, the undervaluation of compensation and its payment in cash, failure to restore lost assets or livelihoods, traumatic and delayed relocation, problems at relocation sites, multiple displacement, and neglect of the special vulnerabilities of the most disadvantaged groups.[70]

It is incumbent upon the operators of the wheel of development to seek the participation of those displaced or to be displaced. It can be done directly or through their formal and informal leaders, representatives and even the NGOs. It would help in understanding the needs and preferences, prevent costly mistakes and reduces the sense of insecurity among the displaced lot. It is already waited for too long to challenge the development model that is biased to certain perceptions and class of society; alternatives for power generation, irrigation, means of production, etc., that do not exert such an enormous toll on human suffering, are now available and which might well be followed to reduce forced displacement.

To achieve the goals of sustainable development and for the development itself to sustain, it must come from the bottom; which is possible only when the third tier of the governance (is functional in its real sense) has determinative rights of participation in policy framing and decision-making when it proposes to affect their interests. Though the structural arrangements in this regard are ensured through 73rd and 74th Amendments of the Constitution and numerous Panchayat Acts in the States, the irony (all too commonplace now) is that the provisions are seldom upheld in practice. A functional gross root democracy and people's participation in decision-making that benefits and harmonises all interests, is probably the best possible way to complete the projects on time and keep the costs from escalating and minimising the miseries of the affected. A good deal of authority in this regard ought to be vested with the local bodies; meaning that their decisions and recommendations be regarded of utmost importance, bearing effectively on the very viability of proposed projects.

However, in the modern contexts, the complexity of representational politics throws up its own set of problems. Elected representatives, NGOs, affected people or their organisation, are all added with their peculiar set of political imperatives, and therefore can rarely if ever act in concert. Political imperatives notwithstanding the initiatives in this regard have to come from the state. Mere lip service such as responding to the popular stress on people's participation by involving NGOs is not the answer. While nongovernmental organisations can play an important supportive role but they cannot substitute the voice of the affected people, nor can they replace what is the basic responsibility of the State. Many NGOs are funded by the government itself which often puts limits to their independence and the ability to speak in opposition to the government line. In any case, meaningful participation of people is a difficult and complicated process which needs meticulous planning, strong will and respect for people's voice. Unless there is a conscious effort to create space for genuine participation at different stages, by building into the process, the modalities for participation and consultation, will not become a reality.[71]

Development which cannot provide the basic necessities of life should be shunned and attempts be made for an alternate mode of development which should aim at providing roads in villages instead of flyovers in cities, schools in all places instead of five star hotels. Protagonists of development should understand that it is not possible for the multinational companies to ameliorate the plight of the starving millions in the country. All present "development" seems hell-bent on impoverishing people and strengthening the hands of the rich sections of society. It is unfortunate that decision-makers are becoming absolutely insensitive to the needs of agriculturists, fishermen, weavers and so on.[72] It is this perception of the marginalised that the state ought to endeavour to reverse and only then can development be imbued with even a semblance of legitimacy. In order to do so, democratisation of the planning process by involving the affected in decisions that so drastically affect their lives seems to be the logical first step. Further, there must also be absolute transparency and accountability at all levels, especially so with regard to the kind of investments made by MNCs, World Bank, IMF, or any other international or national funding agencies, in mega public or private projects.

References

1. Wolfang Sachs, "The Development Dictionary: A Guide to Knowledge as Power", Orient Longman, New Delhi - 1997, pp. 1-7.
2. Richard Holloway, "Doing Development", Earthscan Publications, London - 1989, pp. 1-9.
3. Chris De Wet, "Economic Development and Population Displacement: Can Everybody Win?" Economic and Political Weekly, 15th December, 2001, Vol. 36, Issue 50, p. 4637.
4. Jeremy Seabrook, "Victims of Development, Resistance and Alternatives." London, Verso - 1993, p. VI.
5. Udombana, N. J., N. J. "The Third World and the Right to Development: Agenda for the Third Millennium", Human Rights Quarterly 22, 2000, the John Hopkins University Press, p. 757.
6. Richard Holloway, op. cit. pp. 9-11.
7. Chris De Wet, op. cit. p. 759.
8. Richard Holloway op. cit. p. 11.
9. Srivastava, S.P., (Ed.,) "The Development Debate, Critical Perspectives", Rawat Publications, Jaipur -1998, p. 20.
10. Richard Holloway, op. cit. p. 11.

11. Wolfang Sachs, op. cit. p. 8.
12. Udombana, N. J., op. cit. pp. 22-23.
13. *Ibid.* p. 26.
14. Wolfang Sachs, op. cit. p. 9.
15. Udombana, N. J., op. cit. p. 27.
16. *Ibid.* pp. 24-25.
17. United Nations Millennium Declaration, adopted 8 Sept. 2000, G. A. Res. 55/2, U.N. GAOR, 55th Sess., Supp. No. 49, U.N. Doc. A/RES/55/2, 2000.
18. Philip Alston, "Ships Passing in the Night: The Current State of the Human Rights and the Development Debate Seen through the Lens of the Millennium Development Goals", Human Rights Quarterly 27, 2005, The John Hopkins University Press, pp. 755-757.
19. *Ibid.* pp.798-799.
20. *Ibid.* p. 802.
21. Alf Morten Jerve "Social Consequences of Development in Human Rights Perspective: Lessons from the World Bank", in Human Rights in Development. Global Perspectives and Local Issues, edited by Hugo Stokke and Arne Tostensen, Kluwer Law International, The Haguec- 1999, p. 51.
22. Michael Cernea, "Development's Painful Social Cost Introductory Study" in S. Parasuraman, "The Development dilemma Displacement in India", Macmillan Press Londonc- 1999, p. 3.
23. World Bank Environment Departments Report, 1996.
24. Patrick McCully, "Silenced Rivers, the Ecology and Politics of Large Dams", Orient Longman Limited, Hyderabad -1998, pp. 2-3.
25. *Ibid.* p. 7.
26. Udombana, N. J., op. cit. p. 7.
27. Arundhati Roy, "The Greater Common Good", Frontline, June 4, 1999, p. 7.
28. Udombana, N. J., op. cit. p. 8.
29. *Ibid.* p. 12.
30. *Ibid.* p. 27.
31. Amita Baviskar, "In the Belly of the River", Oxford University Press, New Delhi, 1995, p. 36.
32. Udombana, N. J., op. cit. p. 27.
33. *Ibid.* p. 29.
34. Upendra Baxi, "Notes on Constitutional and Legal aspects of Displacement and Rehabilitation", in Walter Fernandez and Enakshi Gangulay Thakral (Ed.), "Development, Displacement and Rehabilitation", Indian Social Institute New Delhi - 1989, p. 47.
35. Arundhati Roy, op. cit., p. 6.

36. Ramesh, M.K., "Legal Nothings on Involuntary Displacement, Rehabilitation and Large Dams", (unpublished), *www.nlsenlaw.org/wp.../rehabilitating-the-displaced.pdf*
37. Prashant Bhushan, "A Damning Judgement", NAPM Bulletin Vol. 4 No. 5, July-October 2000, p. 6.
38. Chris De Wet, op. cit., pp. 6-7.
39. Morse Bradford, and Berger Thomas, "Sardar Sarover – The Report of the Independent Review", Resource Futures International, (on the Narmada Dam), Chapter 17, June 18, Ottawa, Canada - 1992. pp. 352-353.
40. *Ibid.* p. 356.
41. *Ibid.* pp. 352-353.
42. Dogra, Bharat, "The Debate on Large Dams", Paschim Vihar, New Delhi - 1992. p. 62.
43. "Development must avoid destruction", Deccan Herald, 24-10-1997.
44. Madhu Sarin, "Undoing Historical Injustice to Tribes", From the Lawyers Collective June 2005. p. 8.
45. Ravi Hemadri, *et. al*, "Dams, Displacement, Policy and Law in India", contributing paper for thematic review 1.3: www.dams.org.
46. Arundhati Roy, op.cit. p. 7.
47. www.agragamee.org/discussion_appeal.htm dtd.28-08-2006.
48. Biswaranjan Mohanty, "Displacement and Rehabilitation of Tribes", Economic and Political Weekly, March 26, 2005, pp.1318-1320.
49. Naresh C. Saxena. "Policies for tribal Development Analysis and Suggestions", *www.manupatrafast.com/articles/PopOpenArticle.aspx?ID...dff9.*
50. Ravi Hemadri et al. Op.Cit. www.dams.org.
51. P. McCully, Silenced Rivers, London: Zed Books, 1996; E. Goldsmith and N. Hildyard, "The Social and Environmental Effects of Large Dams", Sierra Club Books, San Francisco - 1984. www.irn.org
52. Malika Basu, in "Where lies the Hope?" Development and Discontent, 5-10-96.
53. Keith Holtermann, Erik Gaull, and Ray Lucas, 1998, "Disaster Dimension." In Saade Abdallah and Gilbert Burnham (Ed.) The Johns Hopkins and Red Cross/Red Crescent Public Health Guide for Emergencies, Baltimore: Johns Hopkins University.
54. Courtland Robinson, W., "Risks and Rights: The Causes, Consequences, and Challenges of Development-Induced Displacement", the Brookings Institution Sais Project on Internal Displacement 2003.
55. "Problems of forest, Land, wildlife and National Parks: Indian case study", B. Ekbal. Kerala Sastra Sahitya Parishad India.

56. McCully, P., "Silenced Rivers", London: Zed Books, 1996; E. Goldsmith and N. Hildyard, "The Social and Environmental Effects of Large Dams", Sierra Club Books, San Francisco - 1984. www.irn.org
57. "A Watershed in Global Governance?" An Independent Assessment of the World Commission on Dams, http://pdf.wri.org/wcd 05-09-06.
58. Krishna Ananth, V., "A New Role for NGOs" www.hinduonnet.com/
59. Report of the Committee on Rehabilitation of Displaced Tribals due to Development Projects, Ministry of Home Affairs, Government of India, New Delhi - 1985.
60. Viegas, Philip, "Encroached and Enslaved – Alienation of Tribal lands and its Dynamics", Indian Social Institute, New Delhi - 1991, p. 36.
61. Kashyap Mankodi *et. al.* "Rehabilitation, the ecological and economic costs, Centre for Social Studies", Surath - 1983, p. 125.
62. Mirdula Singh, "The outees of Pong Dam; Their search for Home Renu Bhanot", in Displacement by Sardar Sarovar and Tehri a Comparative Study of Two Dams", MARG, November, 1992, p. 42.
63. Lokayan, Special Report on Srisailam Dam Oustees, Telugu Version, Hyderabad Book Trust, May, Hyderabad - 1985.
64. Fernandes, Water and Thukral, Emikshi Gangluly (ed), National Development and Tribal Deprivation, Indian Social Institute, New Delhi, 1992, p. 66.
65. Kashyap Mankodi *et. al.* op. cit.
66. Mirdula Singh, op. cit.
67. Declaration on the Right to Development was adopted by the UN General Assembly, resolution 4/128 on December 4, 1986.
68. Arjun Sengupta, "The Right to Development as a Human Right", Economic and Political Weekly, Vol. 36, No. 27, 2001, p. 2527.
69. http://en.wikipedia.org/wiki/Development-induced_displacement.
70. Harsh Mander, "A people savaged and drowned", Frontline, Vol. 20, No. 08, April 12-25, 2003, www.frontline.in/static/html/fl2008/stories/20030425005312400.htm
71. Amrita Patwardhan, "Dams and Tribal Peoples in India" contributing paper prepared for thematic review, World Commission for Dams, accessed from http://www.dams.org/
72. Medha Patkar while addressing a rally in South Karnataka. Deccan Herald 10-10-1999.

Chapter 4

Resettlement and Rehabilitation Policy in India and Andhra Pradesh

The Government of India has at last came out in 2004 with a National Policy on Rehabilitation & Resettlement (NPRR), which would replace the National Policy on Resettlement & Rehabilitation for Project Affected Families, 2003 (NPRRPAF) and amended the Land Acquisition Act, 1894. The benefits to be offered under the policy to PAPs and families would include land-for-land, preference for employment in the project, training and capacity building for suitable jobs and self-employment; scholarships, preference in contracts and other economic opportunities, wage employment in construction work, housing benefits including houses to the landless affected families in both rural and urban areas, etc. A special provision has been made for providing lifetime monthly pension to vulnerable persons, such as the disabled, destitute, widows, old persons, etc who are not provided or cannot immediately be provided with alternative livelihood. The policy provides for grievance redressal mechanism which would include standing R&R Committees at the project/district levels and an Ombudsman duly empowered in this regard. For ensuring transparency, there would be mandatory dissemination of information on displacement, rehabilitation and resettlement, with details of rehabilitation packages. The policy also provides for National Rehabilitation Commission, which empowered to exercise independent overseeing over the rehabilitation and resettlement of the affected families.

Under the new policy, no project involving displacement of families beyond defined thresholds can be undertaken without a detailed Social Impact Assessment (SIA). The SIA report will be examined by an independent multi-disciplinary expert group, which will also include social science and rehabilitation experts. The policy also provides that land acquired for a public purpose cannot be transferred to any other purpose but a public purpose, and that too, only with prior approval of the government. Further, if land acquired for a public purpose remains un-utilised for five years from the date of taking over the possession, the same will revert to the government concerned.

Resettlement and Rehabilitation Policy in India

The Government of India announced National Rehabilitation Policy for Project Affected Families in February 2004, which was pushed forward in near secrecy without allowing little debate or discussion prior to its approval.[1] The policy very high on principles, as mentioned in its preamble, is hollow in reality and regressive in comparison to previous drafts and also some of the existing state or project R&R policies. The policy has also not accommodated the government's own experience of R&R in the past 69 years of dealing with development, disaster, and ethnicity induced displacement. It does very little to address the issues raised in an alternative draft policy submitted on October 5, 1995 in response to the proposed draft policy document by the ministry of rural development in 1994. The alternative policy draft prepared by an alliance of thousands of DPs, PAFs, social movements, civil society organisations and researchers advocated land-based settlement as key to restoration of livelihood, participation of PAFs in project planning, R&R process and other measures for making it sustainable. This policy, as we shall see later, is far from that and has a strong cash-based component, provides space only for consultation with PAFs and has no provisions for addressing second generation problems for making the livelihood sustainable.[2] At best the policy has provision for 'resettlement' or 'relocation' but attempts no 'rehabilitation' even though it admits that displacement has other traumatic psychological and socio-cultural consequences. The policy is nothing more than a document to appease the guidelines laid down by various loan/aid-giving international financial institutions which would ultimately provide legitimacy to the government's power to acquire land at a fast pace and hand it over to big multinational companies, all in the name of *development* and *public interest*. Certainly, it is not aimed at providing a just and quick relocation/resettlement process and opportunity for development to DPs or PAFs who ultimately lose in this game of development and pay the price for it.

The NPRR extends its mandate to include landless agricultural workers, forest dwellers, tenants and artisans in its definition of PAFs, but on the whole remains gender blind. Contrary to the centrality of the idea that, 'avoidance of involuntary resettlement where feasible or minimising it by exploring all alternatives'[3] should be an integral part of any R&R policy, the policy accepts displacement and then appoints the Administrator for R&R who will work to minimise displacement of persons and identify non-displacing or least displacing alternatives in consultation with the requiring body. The overall policy is poor in details and specificity of provisions of R&R and rich only in ambiguities and probableness, leaving much to the interpretation of officials concerned. It has a very restricted mandate and covers only development induced displacement in rural areas and has no provisions for disaster induced or conflict induced displacement. The whole vocabulary of the document is one of welfare and relief rather than of promoting rights to resettlement of PAFs, and creates a situation for their empowerment and a better standard of living. Ironically, it fails to introduce provisions which would allow participation of DPs, IDPs and civil society in the process of planning of the project, seeking non-displacing alternatives, or in sharing intended benefits accruing out of the project.

Displacement, Resettlement and Rehabilitation Policy in India

Displacement due to 'Development' in India is not new, though resettlement and rehabilitation as a policy measure certainly is. The colonial period has produced a vast segment of displaced people. The forest resources, river systems and mineral base that attract the 'developmental projects' have already seen a 'displaced' segment of the Indian society. In the Indian context, it is of interest to note that most of the developmental projects are located in the most backward areas and populated by various small tribes. These segments, with the enactment of land settlement laws, forest laws and commercialisation of forest products and minerals, have undergone a metamorphosis, where legally the access to the various natural resources are denied and these segments are treated as hostages within their environment. Another productive segment was also a part of displacement due to the process of de-industrialisation and forced commercialisation of agriculture these comprise the differentiated peasantry, the artisanal groups and the traditional service groups.[4] Any resistance to the displacement was treated as a 'law and order' problem, so no question of R&R policy. Land was acquired by the draconian provisions of Land Acquisition Act, 1894, which still continues, with some amendments in 1967, 1984, 2004, 2007, 2010 and 2013 with the objective to ensure, in consultation with institutions of local Self-Government and Gram Sabhas established under the Constitution, a human, participative, informed and transparent process for land acquisition for industrialisation, development of essential infrastructural facilities and urbanisation with the least disturbance to the owners of the land and other affected families and provide just and fair compensation to the affected families whose land has been acquired or proposed to be acquired or are affected by such acquisition and made adequate provisions for such affected persons for their R&R and for ensuring that the cumulative outcome of compulsory acquisition should be that affected persons become partners in the development leading to an improvement in their post acquisition social and economic status and for matters connected there with or incidental thereto,[5] but these all acts and amendments are weapon in the hands of Indian state for acquiring land from its citizens.

The situation just after independence was not much different. Independent India's Nehruvian development model based on development of heavy industries found a nationalistic fervour with planners and its privileged citizens. That there would be large-scale displacement was not a hidden fact and Nehru while speaking to displaced persons of Hirakund Dam in 1948, said, '*If you are to suffer, you should suffer in the interest of the nation*'. Barring a few exceptions, most pre-1980 projects did not have a clear-cut resettlement plan. Resettlement was undertaken on a case-to-case basis. To mention a few, there were projects like the Nagarjunasagar, Hirakud, Tungabhadra and Mayurakshi dams; the Rourkela, Bhilai and Bokaro steel plants, several defence establishments, coal mines, etc, which did offer resettlement in the form of house sites to the displaced. Only NTPC, and Coal India Limited (CIL), two government undertakings have formulated an R&R policy and constituted R&R departments to administer it. In addition, resettlement colonies have been demarcated near all their project sites to resettle the displaced.[6] As a result of this ad-hoc approach many of the displaced were left out of the process and even though there is an absence of accurate national database studies on displacement a study for 1951-1995 completed in six states and other research show that their real number 1947-2000 is probably around 60 million.[7]

At the national level, the first policy draft was prepared in 1985 by a committee appointed by the department of tribal welfare when it found that over 40 per cent of the DPs and PAFs 1951-1980 were tribes.[8] The next draft came from the Ministry of Rural Development eight long years later in 1993 and the third in 1994. In response to which the civil society alliance struggling for a national rehabilitation policy proposed its own draft to the ministry in 1995. There was silence till 1998 when another draft came out but the ministry that prepared it also prepared amendments to the Land Acquisition Act 1894. The above alliance found about 50 of the policy acceptable but thought that the amendments rejected all the principles enunciated in the draft policy. So they came together again to dialogue with the ministry and work on alternatives. Many principles evolved out of this interaction. A meeting convened by the minister of rural development in January 1999 ended with an implicit unwritten understanding that a policy would be prepared first and that any amendments to the Land Acquisition Act would be based on the principles it enunciated. However, the newly promulgated policy seems to ignore the whole process.[9] In the scenario of growing unemployment the policy could have revived one of earlier practices where till 1986, the T. N. Singh Formula (1967) stipulated that the parties concerned give one job to every displaced family. But increasing mechanisation has reduced the number of unskilled jobs.[10] This is another instance where the government has failed to take responsibility for PAFs and also making them beneficiary to the supposed benefits of development.

NPRR: Vulnerable Communities

National Policy Resettlement & Rehabilitation in its preamble says, 'the Policy essentially addresses the need to provide succour to the asset-less rural poor, support the rehabilitation efforts of the resource poor sections, namely, small and marginal farmers, SCs and STs and women who have been displaced. A close study of the various provisions, however, doesn't say the same.

To mention the provisions for women, the NPRR defines a family as PAFs consisting of such persons, his or her spouse, minor sons, unmarried daughters, minor brothers or unmarried sisters, father, mother and other members residing with him and dependent on him for their livelihood. It makes provisions for adult sons to get compensation but not for adult females. This has been more or less same in previous drafts of NPRR and also in awards made by NWDTA of 1979, a landmark in R&R policy innovation, which has recognised the male as the head and sole deciding factor for compensation and rehabilitation but, remained completely 'gender blind'.[11] There has been demand that the policy must address itself specifically to the gender question and enunciate the rights of women. The absence of such a provision has meant that the women headed households, unmarried-daughters, widows, and deserted or divorced women are not liable for compensation. There are studies which show that in the villages of Gadher, Kathkadi, Mohkhadi, Surpan, and Vadgam in Gujarat in the submergence zone of Sardar Sarover Project there was cases where widows were not taken care of by their sons. Without land or alternative sources of income generation, they were the most vulnerable sections of the society.[12] This results in further marginalisation and disempowerment of women and decline in their social, physical and economic status. In fact, women suffer the most because of loss of their customary rights over land and supplementary income from the Common Property Resources (CPRs).[13] The loss of customary rights over forest and land means they have to work hard to collect fuel, wood, and water which was earlier easily available in surroundings but is not in the rehabilitation sites where hand pumps for providing water are few in number.

The World Bank, one of the first in developing and initiating wide ranging socio-economic studies on the cases of displacement and rehabilitation, also did not include any special provision for land allotment to women in studies conducted in the early nineties.[14] In a study by Tata Institute of Social Sciences (TISS), 1993 it was pointed out that the absence of employment opportunities and adverse conditions at the rehabilitation sites in Gujarat where PAFs of Sardar Sarover Project were resettled forced the women to join casual labour market to earn and supplement family income, mainly in the sugar plantation, where they were paid less than male workers. The experience also shows that since most of the tribal communities are not familiar with the monetary economy more often than not, their money is wasted on buying consumer goods or liquor which increases the burden on women. Though[15] writing, before the policy was finalised do hint that land for adult daughters did not find much favour either with the PAFs or activists which may be true in some areas but is not desirable. The policy also fails to address the issues of gender equity and provisions for empowerment of women. To pay lip service, however, it makes provision for a representative of women residing in the affected zone to be included in the R&R Committee to monitor and review the progress of implementation of scheme/plan of R&R of PAFs.

NPRR has special provisions for PAFs of STs, but treats SC families with general PAFs. The policy merely reiterates the fact that the PAFs of SC category enjoying reservation benefits in the affected zone shall be entitled to get the reservation benefits at the resettlement zone. For STs the policy says each PAF of ST category shall be given preference in allotment of land and will be re-settled close to their natural habitat in a compact block so that they can retain their ethnic, linguistic and cultural identity and very generously mentions free of cost land for community and religious gathering.

The price paid by the government for the loss of CPRs and customary rights/usages of forest produce to each tribal PAF shall be additional financial assistance equivalent to 500 days minimum agriculture wages, i.e., Rs 43,310. It is difficult to think of a sustainable livelihood for tribes without forest. The forest is not just the source of fuel wood or other minor forest products, but is their natural habitat and central to their existence and cultural heritage. The government probably expects them, who are not used to monetised economy and urban ways of living to buy cooking gas stoves and build concrete houses with the money provided. This is enough to show the ignorance of the tribal way of life and their culture and the government on its part has learnt nothing from its own R&R experience of dealing with various kinds of displacement in the last 50 years. The government's sincerity in resettling tribes in their natural habitat is visible from the fact that it would have to pay only 25 per cent higher R&R benefits in monetary terms if it fails to do so.

The policy very categorically mentions that the rehabilitation grants and other monetary benefits proposed would be minimum and applicable to all project affected families whether belonging to Below Poverty Line (BPL) or Non-Below Poverty Line category. States where R&R packages are higher than proposed in the policy are free to adopt their own packages. However, it is a known fact that the states would always prefer to choose where their obligation is minimal. So, no doubt if Gujarat Government which has a provision for maximum five acres of land backtracks on its promise and Madhya Pradesh Government, which has a ceiling of 50 families, chooses to use it only when a project displaces 500 families in the plains and 250 in hilly areas, DPD, and scheduled areas.

The government's sincerity and the cash component of the policy are further visible in these provisions. It says any PAF owning house and whose house has been acquired may be allotted free of cost house site to the extent of actual loss of area of the acquired house but not more than 150 sq. meters of land in rural areas and 75 sq. meter of land in urban areas. However, only PAF of BPL category shall get a one-time financial assistance of Rs 25000 for house construction and Non-BPL families shall not be entitled to receive this assistance (emphasis added). There is no compensation for loss of the house except for the fact that government would provide one-time financial assistance of Rs 5000 as transportation cost for shifting of building materials, belongings and cattle etc. from the affected zone to the resettlement zone.

It is a commonly known fact that BPL families are generally landless, casual labourers, and sharecroppers and still the policy makes provision for a one-time financial assistance equivalent to 625 days of the minimum agricultural wages. In case of displacement a Displaced PAF shall get a monthly subsistence allowance equivalent to 20 days of minimum agricultural wages per month for a period of one year up to 250 days of MAW. A generous estimate of minimum agricultural wage at the rate of Rs 86.62 per day would add up to Rs 37,500 or Rs 15,000 depending on the category to which one belongs. This is the price the government proposes for livelihood of its citizens who are already at the margins of development. There is no attempt on part of the government, visible from these policy guidelines at making the life of DPs or PAFs sustainable, except for increasing their risk of impoverishment and disempowerment. The past experience has been that many a time the small-scale farmers, sharecroppers, and casual labourers in absence of any employment, adequate land, credit facilities, technology, seeds, etc., fail to adapt to the new conditions at the resettlement zones and are forced to marginalisation and become casual labourers at the project itself, if nearer, or further migrate to any other place.

The policy provides no safeguard against double or triple displacement which has happened in the past due to poor planning of resettlement process and project assessment, especially in the Dam related submergence and displacement. This is one of its major lacunae, in absence of such a safeguard chances are that these communities can be displaced again and again over a period of time.

The instances above suggest a greater thinking and study on the part of the government towards R&R measures of the tribes and other vulnerable sections to understand their needs better. The policy needs to be made more participatory and transparent in order to instil self-confidence and pride within PAFs because more often than not displacement and R&R has been a disempowering process due to sheer apathy of the officials and absence of a genuine effort on the part of the state in helping rebuild and rehabilitate their livelihood. In fact, the whole process needs to be seen not as welfare and relief, as in times of natural disasters, but as their right to resettlement and rehabilitation.

Absence of any provision of penalisation for R&R officials in the policy is another serious lacunae and is clearly visible where it says, "It is expected that the appropriate Government and Administrator for R&R shall implement this policy in letter and spirit in order to ensure that the benefits envisaged under the policy reaches the PAFs, especially resource poor sections including SCs/STs".[16] Whereas the Land Acquisition Act, 1894 categorically mentions that 'any person or agency obstructing the process of acquisition on conviction before a magistrate is liable to imprisonment, for any term not exceeding one month, or to fine not exceeding five hundred rupees or both.' What are we supposed to make of this? Simply interpreted, it means the government can displace its citizens whenever it wants on the pretext of 'development' or 'public interest,' but is not accountable for their resettlement.

The NPRR in turn sets up a 'Disputes Redressal Mechanism' (DRM) and 'Grievance Redressal Cell,' (GRC) the terms of which are to be fixed by the appropriate government. Even there, only the DRM has provisions for accommodating the representatives of PAFs and specifically mentions women, SCs and STs, NGOs and MP/MLA of the area, but not in GRC. In a way no PAFs can move to court unless and until government decides to give them the power to do so or at the most they can appeal to the National Monitoring Committee at the Centre.

NPRR: Development (rural and urban), Disaster, and Ethnicity Induced Displacement

Displacement in India has been caused by various kinds of development projects, ethnic conflicts, and natural disasters such as earthquake, cyclone, flood, riverbank erosion, drought, landslide, desertification, etc. The displacement by dams is only one kind which contributes around 50 per cent of the total DPs and IDPs population. But the provisions of the NPRR drafted by the Ministry of Rural Development are in no way appropriate to address all kinds of displacement and subtle differential impacts of displacement in each of the cases. The policy draws heavily from the existing rehabilitation policies for water resources PAFs of Gujarat, Odisha, Rajasthan, Maharashtra, Madhya Pradesh and Karnataka and covers only development projects and leaves others. The policy privileges the displacement by dams and fails to address the issues arising out of other kinds of displacement-related cases. Unfortunately, dam related displacement has been mistaken to be coterminous with all development-related displacement and this error has influenced the provisions for rehabilitation.[17]

The policy makes no provisions for dealing with urbanisation and semi-urban situation arising out of projects such as railways, highways, mines, industrial townships etc. It mentions, 'In case of projects relating to Railway Lines, Highways, Transmission Lines and laying pipelines wherein only a narrow stretch of land extending over several kilometres is being acquired, the PAFs will be offered an ex-gratia amount of Rs 10,000 per family, and no other R&R benefits shall be available to them'. The policy gives no guidelines of calculating the cost or damage to a family but arbitrarily fixes an amount which, given the past experience would ultimately harm the interests of the affected family.

The PAFs, especially vulnerable groups in absence of any social security measures in general and in R&R provisions are left to themselves and are directly exposed to the market-like situations. The fact that most DPs and PAFs, especially vulnerable groups of SCs and STs, are CPR dependent and are service providers to the villages and exist precariously in a semi-monetised informal economy, sudden overnight change to a monetised economy often makes them vulnerable to outsiders influence spending their money on cheap trinkets and forces them in to dominant economy as cheap labour in mines, household, market, construction work, etc. leading to further disempowerment and impoverishment.

It has further been observed that even though projects like NTPC and CIL did allot land for houses for PAFs around its own township. Many a time tribes refused to settle themselves there. An example would be the resettlement colonies of the Mayurakshi dam project in Dumka district of Jharkhand (erstwhile Bihar), which was completed in the 1950s. Whereas one finds DPs from other social groups residing in the Mayurakshi resettlement colonies, not a single tribal family is to be found there, though more than half of the displaced were tribes. Similarly, the efforts of the Odisha forest department to shift two tribal villages from within the Simlipal wildlife sanctuary to resettlement colonies located outside the sanctuary boundaries proved futile because the tribes returned to the forest villages after some time.[18] This suggests a greater thinking required in dealing with displacement of different kinds and socio-economic aspects of DPs and PAFs. It also needs to assess the differential changes brought by projects other than the dams in the region which sometimes not only raises the standards of living of the DPs and provides new opportunities of social mobility but also brings in associated evils of development.

NPRR: Economic Liberalisation

There are indications that the previous draft policies in 1985, 1993 and 1994 formulated by the centre and other state policies and Acts, except the one by Maharashtra, were prepared only under pressure of World Bank.[19] In 1980, the World Bank became the first development agency to adopt an explicit policy concerning involuntary resettlement, through a policy formulated by social scientists and grounded in social research.[20] Responding to the sharp criticism regarding the devastating social impact of poorly planned population relocation, it was forced to take steps to make resettlement of relocated population an integral rather than peripheral part of project planning and implementation. The policy paper was updated from time to time and after a lengthy consultation it issued a revised 'Operational Policy on Involuntary Resettlement, OP 4.12' in December 2001.[21] Michael, M., Cernea, senior adviser to World Bank also observed, "Our study found that impoverishment and brutal violation of basic human rights happen most frequently in programmes that are not subject to agreements on policy guidelines and to professional outside review, supervision and evaluation. Such domestic projects account for overwhelming majority at least 95 per cent of the millions and millions of people forcibly displaced worldwide. This fact is irrefutable argument for adoption of national policies and legal framework for resettlement in all developing countries".

The current policy document is a result of such pressure tactics and exigencies because the government in its bid to privatise Public Sector Undertakings (PSUs), selling out basic services providing utilities and inviting Foreign Direct Investment (FDI) needs land at an unprecedented scale. The policy in fact gives every indication of being a response to liberalisation. One can see it, among others, from the extent of land most states acquire for private companies. For example, Odisha had acquired 40,000 ha for industries during 1951-1995 but plans to acquire 100,000 ha in a decade. AP has acquired in five years half as much land for industry as it did in 45 years. Similar quantities are being acquired in Jharkhand for mines that foreign companies are eyeing. Goa had acquired 3.5 per cent of the state's landmass 1965-1995 and plans to acquire 7.2 per cent of it during this decade.[22]

This is not a hidden agenda. In 1999, a loan given by the Asian Development Bank (ADB) to the Madhya Pradesh government in order to enable private sector takeover of public infrastructure required that the state government first frame a rehabilitation policy. There is no doubt that the NPRR is also the consequence of a conditionality of the World Bank or some other multilateral institution, in order to facilitate the same processes of the corporate takeover of our resources.[23] The very fact that the Indian government refused to discuss the report of the WCD, Supreme Court judgement on the Narmada and the proposed interlinking of rivers all go in the same direction.[24] Since the policy doesn't guarantee 'land-for-land' to PAFs and remains ambiguous by including guidelines such as, "Each PAF owning agricultural land in the affected zone and whose entire land has been acquired *may be* allotted agricultural land or cultivable waste land to the extent of actual land loss subject to a maximum of one hectare of irrigated land or two hectares of un-irrigated land/cultivable waste land subject to availability of government land in the districts",[25] it is easier for government to displace people and complete R&R by paying cash compensation. This is no hidden fact, land being a fixed commodity, that ultimately all the DPs and PAFs can't be provided land because of unavailability of land. In case of R&R of Sardar Sarover Project oustees Madhya Pradesh Government had categorically stated that it didn't have land to rehabilitate oustees from 193 villages. Any land acquisition will happen only by confiscating CPRs being used by other communities causing tension between host communities and oustees, and culturable waste land which will need investment of an unusually higher order than the amount of compensation paid by the government.

The provision that this policy will be applicable to projects displacing 500 families or more en masse in plain areas and 250 families' encases in hilly areas, Desert Development Programme (DDP) blocks, and areas mentioned in Schedule V and VI of the Constitution of India is also of grave concern. No draft has ever mentioned the minimum number of families for the policy to apply. It is ironic because Madhya Pradesh and Maharashtra state Acts make rehabilitation applicable to projects that displace 50 families or a full village with fewer families than that. So, it is for the first time that the government introduces a ceiling to the number of PAPs. This is not without attributed motives, in recent years many large projects have been acquiring only land that is the people's livelihood but leaving their houses untouched. Others focus on the CPRs that are crucial to people's sustenance. It has happened in the Kashipur mines in Odisha. By official count the Lower Subansiri dam in Arunachal Pradesh displace only 38 families but several thousand will lose their CPRs to it. The policy will not apply to them. Many large projects like the Golden Quadrangle and huge mines to be owned by private companies have been splitting land acquisition into small bits, each of them displacing fewer than 500 families. Each of them can be called a project and deprive the affected families of the benefits of this policy.[26]

The 1998 policy draft had made land for land mandatory for tribes and had applied it to non-tribes "as far as possible". The final policy, however, ignores the tribes and finds a bigger escape route by saying that those who lose their land will get some if it is available with the government in that district. They will also be given Rs 10,000 per ha for land development and Rs 3,000 for building a cowshed. This is important to note because as the projects are now penetrating hitherto untouched areas for exploitation of its natural resources it becomes essential for the government to remove obstacles in the way because most of these regions are covered by the Schedule 5 or 6 of the Constitution. So, the policy with a greater cash component will facilitate quick displacement and act as a tool to legitimise resource alienation and to strengthen corporate control over land, without offering any protection to the affected communities.

The complicity of the government and international financial institutions is also visible in promoting the globalisation agenda by the fact that the World Bank has, meanwhile, announced its intention to dilute its own rehabilitation norms, and as a precursor to renewed large-scale lending to middle income countries such as India, it has stated that it would replace its policies, which have come into being as a result of struggles all over the world, with the national safeguard policies of the respective countries. No doubt this vacuous and damaging rehabilitation policy of the Indian government would count as a national safeguard for the World Bank. It may even be the reason why the policy was designed in the first place.[27] It is also learnt that another institution, Barclays Bank, is considering financing the Omkareshwar Project through National Hydroelectric Power Corporation (NHPC), whose role concerning human rights violations in R&R is far from desirable. However, the Bank seems to gloss over the human rights record and is considering granting loan to the company even by neglecting its own corporate social responsibility (CSR) clause.

NPRR: Human Rights

Displacement from one's habitual residence and the loss of property without fair compensation can, in itself constitute a violation of human rights. In addition to violating economic and social rights, arbitrary displacement can also lead to violations of civil and political rights, including arbitrary arrest, degrading treatment or punishment, temporary or permanent disenfranchisement and the loss of one's political voice. Finally, displacement carries not only the risk of human rights violations at the hands of state authorities and security forces but also the risk of communal violence when new settlers move in amongst existing populations.[28]

Ironically, NPRR makes no attempt at addressing various rights violations, which are common in these circumstances especially that of vulnerable groups whose vulnerability increases manifold in these situations. NPRR is just silent on these issues. It uses the word rights in two instances, once to give cash compensation to tribes in lieu of loss of their customary rights over forest produce and secondly to grant them fishing rights in the reservoir. This shows the true nature of NPRR and the respect shown by the government to fundamental rights of its citizens.

Balakrishnan Rajagopala of Massachusetts Institute of Technology has noted five 'human rights challenges', (a) Right to Development and Self Determination, (b) Right to Participation, (c) Right to Life and Livelihood, (d) Right of vulnerable groups, and (e) Right to Remedy, that arise in relation to development induced displacement. Indian Constitution also mentions some of these rights explicitly or implicitly within Fundamental Rights (Arts. 19, 21, 29, 31), guiding principles of state policy (38, 41, 46, 47, 48A), special provisions relating to certain clauses (Arts. 330, 342), and right to Constitutional

Remedies (Art. 32). So, if the government is serious to address the problems of R&R process, it has to introduce a rights-based approach to NPRR.

NPRR: Impoverishment Risk and Reconstruction Model

Cernea, developed this model using the primacy of risk analysis as one of the sophisticated instruments employed in economic analysis for designing and financing development projects. He argued that conventional economic risk analysis evaluates the sources, magnitude, and effects of risks that may reduce the rate of return to capital investments in development projects. And it is also common practice for governments to provide guarantees against various risks incurred by investors in infrastructure projects. The state takes responsibility for such risks in order to protect and encourage the private investors. Yet when the same private investments create risks to such primary stakeholders as the residents of the project area, by expropriating and displacing them, the state does not provide comparable protection against risks to these affected people. Except compensation, most governments do not use any refined economic and legal methodology to institute risk insurance measures for such primary stakeholders. In conclusion, he notes that while economic analysis and sensitivity tests are generally designed to identify, measure, and counteract risks to the project and project investors, they are not conversely designed to measure the risks posed by the project to the other project actors, such as the displaced people. He emphasised that these specific project risks must be pondered from both perspectives economic and socio-cultural, for which it is necessary to understand how impoverishment risks occur, and, equally important how to counter them which requires deconstructing the anatomy of impoverishment and defining the key determinants of income re-construction. After synthesising much empirical evidence, he concluded that the onset of impoverishment could be represented through a model of eight interlinked potential risks intrinsic to displacement, as shown in the following table.[29]

This model already has been used to analyse several situations of internal displacement. Lakshman Mahapatra applied the model to Indian condition before the NPRR was framed, and concluded "detailed examination of India's resettlement experiences confirms empirically and theoretically the validity of the conceptual model of risk and

Table 4.1: Comparison between NPRR and Cernea's Model

Sl. No.	*Various Impoverishment Risks*	*Remedies*	*NPRR - 2003 Provisions*
1.	Landlessness	to land based rehabilitation	(6.4) Each PAF owning agricultural land in the affected zone and whose entire land has been acquired may be allotted agricultural land or cultivable waste land to the extent of actual land loss subject to a maximum of one hectare of irrigated land or two hectares of un-irrigated land/cultivable waste land subject to availability of government land in the districts.
2.	Joblessness	to re-employment	(6.17) ...wherein only a narrow stretch of land extending over several kilometres is being acquired, the PAFs will be offered an ex-gratia amount of Rs 10,000 per family, and no other Resettlement and Rehabilitation benefits shall be available to them (emphasis added).
3.	Homelessness	to house reconstruction	(6.14) Each PAF belonging to the category of 'agricultural labourer', or 'non-agricultural labourer' shall be provided a onetime financial assistance equivalent to 625 days of the minimum agricultural wages.
4.	Marginalisation	to social inclusion	(6.18) The PAFs shall be provided necessary training facilities for development of entrepreneurship to take up self-employment projects at the resettlement zone as part of R&R benefits.
5.	Food	to adequate nutrition security	(6.2) ...may be allotted free of cost house site... (6.3) one-time financial assistance of Rs 25000 for house construction, only for BPL categories and (6.14) ... transit accommodation, pending resettlement and rehabilitation scheme.
6.	Insecurity	to adequate health care	(6.21.4) Tribal PAFs will be re-settled close to their natural habitat in a compact block so that they can retain their ethnic, linguistic and cultural identity.
7.	Increased morbidity and mortality	to restoration of community assets	(6.11) Each PAF owning agricultural land in the affected zone and whose entire land has been acquired shall get one-time financial assistance equivalent to 750 days minimum agricultural wages for "loss of livelihood" where neither agricultural land nor regular employment to one member of the PAF has been provided.
8.	Loss of	to community reconstruction	(6.15) Each displaced PAF shall get a monthly subsistence allowance equivalent to 20 days of minimum agricultural wages per month for a period of one-year upto 250 days of MAW.
9.	access to	to ensure access and provisions to community services	(6.22.2)
10.	CPRs	to respect and restore human rights	(6.21.3) Each tribal PAF shall get additional financial assistance equivalent to 500 days minimum agriculture wages for loss of customary rights/usages of forest produce...
11	Social disarticulation/ disintegration	to empower protect their rights	(6.21.9) shall be given fishing rights in the reservoir area.

Source: 1. The first eight impoverishment risks has been taken from (Cernea, 1999), next two from (Robinson, 2003) p. 13 and the last point added by me considering the special needs in the situation like this. 2. First eight points as proposed by Balaji Pandey, 1998 quoted in (Bandyopadhyay, 2004) and next three mentioned in the NPRR-2003, Government of India, 2004.

reconstruction as an analytical, explanatory, and strategic tool".[30] Below is a comparison of NPRR vis-à-vis the model to see how its provisions addressed the potential risks as suggested by Cernea.

Resettlement and Rehabilitation Policy in Andhra Pradesh

Millions of people since independence have been displaced by various projects in India and Andhra Pradesh in the name of development and progress. Displacement means people forgoing their villages, lands, work, income, culture and the way of life established and accumulated since the time immemorial. It amounts to a total destruction of the existing economy in the process of creating a new one for a new set of people and regions. Consequently a set of losers and gainers has been created. Losers are those who are displaced and the gainers are those who live in command area of an irrigation projects, industrialists, bureaucrats, contractor-politician combine.

R&R during Pre-State Formation

Several development Projects, unlike in most of other states in India, were initiated in the erstwhile Nizam State. Nawab Ali Jung Bahadur formed an Irrigation Development Department in 1886 to combat the problems of floods and famines. By 1925 the department has provided irrigation to 7,000 acres through minor irrigation works and launched an intensive drive to construct large and medium dams.

Two major irrigation projects, viz., Nizam Sagar and Tungabhadra are chosen for the present purpose. These two projects were initiated under the regimes of Nizam and the British respectively. However, the popular government of Hyderabad state in Telangana undertook the rehabilitation of displaced people of Tungabhadra project.

Nizam Sagar Project (one river Manjira lower tributary of river Godavari) was constructed during the period 1923-31 by the erstwhile Princely State of Hyderabad, in Banswada taluk Nizamabad district. At the time of conception and execution it was not only the largest in the State but also one of the biggest projects in India. It was proposed to irrigate 2,75,000 acres serving 326 villages spread over four taluks in Nizamabad district.[31]

Submergence: The construction of the dam and the creation of the reservoir affected forty villages in two taluks, viz., Yellareddy and

Andole. A total of 5,037 houses in these villages were submerged. In addition, lands to the extent of 20,140 acres were acquired. In all 35,274 acres of land, including 15,135 acres of crown waste was inundated.[32]

Rehabilitation Policy: Physical Rehabilitation Method (PRM) was adopted by the then government to make the displaced people to resettle, which means providing land to land and village to village for those displaced. The salient features of the PRM are as follows:

1. To offer the displaced ryots lands of their choice under canal;
2. To offer lands for construction of a new village;
3. To help them obtain necessary building materials;
4. To give them proper design for houses after making decent layouts with all facilities and amenities;
5. To make some cash payments for purchase of agricultural implements for agriculture, manure and others; and
6. To construct model houses economically.

Though, the government's policy was to provide land under canal and new village with all infrastructure facilities some of the DPs thought that the government would not make suitable arrangements for their accommodation. Some other persons felt that if they were paid cash compensation they would make their own arrangements to purchase lands at the place of their choice at a future date. Thus, the government, on force had to accept for the payment of cash compensation for lands. Therefore, for about one-third of the total displaced persons, government had to pay compensation for lands along with the houses. But the government was not happy over it, and recorded its displeasure on cash compensation as: "that the people receiving compensation will fritter away the amounts and find themselves in the lurch with no house to live-in and no land to cultivate and live-on.

Further, the government was serious in implementing the above rehabilitation programme, within a specified time frame. In this connection the government felt that "the above (salient features) were to be got done as soon as the expropriation process is completed so that there may be no time left which would inconvenience the ryots and in turn delay the rehabilitation of ryots and development of ayacut and the government officers of outstanding ability to all concerned, be chosen so that it can be got over satisfactorily".[33] Right from the beginning of the project the concern for displaced people and earnestness in the implementation of the programme by mobilising the officers of proven integrity were striking features of rehabilitation policy.

Tungabhadra Project: It is an inter-state project actually proposed by the Madras Government to the Indian Irrigation Commission of 1901-03. It is this commission, which had recommended that water should be shared with the Hyderabad State (Nizam). The project was delayed by 50 years of prolonged negotiations for sharing water between the two states and due to long delay in project design, while the notification for land acquisition was issued by the Government of Madras in 1941, Hyderabad Government did so in 1945.[34]

Submergence: Three districts were affected by this project. The districts are Bellary, Raichur and Dharwar. While Bellary district was under Madras Presidency, parts of Raichur and Dharwar were under Nizam regime. Hyderabad state has emerged in 1948. It is the Hyderabad Government (1953-54) which has formulated and implemented R&R programme. Thirty-seven villages were submerged in Hyderabad State. The number of families and persons affected in these 37 villages is 5,225 and 30,000 respectively.[35]

Rehabilitation Policy: The spirit of rehabilitation policy followed under Nizam Sagar Project was reflected in rehabilitation of persons displaced in the project too: policy of land to land village to village. Nineteen rehabilitation centres were established to resettle the DPs. A scheme was prepared to acquire excess lands and lands of non-cultivating owners for the purpose of allotting them to displace. The important aspect of the policy was the provision of land for cultivation and house to live-in to all the displaced families including tenants and agricultural labour. Another striking aspect of the policy was involvement of army in transportation of men and material of displaced families to new centres and in the construction of houses at new sites. The army men have put their best efforts to build one house a day on an average.[36]

All the model houses were constructed at hurricane speed, so that the displaced were resettled in their new houses by June 1953 when the villages evacuated had submerged. Besides, the government also took several steps to create an environment to develop the allotted lands. The important among them were:

1. Making available thakavi loans in cash and in the form of housing materials and agricultural implements.
2. Establishment of multipurpose cooperative societies and setting up of a Debt Conciliation Board.

Though some families preferred cash compensation to settle on their own, most of the displaced settled down in the 19 rehabilitation centres, as stated earlier, in the ayacut area to their satisfaction. A reporter of Hyderabad today writes, "I try myself to get reactions from the villagers themselves. Nowhere could I find a word against government undertaking the solution of thorny problem."[37] The rehabilitation policies adopted and implemented by both the regimes prior to the formation of Andhra Pradesh State were done to the satisfaction of the displaced.

R&R Policy during Post-State Formation

Nagarjuna Sagar: Nagarjuna Sagar Project was launched in 1955 as a joint project between Andhra and Hyderabad States. It was completed in the mid 1960s.

Submergence: The dam affected 57 villages in two districts, viz., Nalgonda and Guntur. In all 25,000 people comprising 5,098 families were displaced. Most of them belonged to the tribal communities, viz., Lambada and Chenchu. About 2,05,948 acres of land was acquired for the project.

Private lands were acquired as per provisions of the Nagarjuna Sagar project (Acquisition of Land) Act XXXII of 1956. Land acquisition process was started in 1962 and it went on till 1966. But the compensation was, however, paid at the market rates prevailing as on 1st July 1953 which is against the principle of the Land Acquisition Act, 1894. The reason for fixing 1st July 1953 as the basis for market rates, as stated in the State Assembly in the Course of a debate on this subject, is rather ingenious.[38] It appears that people came to know of this project in July 1953 and therefore this date was considered suitable for fixing the market rate. This Act turned out to be worse than the

1894 Act as far as compensation is considered. As a result the displaced households received compensation, which was as low as Rs 25 per acre of land. [39]

Rehabilitation Policy: Physical rehabilitation policy followed by earlier regimes was continued under Nagarjuna Sagar Project. The following ground rules were laid down by the Nagarjuna Sagar Control Board to regulate the assignment of lands to the displaced families:

1. The grant of free lands to a displaced family should not exceed five acres of dry land;
2. Only families that have been living by cultivation for the last three years should be eligible for free grant;
3. In respect of owners of the land, only those owning 20 acres or less, taking their holding both;
4. In respect of the owners of the land, the rent should be just enough to make up for their total possession elsewhere and in new centres, subject to a maximum of 10 acres;
5. An assignee will not be entitled to transfer the land given to him for a period of five years from the date of allotment;
6. In addition to any free grant of dry land which a family may be entitled to as above, each displaced family living by cultivation for the last three years and each owner of the land, whether owning less than 20 acres or more, may be assigned dry land on payment of market rate, subject to the condition that the total holding in the new village did not exceed 20 acres;
7. The following order of priority should be observed in the assignment of land at market value:
   (a) Families with no land left after submergence; and
   (b) In the case of families with lands left over after submergence, priority should be given to families with smaller holdings over families with larger holdings.

Apart from the above, facilities to be provided at the new rehabilitation centres included.

1. Grant of house sites;
2. Provision of transport for shifting to the new centre;

3. Provision of water supply;
4. Roads and common facilities;
5. Renewal of temples; and
6. Construction of chawadies-cum-community centres.

Twenty-four main and ten subsidiary rehabilitation centres were established in Guntur and Nalgonda districts. Nearly 5,292 acres (2,812 in Guntur and 2,480 in Nalgonda) of forest land was reserved for the purpose.

The rehabilitation of Nagarjuna Sagar Project has some additional policy provisions which were not there in the earlier policies of previous regimes such as:

(i) Allotment of excess land on payment which is over and above five acres of free land which was already allotted under rehabilitation package;

(ii) Permitting displaced farmers to cultivate already acquired land on lease till submergence takes place.

The earlier regimes allowed the displaced farmers to make use of the land free of cost i.e., without any lease amount. Further the actual implementation of the policy did cause a number of problems to the affected people. For example, the displaced families of Elleshwaram village of Nalgonda district were allotted lands and house sites in some other village where, much to their dismay the allotted lands were already encroached by the local people. Then an alternative site was allotted, which was found not suitable for human settlement as it was rocky and no water was available. All these caused delay in their resettlement. Meanwhile, the reservoir was filled with water due to sudden floods in the river as a result of which the village was submerged forcing the people to take refuge on a nearby hillock. They lost all their belongings including some cattle in the floods. The people were driven from pillar to post in the process of finding a place to settle down.

In retrospect, the Nagarjuna Sagar Project remains one of the worst rehabilitation experiences yet did not draw much attention because of relatively smaller magnitude of displacement, greater proportion of the affected being tribes and also because of lack of public awareness on the problem in 1960s.[40]

Sri Ram Sagar: It is a major irrigation project meant to serve six districts of Telangana region of the state. The project is proposed to irrigate a total area of 16,109 lakh acres in Stage-I and 8,930 lakh acres in Stage II.[41] Of course, after more than three decades of completion of the reservoir it is only providing irrigation for about five lakh acres.

Submergence: As many as 91 villages of two districts, Nizamabad and Adilabad, were affected due to the project main dam. In addition, 26 villages were affected under the balancing lower Maner Dam reservoir. In all 117 villages with 47,599 families were affected. An area of 1,52,493 acres was acquired.

Rehabilitation

1. **Compensation**: No uniform method has been followed in the valuation of lands and arriving at compensation. Each Special Duty Collector, who was engaged in land acquisition, followed his own method of valuation, as there was no clear stipulation about any particular method in the form of government direction. However, in a majority of cases registration statistics were used as basis for the valuation of land.
2. **Rehabilitation**: Two rehabilitation methods were followed under this project:
   (i) Physical Rehabilitation Method (PRM) as in the case of earlier projects, and
   (ii) Cash Grant Method (CGM).

Under the former, land was given in lieu of land, though not to the full extent. The method was proposed as an alternative to PRM.

Physical Rehabilitation Method

1. Displaced families would be granted, free of cost, land equal to the extent acquired subject to a maximum of five acres of dry land or two acres of wet land per family. Families who were living by cultivation for at least three years prior to displacement shall be eligible for such a grant. No further land will be assigned to the displaced families even on payment of market value.

2. The displaced families who desire to get themselves rehabilitated at the centre established by government were to have ten cents of land, free of cost, as house site, in the case of those whose lands have been acquired and five cents in the case of those whose lands were not acquired.

Cash Grant Method (CGM): Displaced families who desired to get themselves rehabilitated in places other than the rehabilitation centre established by the government would be allowed a cash grant of Rs 5,000 per family, in cases where lands but no house properties were acquired, a cash grant equivalent to 50 per cent of the compensation paid for such properties subject to minimum of a Rs 500 and a maximum of Rs 2,000 per family.

The PRM was replaced by the CGM in 1978 under the pretext that the contractors were reluctant to make up civil works at the rehabilitation centres.[42] Thus, there is a clear departure from the R&R policy of the earlier years. The humanitarian and compassionate approach, one observes in the Nizam Sagar and Tungabhadra resettlement, was replaced by a mechanical and bureaucratic approach. Other amenities of course, like drinking water, community hall, temple, school building, etc., were not disturbed.

However, until 1978, before the change in the policy, the government had established 19 rehabilitation centres for 26 submerged villages of Nizamabad district and 12 rehabilitation centres for 26 villages of Adilabad district. For the purpose of allotment to the displaced the government secured about 36,428 acres from forest department and 2,373 acres from government waste lands. Out of this about 1,934 acres of land was demarcated as village sites and 23,428 acres for cultivation. On an average a family was provided 2.9 acres for cultivation. Even under this project as in the case of Nagarjuna Sagar the displaced had to encounter the encroachment problem. About 461 acres of land granted to the displaced was already under occupation of local people. And this has resulted in big quarrel between the displaced that came from faraway places to resettle and the local scheduled caste families.[42]

Srisailam: As far as Srisailam Project is concerned the state government had appointed a committee to suggest an appropriate rehabilitation policy. The committee recommended the policy which was followed in the Nagarjuna Sagar Project for the rehabilitation of displaced. But, the government disagreed with the above recommendations and stuck to the CGM already introduced in the case of Sri Ram Sagar (Pochampad) project in 1978 in the place of PRM. The provisions under the CGM are as follows.[43]

1. Displaced families whose lands alone were acquired might be granted 50 per cent of the compensation subject to a maximum of Rs 1,000;
2. Displaced families whose houses alone were affected might be granted 50 per cent of the compensation paid for the acquisition of the house property subject to a maximum of Rs 1,000;
3. In case of displaced families whose lands as well as houses were acquired they might be paid 50 per cent of compensation paid for the acquisition of land and house properties, subject to a maximum of Rs 5,000.

Indira Sagar (Polavaram) Multipurpose Project

The Polavaram project, also known Indira Sagar Project is conceived as a multipurpose major irrigation project. This project assumes importance for two reasons.

1. In terms of displacement of lakhs of people and submergence of large tracks of land it scores a point over all other major irrigation projects undertaken in Andhra Pradesh.
2. Polavaram project happens to be the first multipurpose project in which R&R policy, 2005 of Government of Andhra Pradesh is applied while dealing with the problem of displacement.

An attempt is made in the following section to assess the effectiveness of the government policy in tackling the issue of resettlement and rehabilitation within the frame work of the R&R policy, 2005, preceded by a brief description of the physical magnitude of direct benefits and costs. The figures shown in this regard are taken from the report on "Resettlement and Rehabilitation, Project Affected Families, Economic Rehabilitation Plan" (R&R-PAFERP).

The project would benefit East Godavari, West Godavari, Krishna and Visakhapatnam districts of Andhra Pradesh by providing drinking water to people and industry apart from irrigation of land in the above districts. In addition, the project will generate 960 MW of power. It is contemplated to save 62,000 acres of existing ayacut in Krishna district and provide additional irrigation for seven lakh acres of new ayacut in the upland areas of East and West Godavari districts and Visakhapatnam under right and left main canals (report on R&R-PAFERP 2005).

Submergence: The project submerges 44,763,84 hectares of land including 3,223 hectares of forest land. In addition to this 9,489.31 hectares is required for canal networks. Thus, the total land required for the project would be 54,253.15 hectares.

Displacement: The project will affect 276 villages in three districts, viz., Khammam, West Godavari and East Godavari, East and West Godavari districts are marginally affected with 42 and 29 villages respectively while Khammam district would be affected heavily with a displacement of 205 villages in seven mandals. In all these 276 villages, 44,574 families/households have been estimated to be affected by land acquisition for canal network. However, the number of persons affected would be around 2.5 lakhs, according to people's perception. But according to a survey the number of persons affected is estimated as 1,77,275, based on an average family size of 3.98 persons among affected households. The percentage of tribal households to be displaced constitutes 15.42 per cent. The remaining 37.22 per cent related to BC and FC categories (BC – 17.20 per cent and FC – 19.20 per cent). Further, 76.60 per cent of the households estimated to be displaced in Khammam district of Telangana region which does not derive any benefit from the said project. The share in the displacement of households of East and West Godavari district is 7.79 and 15.61 per cent respectively. This adds to the already existing problem of regional imbalances and inequalities, an undeniable basis for the demand of separate statehood for Telangana.[44]

National Resettlement and Rehabilitation Policy 2003

Until 2003, there was no national-level policy on resettlement and rehabilitation of displaced people due to various developmental projects. After years of mulling on a draft policy, Government of India released NPRR in early 2003. This policy is a pro-active effort of Government of India and provides a broad framework for taking up resettlement and rehabilitation works in development projects. This broad policy essentially attempts to provide a common ground and align the rehabilitation efforts of various States in a holistic sense.

But, the policy also has its own lacunae. One major gap is that, this policy does not stipulate the need for a definite "time-frame" for implementation of rehabilitation plans in relation with the progress of construction. Therefore, the policy would, in all probability, fail to discourage the present practice of starting project construction without much attention to rehabilitation needs of displaced people. Secondly, the policy dilutes the spirit of "discouraging projects that disturb tribals and their livelihoods" clearly sounded in earlier instructions such as G.O. No. 64 of Government of Andhra Pradesh. This policy document failed to pool the best provisions and practices from various states in India.

The effect of this national policy is yet to be seen in "practice". At best, this policy may prompt State Governments to come up with more attractive rehabilitation plans in order to get clearances from various ministries of Central Governments.

Narmada Award and Court Verdicts

Recent award of Supreme Court in the case of Sardar Sarovar Project on rehabilitation practice does exactly point out the gap in "policy" and "practice" of resettlement and rehabilitation. The award delivered on 15th March 2005 categorically says that rehabilitation shall be completed before the submergence takes place (Sub-clause IV(6) (ii) of Clause XI of the Award). This award, in fact, upholds the spirit of Narmada Water Disputes Tribunal Award (1979), which in essence states that "rehabilitation before submergence".

Though this judicial intervention may contribute to the betterment of rehabilitation practice in Sardar Sarovar Project in Gujarat, the extent of its influence on other projects, especially on the irrigation projects, in several other States is a matter of larger policy concern. In most cases, States accept them as project specific awards and do not extend them logically to other projects, at least on moral grounds, in spite of close similarities. Another example is the judgment of High Court of Andhra Pradesh on a (Public Interest Litigation) PIL filed during the year 2004 to stop construction activity of Pulichintala Irrigation Project until obtaining environmental clearance from Ministry of Environment and Forest, Government of India. While obeying the court orders in case of Pulichintala Project, Government is proceeding with the construction work on Polavaram Project, which also lacks various clearances.[45]

G.O. Ms. No. 64 of 1990 issued by Government of Andhra Pradesh

Consolidating the instructions of various earlier G.Os related to displacement of tribes, Social Welfare Department, Government of Andhra Pradesh released G.O. Ms. No. 64 of 1990. The G.O. says that "the dispossession and displacement of tribes on numerous counts is mounting in these sensitive areas, which is creating conditions of discontent and unrest in some of the scheduled areas". Saying that, "the government has carefully considered the entire question of acquisition of land for public purposes and rehabilitation of tribal people in the scheduled areas to ensure that the tribal people in scheduled areas enjoy the safeguards envisaged for them under the Constitution of India and their interests are not compromised on any count whatsoever", the G.O. contains the following major provisions:

- There should be no displacement of tribes nor any disturbance of tribal way of life execution of any developmental project.
- Construction of new major and medium irrigation projects shall be avoided to the extent possible so as to avoid submergence of tribal lands.
- Plans for rehabilitation shall be prepared in association with the people adversely affected and it must be ensured that the people are fully compensated and rehabilitated completely.
- Entire cost of rehabilitation shall be in the first charge on the project. In other words, rehabilitation shall be completed first before project execution.
- Wherever it is unavoidable to take up a scheme involving submergence of tribal lands, rehabilitation shall be taken up

on land-to-land basis, at least for a part of the land lost in submergence.

- If adequate land cannot be provided, employment (in the project or in other projects or in government) should be provided atleast to one of the members of each family displaced.
- A substantial training programme of entrepreneurial skills for displaced tribes, with follow-up in helping and getting financial support, marketing outlets, supply of raw materials etc., shall be built up at the time of execution of the project.

Though the G.O. clearly states that the instructions apply to all those projects already executed or being executed in tribal areas, no effort was made to implement this G.O. in any project during later years. Some of the submergence villages in Yeleru project, viz., D. Kristavaram in Addatheegala Mandal, Ramuladevapuram and Lingavaram in Gangavarammandal, were under Notified Scheduled Areas. Neither a comprehensive rehabilitation plan nor any one of the above provisions was implemented in these villages. Still, authorities did not bother to apply the provisions of this Government Order to compensate the sacrifice of people of that villages.[46]

Resettlement and Rehabilitation Policy 2005

The Government of Andhra Pradesh in 2005 brought out a Policy on Resettlement and Rehabilitation for Project Affected Families (RRPAFs) in the form of a Government Order (G.O. Ms. No.68, dated 8th April, 2005). The Government of Andhra Pradesh claimed the policy as first of its kind in the state. It also has given an impression that it is the best policy in the entire country. It is true as far as the Preamble of the policy is concerned. The Preamble notes, "apart from depriving them of their lands, livelihoods and resource base, displacement has other traumatic, psychological and socio-cultural consequences'. Further, it also records: "The Government of Andhra Pradesh recognised the need to minimise large-scale displacement to the extent possible and where displacement is inevitable, the need to handle with utmost care, human touch and forethought, issues related to RRPAFs." However, the contents of the present policy on R&R are required to be studied before any meaningful comment is made on this.

Chapter VI of the R&R Policy, 2005 provides for the following benefits for PAFs under different heads such as:

1. Free house site,
2. Grant for house construction,
3. Allotment of government land to PAFs, who become small or marginal farmers or landless after acquisition,
4. Grant for cattle shed,
5. Grant for transporting materials,
6. Income generating schemes,
7. Minimum agricultural wages for a specified number of days depending on their being small, marginal farmers or agricultural labourer after land acquisition,
8. Subsistence allowance, and
9. Amenities at settlement.

The policy also envisages special benefits to ST PAFs.

1. The ST PAFs will be allotted land in the project benefitted area which consideration is not applicable to other PAFs,
2. The ST category shall be given preference in allotment of land,
3. An additional financial assistance equivalent to 500 days minimum agricultural wages,
4. They will be resettled close to their natural habitat of their choice, to the extent possible, in compact blocks,
5. The ST PAFs resettled out of the district or outside tribal area will get 25 per cent higher R&R benefits in monetary terms,
6. R&R benefits would be available only to the original tribal land owner and not to the one who appropriated the land in violation of laws prevailing, and
7. The ST PAFs shall be given fishing rights in the reservoir area if they had such rights in the river/pond/dam earlier.

Table 4.2: Benefits to Displaced Persons

Prescribed Item	*A.P. State Policy, 2005*
House site	202 Sq.mts (Rural) 75 Sq.mts. (Urban)
Transportation charges	Rs 5000
Financial Assistance for cattle shed	Rs 15000
Financial Assistance for construction of Work shed / shops	Rs 25000
House construction grant for BPL families	Rs (50000+3000)
Allotment of land against land acquired	2.5 Ha of dry land OR 1.25 Ha of wet land
Financial assistance for 1 Ha waste/degraded land for land development	Rs 10000
Financial assistance for 1 Ha wet land for agriculture production	Rs 5000
PAF (land less) – Minimum Agricultural Wages	750 days
PAF (marginal farmers) – Minimum Agricultural Wages	500 days
PAF (small farmers) – Minimum Agricultural Wages	375 days
Agriculture labour - Minimum Agricultural Wages	625 days
Subsistence allowance to displaced families - Minimum Agricultural Wages	240 days
Vulnerable persons (Annuity Policy)	Rs 500 monthly pension
Each non-tribal PAF who is a member of registered Fishermen co-operative Society/ Fishing license holders in the affected zone and who lost fishing rights and livelihood shall get additional financial assistance for loss of fishing rights.	500 days minimum agricultural wages
The non-tribal families in the project affected areas having fishing rights in the river/pond/dam who is a member of registered Fishermen cooperative Society/ Fishing license holders shall be given fishing rights in the reservoir	Fishing rights in the reservoir

R&R Benefits for Project Affected Families of Scheduled Tribes	
Govt. shall acquire land in the project benefitted area in lieu of acquired land restricting to the extent	2.5 Ha dry or 1.25 Ha wet land or to the extent of land acquired whichever is lower
Additional financial assistance for loss of their customary rights/usage of forest produces. Eachnon-tribal PAF Each non-tribal PAF who is a member of registered Fishermen co-operative Society/Fishing license holders in the affected zone and who lost fishing rights and livelihood shall get additional financial assistance equivalent to 500 days minimum agriculture wages for loss of fishing rights.	500 days minimum agricultural wages
Tribal PAFs resettled outside the district or outside tribal area will get higher R&R benefits in monetary terms	25 per cent
The Tribal families residing in the Project Affected Areas having fishing rights in the river/pond/dam shall be given	Fishing rights in the reservoir

Source: Documents on R&R: Commissioner for R&R, Government of Andhra Pradesh.

There is a gap between the recognition of PAFs distresses and the way their grievances are sought to be redressed by the government. For example, the Preamble of R&R Policy, 2005 mentions the following:

Compulsory acquisition of land for public purpose including infrastructure projects displaces people, forcing them to give up their home, assets and means of livelihood, apart from depriving them of their lands, livelihoods and resource-base, displacement has other traumatic psychological and socio-cultural consequences. The Government of Andhra Pradesh recognises the need to minimise large-scale displacement to the extent possible and, where displacement is inevitable, the need to handle with utmost care, human touch and forethought, issues relating to R&R of PAFs. Such an approach is especially necessary in respect of tribal, small and marginal farmers and women.

The system of extending cash compensation does not, by itself, in most cases, enable the affected families to obtain cultivable agricultural land, homestead and other resources, which they have to surrender to the state. The difficulties are more acute for persons who are critically dependent on the acquired assets for their subsistence/livelihoods, such as landless agricultural workers, forest dwellers, tenants and artisans, as their distress and destitution is more severe, and, yet they are not eligible for cash compensation.

The Policy essentially addresses the need to provide succor to the asset-less rural poor, support the rehabilitation efforts of the resource poor sections, namely, small and marginal farmers, SCs/STs and women who have been displaced, besides, it seeks to provide a broad canvas for an effective dialogue between the PAFs and PDFs and the Administration for R&R. Such a dialogue is expected to enable timely completion of projects with a sense of definiteness as regards costs and adequate attention to the needs of the displaced persons especially the resource poor sections. The intention is to impart greater flexibility for interaction and negotiation so that the resultant Package gains all-round acceptability in the shape of a workable instrument providing satisfaction to all stakeholders/ requiring bodies.

The Government of Andhra Pradesh Policy on the R&R of PAFs and PDFs will be applicable to the projects as defined in this policy and upon notification under this policy.

Administrator for R&R shall implement this Policy in letter and spirit in order to ensure that the benefits envisaged under the policy reaches the PAFs and PDFs, especially resource poor sections including SCs/STs.

Objectives of the Policy

1. To minimise displacement and to identify non-displacing or least-displacing alternatives;
2. To Plan the resettlement and rehabilitation of PAFs/PDFs including special needs of Tribal's and vulnerable sections;
3. To provide better Standard of living to PAFs and PDF's; and
4. To facilitate harmonious relationship between the Requiring Body and PAFs through mutual cooperation.

Although the philosophy behind the R&R effort as incorporated in the Preamble echoes the concerns of well-informed public and voluntary organisations, the very fact that the Government of Andhra Pradesh has come forward to fashion its public policy on the lines indicated in the Preamble is definitely a laudable exercise. It is much more praiseworthy when there is no mismatch between the latter and spirit of the policy content while administering it for the benefit of the resource-poor sections. But this does not appear to be the case. The concern shown in the Preamble got diluted in chapter VI of the R&R Policy, 2005 which lists out the package of benefits to PAFs and PDFs. A case in point is: allotment of land to affected families. The compensation for loss of land is apparently in terms of land only in and around the project benefited area. But this benefit is extendable subject to availability of government land in the district. Even if available, it will be restricted to either 2.5 hectares of dry land or 1.25 hectares of wet land or to the actual extent of land acquired from the affected family whichever is lower. Non availability of the required type of land in the district leaves the affected families completely unsettled as their basic occupation is not protected in the post-project period. The government, on its part, pays them cash compensation for the lands acquired from them and the onus of rehabilitating oneself in such condition rests on the affected individual family. It has been noted in the past that in such cases the affected families go on hunting for land.

Two possibilities were reported from the experience of the earlier projects: one the affected family even if successful in buying land need not necessarily settle down at the government-sponsored resettlement zone. Worse still is the possibility of land prices soaring high leaving the displaced or vulnerable section of the farming community outside the fringe of the land market? Thus, non-allotment of land has an unsettling effect in the project area where resettlement of oustees ought to have been the strict principle in letter and spirit. Moreover, the government by not accepting the alternative proposal of the project prepared by senior retired engineers going against its own policy objective stated in R&R Policy, 2005 as "to minimise displacement and to identify non-displacing or least displacing alternatives." This raises doubts in the minds of public about the government's claim that the R&R Policy, 2005 of the government is by far the best in attending to the resettlement and rehabilitation requirements of PAFs.

State Mission for Resettlement and Rehabilitation (SMRR)

The government has established the R&R Commissionarate for planning, Monitoring and effective implementation of R&R of PDF and PAFs of Irrigation Projects taken up under Jalayagnam and also delegated financial powers by declaring the Commissioner (R&R) as the Head of the Department. Further, the government has approved the proposal of World Bank on Non Lending Technical Assistance (NLTA) for strengthening and transforming institutions for management of Land Acquisition and R&R along with action plan and time table and authorised the Commissioner (R&R) to carry the activities forward. In pursuant to the above, the government has permitted the Commissioner (R&R) for setting up of an R&R Society as an executing agency with a flexible organisational structure, operational procedures and financial autonomy which would work under the overall control of the State level R&R Commissioner. Subsequently, the government approved the Memorandum of Articles for SMRR and request to take necessary action for Registering a Society. Accordingly, a Society is formed and registered under the name of SMRR under Andhra Pradesh Societies Registration (204 of 2009) with the following objectives and functions.

Objectives

1. To bring flexibility in planning, implementation and monitoring of R&R programmes considering the local conditions like scarcity of land, population density, extensive rural poverty (Wherever needed);
2. To develop alternate lands, villages and townships for the PDFs and PAFs on its own or through government/non-government /private sector agencies;
3. To engage required technical expertise from outside the government and external agencies and thus reduce pressure on the existing government machinery;
4. To develop NGOs/CBO partnership to work with the affected communities;
5. To mobilise and promote partnership of private/public sectors in the implementation of R&R programmes;

6. To mobilise resources, in addition to regular budgetary allocation by the State, for R&R programmes;
7. To put in place a suitable financial management structure to meet the challenges of long term process of planning and implementation of R&R activities with flexibility in terms of financial operations to ensure that funds are available throughout the year;
8. To reduce fiduciary risks through increased transparency and accountability;
9. To plan and implement effective information, education and communication (IEC) strategies;
10. To ensure improved monitoring and tracking mechanisms and build partnership with civil mission;
11. To evolve Strategies and approaches for the empowerment of the displaced persons through social mobilisation and institution building for the community participation or to develop a working mechanism with the existing institutions;
12. To be a centre for research, documentation and information dissemination on all aspects of R&R and to act as a forum of advocacy for the formulation and implementation of pro-poor policies, plans and programmes;
13. To facilitate to conduct Social Audit;
14. To undertake any other activity to further the cause of and empower and build the organisations of the PAFs and PDFs;
15. To acquire movable and immovable assets to facilitate in achievement of Mission objectives;
16. To borrow/raise funds for the fulfilment of its objects, wherever necessary;
17. To accept donations, transfer of assets, devolutions for the fulfilment/furtherance of its objects.

Functions

The Mission undertakes such functions, programmes and activities as required in fulfilling the objectives listed in Art. 4. It may take up these functions either through its own staff, Specialists of Different Fields, grass-roots community organisations, NGOs, government departments/agencies, Other Institutions, Agencies or Individuals as deemed fit.[47]

Grievance Redressal Cell

(a) In respect of every project to which this Policy applies, the State Government shall constitute a GRM under the Chairmanship of the Commissioner for R&R for redressal of grievances of the PAFs.

(b) The composition, powers, functions and other matters relating to the functioning of the GRM shall be such as may be prescribed by the Appropriate Government.

Table 4.3: Projects in Telangana Region and PAFs

Sl. No.	*Project*	*District*	*PAFs*			*PDFs*		
			BPL	*APL*	*TOTAL*	*BPL*	*APL*	*TOTAL*
1.	Aliminate Madhava Reddy Project (AMRP)	Nalgonda	2154	594	2748	2154	594	2748
2.	Sri Rama Sagar Project Stage-II Mylaram Balancing Reservoir	Warangal	322	2	324	322	2	324
3.	J.Chokkarao Devadula Lift Irrigation Scheme Phase-II		82	1	83	82	1	83
4.	Mid Manair Reservoir Project	Karimnagar	10612	511	11123	10612	511	11123
5.	Sripada Sagar Project, Stage-I, Phase-I		6816	736	7552	6816	736	7552
6.	Sripada Sagar Project, Stage-I, Phase-I	Adilabad	5077	183	5260	5077	183	5260
7.	Gaddennavagu Project, Bhainsa	Adilabad	2227	245	2472	2227	245	2472
8.	Neelwai Project		371	3	374	371	3	374
9.	Gollavagu Project		158	11	169	158	11	169
10.	Sri Komaram Bheem Project, Asifabad		2080	11	2091	2080	11	2091
11.	Bazarhatnoor Project		151	0	151	151	0	151
12.	Chickman Vagu Project		63	0	63	63	0	63
13.	Jawahar (Nettampadu) Lift Irrigation Scheme	Mahbubnagar	2471	104	2575	2471	104	2575
14.	Mahathma Gandhi (Kalwakurthy) Lift Irrigation Project		242	10	252	242	10	252
15.	Rajiv Bheem Lift Irrigation Scheme		3587	404	3991	3587	404	3991
16.	Priyadarshini Jurala Project (PJP)		163	0	163	163	0	163
	Telangana Region Total		**36576**	**2815**	**39391**	**36576**	**2815**	**39391**

Source: Documents on R&R: Commissioner for R&R, Government of Andhra Pradesh and G.O. MS No: 68, dt 08-04-2005.

Table 4.4: Community-wise PAFs in Telangana Region

Sl. No.	Project	District	S.C	S.T.	B.C.	O.C.	TOTAL	PAF	PDF	BPL	APL	TOTAL
1	AMRP Project	Nalgonda	723	28	1246	751	2748	2748	2748	2154	594	2748
2	Sri Rama Sagar Project Stage-II Mylaram Balancing Reservoir	Warangal	163	75	86	0	324	324	324	322	2	324
3	J.Chokkarao Devadula Lift Irrigation Scheme Phase-II at Donga Chelimi Thanda, H/o Gandiramram (V) of Narmetta		0	83	0	0	83	83	83	82	1	83
4	Mid Manair Reservoir Project	Karimnagar	1960	64	7563	1536	11123	11123	11123	10612	511	11123
5	Sripada Sagar Project		1882	14	5169	487	7552	7552	7552	6816	736	7552
6	Sripada Sagar Project	Adilabad	757	0	2317	654	3728	3728	3728	3375	353	3728
7	Gaddennavagu Project, Bhainsa		521	69	1425	457	2472	2472	2472	2227	245	2472
8	Neelwai Project		73	99	191	11	374	374	374	371	3	374
9	Gollavagu Project		27	17	125	0	169	169	169	159	10	169
10	Sri Komaram Bheem Project, Asifabad		167	386	1375	36	1964	1964	1964	1939	25	1964
11	Bazarhatnoor Project		0	0	151	0	151	151	151	151	0	151
12	ChickmanVagu Project		63	0	0	0	63	63	63	63	0	63
13	Jawahar (Nettampadu) Lift Irrigation Scheme	Mahbubnagar	375	8	1904	288	2575	2575	2575	2471	104	2575
14	Mahathma Gandhi (Kalwakurthy) Lift Irrigation Project		48	1	95	108	252	252	252	242	10	252
15	Rajiv Bheem Lift Irrigation Scheme		789	19	2345	838	3991	3991	3991	3587	404	3991
16	Priyadarshini Jurala Project (PJP)		30	0	103	30	163	163	163	163	0	163
Total			**7578**	**863**	**24095**	**5196**	**37732**	**37732**	**37732**	**34734**	**2998**	**37732**

Source: Documents on R&R: Commissioner for R&R, Government of Andhra Pradesh and G.O. Ms No: 68, Dt 08-04-2005.

Table 4.5: Status of R&R Villages in Telangana Region as on 31-07-2012

Sl. No.	*District Name*	*Project Name*	*Project Adminis-trator*	*No. of Villages submerged fully*	*No. of villages submerged Partially*	*Total No. of Villages*	*No. of villages Notified*	*No. of villages Socio economic Survey Completed*	*No. of villages Socio economic Survey Published*	*No. of Villages Draft plan Scheme submitted*	*No. of Villages Draft plan Scheme Approved*	*Draft Plans to be Prepared*
1.	Nalgonda	Aliminate Madhava Reddy Project	Jt. Collector	2	1	3	3	3	3	3	2	0
2.	Warangal	Sri Rama Sagar Project Stage - II	Jt. Collector	0	3	3	3	3	3	1	0	2
		J.Chokka Rao Devadula Lift Irrigation Project		0	2	2	2	2	2	1	0	1
3.	Karim-nagar	Sripada Sagar Project, Stage-I, Phase-I	Jt. Collector	10	3	13	13	12	12	12	12	1
		Mid Manair Reservoir Project		18	5	23	23	11	11	11	11	12
4.	Adilabad	Gaddenavagu Suddavagu Project	Jt. Collector	7	1	8	8	8	8	8	8	0
		Komaram Bheem Project	Jt. Collector	5	1	6	6	6	6	6	6	0
5.	Adilabad	Gollavagu Project,	Jt. Collector	0	1	1	1	1	1	1	1	0
		Neelwai Project		2	1	3	3	3	3	3	3	0
		SripadaSagar Project, Stage-I, Phase-I		9	0	9	9	9	9	9	9	0
		Bazarhatnoor Project		0	1	1	1	1	1	1	1	0
		Chickman Vagu Project, Indervelly		1	0	1	1	1	1	0	0	1
6.	Mahbub-nagar	Rajiv (Bhima) Lift Irrigation Scheme	Jt. Collector	7	1	8	8	8	6	3	0	5
		Mahathma Gandhi (Kalwakurthi) Lift Irrigation Scheme		1	0	1	1	1	1	1	0	0
		Jawahar (Nettampadu) Lift Irrigation Scheme		3	0	3	3	3	3	3	0	0
		PriyadarshiniJurala Project		0	1	1	1	1	1	0	0	1
		Total		**65**	**21**	**86**	**86**	**73**	**71**	**63**	**53**	**23**

Source: Documents on R&R: Commissioner for R&R, Government of Andhra Pradesh.

(c) Any PAF, if aggrieved, for not being offered the admissible R&R benefits as provided under this Policy, may move an appropriate petition for redressal of his grievances to the GRM.

(d) The form and manner in which and the time within which complaints may be made to the GRM and disposed of shall be such as may be prescribed by the appropriate Government.

Table 4.6: Status of R&R Centres in Telangana Region as on 31-07-2012 in Telangana Region

Sl. No.	*District Name*	*Project Name*	*No. of R&R Centers Contemplated*	*No. of Centers R&R land Acquired*	*Balance land to be Acquired*
1.	Nalgonda	Aliminate Madhava Reddy Project (A.M.R.P)	3	3	0
2.	Warangal	Sri Rama Sagar Project Stage - II	3	3	0
		J.Chokka Rao Devadula Lift Irrigation Project	3	2	1
3.	Karimnagar	Sripada Sagar Project, Stage-I, Phase-I	12	12	0
		Mid Manair Reservoir Project	12	12	0
4.	Adilabad	Gaddenavagu Suddavagu Project	9	9	0
		Komaram Bheem Project	10	10	0
5.	Adilabad	Gollavagu Project,	1	1	0
		Neelwai Project	1	1	0
		Sripada Sagar Project, Stage-I, Phase-I	5	5	0
		Bazarhatnoor Project	1	1	0
		Chickman Vagu Project, Indervelly	-	-	-
6.	Mahbub-nagar	Rajiv (Bhima) Lift Irrigation Scheme	8	7	1
		Mahathma Gandhi (Kalwakurthi) Lift Irrigation Scheme	1	1	0
		Jawahar (Nettampadu) Lift Irrigation Scheme	3	3	0
		Priyadarshini Jurala Project	1	1	0
		Total	**73**	**71**	**2**

Source: Documents on R&R: Commissioner for R&R, Government of Andhra Pradesh.

Table 4.7: Status of R&R B.P.L. Housing Units as on 31-07-2012 in Telangana Region

Sl. No.	*District Name*	*Project Name*	*No. of Housing Units for Contemplated*	*No. of Housing Units Completed*
1.	Nalgonda	Aliminate Madhava Reddy Project	2748	1049
2.	Warangal	Sri Rama Sagar Project. Stage – II	324	74
		J.Chokka Rao Devadula Lift Irrigation Project	83	-
3.	Karimnagar	Sripada Sagar Project, Stage-I, Phase-I	7552	1448
		Mid Manair Reservoir Project	11123	96
4.	Adilabad	Gaddennavagusuddavagu Project	2472	1274
		Komaram Bheem Project	2091	1995
5.	Adilabad	Gollavagu Project,	169	0
		Neelwai Project	374	-
		Sripada Sagar Project, Stage-, Phase-I	5260	-
		Bazarhatnoor Project	151	151
		Chickman Vagu Project, Indervelly	63	-
6.	Mahbubnagar	Rajiv (Bhima) Lift Irrigation Scheme	3991	-
		Mahathma Gandhi (Kalwakurthi) Lift Irrigation Scheme	252	-
		Jawahar (Nettampadu) Lift Irrigation Scheme	2575	-
		Priyadarshini Jurala Project	163	-
	Total		**39391**	**6087**

Source: Documents on R&R: Commissioner for R&R, Government of Andhra Pradesh.Note: The Housing units are revised as per GOMS No.08, dt: 10.02.2012.

Table 4.8: Status of R&R Centres Infrastructure as on 31-7-2012 in Telangana Region

Sl. No.	*District Name*	*Project Name*	*Infrastructure*						
			No. of Centers	*Site marking*	*Leveling*	*Roads*	*Water*	*Electricity*	*Others*
1.	Nalgonda	Aliminate Madhava Reddy Project (A.M.R.P)	3	3	3	3	3	3	3
2.	Warangal	Sri Rama Sagar Project Stage - II	3	3	3	1	3	3	-
		J.Chokka Rao Devadula Lift Irrigation Project	2	2	2	-	-	2	-
3.	Karimnagar	Sripada Sagar Project, Stage-I, Phase-I	12	8	8	8	8	5	5
		Mid Manair Reservoir Project	12	11	11	4	4	1	4
4.	Adilabad	Gaddenavagu Suddavagu Project	9	9	9	8	8	8	5
		Komaram Bheem Project	10	10	10	10	10	10	10
5.	Adilabad	Gollavagu Project,	1	1	1	1	1	1	-
		Neelwai Project	1	1	1	1	1	1	-
		Sripada Sagar Project, Stage-I, Phase-I	5	5	3	3	3	3	-
		Bazarhatnoor Project	1	1	1	1	1	1	-
		ChickmanVagu Project, Indervelly	-	-	-	-	-	-	-
6.	Mahbub-nagar	Rajiv (Bhima) Lift Irrigation Scheme	7	6	7	4	1	1	-
		Mahathma Gandhi (Kalwakurthi) Lift Irrigation Scheme	1	1	1	-	1	1	-
		Jawahar (Nettampadu) Lift Irrigation Scheme	3	1	1	-	-	-	-
		Priyadarshini Jurala Project	1	1	1	1	-	-	-
	Total		**71**	**63**	**62**	**45**	**44**	**40**	**27**

Source: Documents on R&R: Commissioner for R&R, Government of Andhra Pradesh.

Table 4.9: Status of R & R Financial Status as on 31-07-2012 in Telangana Region

Sl. No.	*District Name*	*Project Name*	*Amount Required*	*Amount Released*	*Expenditure Incurred*	*Balance available*
			in Crores	*in Crores*	*in Crores*	*in Crores*
1.	Nalgonda	Aliminate Madhava Reddy Project	53.050	53.050	50.130	2.920
2.	Warangal	Sri Rama Sagar Project Stage – II	9.080	5.581	3.404	2.177
		J. Chokka Rao Devadula Lift Irrigation Project	2.550	1.750	1.115	0.635
3.	Karimnagar	Sripada Sagar Project, Stage-I, Phase-I	194.840	149.490	149.490	0.000
		Mid Manair Reservoir Project	325.630	135.840	135.840	0.000
4.	Adilabad	Gaddenavagu Suddavagu Project	62.500	61.970	61.870	0.100
		Komaram Bheem Project	69.500	66.030	62.600	3.430
5.	Adilabad	Gollavagu Project,	3.210	3.210	3.200	0.010
		Neelwai Project	12.07	12.040	11.400	0.640
		Sripada Sagar Project, Stage-I, Phase-I	147.830	105.200	101.000	4.200
		Bazarhatnoor Project	2.920	2.920	2.820	0.100
		ChickmanVagu Project, Indervelly	5.370	0.000	0.000	0.000
6.	Mahbubnagar	Rajiv (Bhima) Lift Irrigation Project	29.000	23.871	21.291	2.580
		Mahatma Gandhi (Kalwakurthi) Lift Irrigation Project	3.000	0.037	0.037	0.000
		Jawahar (Nettampadu) Lift Irrigation Project	15.510	3.027	3.027	0.000
		Priyadarshini Jurala Project	1.781	1.781	1.781	0.000
	Total		**937.841**	**625.797**	**609.005**	**16.792**

Source: Documents on R&R: Commissioner for R&R, Government of Andhra Pradesh.

Summing Up

Since Independence, many irrigation projects were constructed and several other are being constructed in India. In all, millions of people were affected by displacement caused due to submergence of their native habitations. Most of these people were deprived of satisfactory resettlement and rehabilitation due to the absence of comprehensive policies and lack of commitment in practice. Policies of governments on R&R released over last few years stand as examples to say that governments are becoming sensitive to the displacement issue. But, what is essential and yet to be proved is the commitment of governments in establishing "best practices" in resettlement and rehabilitation.

Though injustice done to displaced population since Independence cannot be undone, following specific steps will help in minimising human suffering and achieving sensible development in future:

1. Discourage projects that seriously affect tribal population. Explore least displacing alternatives to each and every irrigation project proposed.
2. Recognise that displacement and suffering is avoidable. Consider constructing a Barrage instead of a Dam in case of Polavaram Project and save lakhs of people from displacement.
3. Prioritise projects that benefit the tribal communities rather than submerge them, in order to address the disparities in development.
4. Secure all clearances from appropriate authorities before starting the construction work. Implement the rehabilitation package before project construction.
5. Consult the people facing displacement and get the consent from local Panchayat Raj Institutions (PRIs) before contemplating any project as stipulated by R&R Policies; 73rd Amendment to Constitution and various State Panchayat Raj Acts.
6. Recognise the sacrifice of project displaced people by displaying their details at each and every project location along with usual engineering details and persons associated with it.

In conclusion, the comparison above clearly shows the inadequacies of the policy in its current form to deal with the impoverishment risks, and socio-cultural and politico-economic needs of the DPs and IDPs. What is needed, as suggested by the WCD, is that "an approach based on 'recognition of rights' and 'assessment of risks'...be developed as a tool for future planning and decision making".[48] Secondly, in line with the point emphasised in the guiding principles for IDPs that "the *Primary duty* and *responsibility* for providing humanitarian assistance to internally displaced persons lies with national authorities", and project authorities (MNCs and private companies) as is the case in era of economic reforms. Finally, there is also a need, as suggested by Medha Patkar of Narmada Bachao Andolan, to link development with displacement policy which assumes greater importance in view of the onslaught of national and international capital in the age of so-called liberalisation, globalisation and privatisation" to protect the rights of vulnerable communities to be an equal partner in developmental process.

The Andhra Pradesh experience of R&R throws up the following aspects:

1. Struck by the continued degeneration and volatility of the policy in the post-state formation period till the government came up with a policy on R&R in 2005.
2. The policy formulation and implementation are apathetic to and least informed by the growing public concern for the displaced families as much as by the questions raised in challenging the received models of development, demanding alternatives.
3. There has been a shrinking of space for human problem and human rights of displaced people in state policy.
4. A matter of serious concern is the growing legislative apathy to the rehabilitation of the involuntarily displaced people either as a part of the legislative process or otherwise. As a consequence, there has been growing room for fraud and corruption as well as emergence of a class of political-lawyer-contractor-bureaucrat combines with a tendency to earn profit on the adversity of the displaced and dispossessed.

The failure of the state and the resultant loss of faith in the policy pronouncements and methods of implementation find expression in the form of activist and voluntary intervention (if not in Andhra Pradesh) in the country in the context of major projects like Sardar Sarovar. The churning out of oustees' woes time and again by themselves and by well informed people and fact finding groups made the Central government ponder over the distress of displaced people and the need to minimise it by appropriate measures. The national policy guideline on R&R is a direct outcome of this. The present policy on R&R, 2005 of Andhra Pradesh government is a derivate of the national policy. Both the policies, however, have roots in the conscious efforts of voluntary groups and NGOs who brought the issues of displacement and R&R to the knowledge of the world.

However, the Policy 2005 does leave many a gap between the actual concerns expressed by the government and the actual benefits suggested for their resettlement and rehabilitation. This does not end here. There is also a gap between what is proposed to be done for the oustees of Indirasagar Project and what was already done under projects executed in (a) Pre-state formation period and (b) post-state formation period. It has been recorded time and again that the policy of rehabilitation was well articulated and well executed in pre-state formation period than in the post-state formation period.

The concern and the vision towards involuntarily displaced people demonstrated by the earlier regimes of pre-state formation are reflected in "if the ryots are left to their discretion after paying cash compensation without making any arrangements for their welfare; (a) it will reflect on the administration, (b) it will case great inconvenience and trouble to riots to themselves." But this concern is no longer seen in the later regime. The politicians who declared themselves as great visionaries have done precious little in attending to the problems of the ousted families/persons which get solved only when they are rehabilitated in physical terms.

As long as this remains unfulfilled, the policy-makers have to necessarily draw lessons from the experiences of projects of pre-state formation period instead of dubbing the voices of public and voluntary organisations as anti-dam and anti-development. As long as the apathy towards displaced is visible the social activism and the voluntary intervention would be there.

References

1. Chittaroopa Palit, "Short-changing the Displaced: National Rehabilitation Policy", Economic and Political Weekly, Issue July 3 2004, pp. 2961-2963.
2. Sah, D C., "Involuntary Migrations." Rawat Publications, Jaipur - 2003.
3. Courtland Robinson, W., "Risks and Rights: The Causes, Consequences, and Challenges of Development-Induced Displacement", The Brookings Institution-SAIS Project on Internal Displacement, May, Washington D.C. - 2003.
4. Bharathi, M., and R S Rao, "Linking Development to Displacement", Economic and Political Weekly, Issue July 10-16, 1999.
5. The Right to Fair Compensation and Transparency in Land Acquisition, Rehabilitation and Resettlement Act, 2013.
6. Mohammed Asif, 'Why Displaced Persons Reject Project Resettlement Colonies", Economic and Political Weekly, Issue June 10 2000, pp. 2005-2008.
7. Walter Fernandes, "Rehabilitation Policy for the Displaced", Economic and Political Weekly, Vol 39, Issue 12, March 2004, pp. 1191-1193.
8. Report of the Committee on Rehabilitation of Displaced Tribals due to Development Projects, Ministry of Home Affairs, Government of India, New Delhi - 1985.
9. Walter Fernandes, op. cit.
10. Walter Fernandes, "Pawns in the 'Development'", in S Parasuraman and P. V. Unnikrishnan, (Ed.), India Disasters Report Human - Instigated Disasters, 2000, pp. 276-279.
11. Roopee Sahaee, "National Rehabilitation Policy: Many Loopholes", in Economic and Political Weekly, Issue February 8, 2003, pp. 510-512.
12. Bela Bhatia, "Forced Evictions in the Valley", in Jean Dreze, Meera Samson, and Satyajit Singh (eds), The Dam and the Nation: Displacement and Resettlement in the Narmada Valley, 1997.
13. Renu Modi, "Sardar Sarovar Oustees: Coping with Displacement", Economic and Political Weekly, Vol. 39, Issue 11, March 2004, pp. 1123-1126.
14. *Ibid.*
15. Vasudha Dhagamwar, Subrata De, and Nikhil Verma, "Industrial Development & Displacement: The People of Korba", Sage Publications, New Delhi - 2003. p. 211.

16. National Policy on Resettlement and Rehabilitation for Project Affected Families.2003, New Delhi: Ministry of Rural Development, Department of Land Resources. Chapter1, p. 5.
17. Vasudha Dhagamwar, Subrata De, and Nikhil Verma, op. cit.
18. Mohammed Asif, June, op. cit.
19. Sah, D.C., "Involuntry Migrations, Jaipur: Rawat Publications, New Delhi - 2003.
20. Roopee Sahaee, February 2003, op. cit.
21. Bandyopadhyay, D., "Rayagada Story Retold : Destitutes of Development", Economic and Political Weekly, Vol. 39, Issue 5, January 2004, pp. 408-411.
22. Walter Fernandes, op. cit.
23. Chittaroopa Palit, op.cit.
24. Renu Modi, op. cit.
25. NPRR (2003), op. cit. Chapter 6, p. 3.
26. Renu Modi, op. cit.
27. Chittaroopa Palit, op.cit.
28. W Courtland Robinson, op. cit.
29. Michael M Cernea, 'Why Economic Analysis is Essential to Resettlement: A Sociologist's view', Economic and Political Weekly, Issue July 31-August 1999.
30. W Courtland Robinson, op. cit. pp.13-14.
31. Government of Andhra Pradesh, 1965, Nizamsagar Project, Public Works Department, Vol.1.
32. *Ibid*, p. 76.
33. *Ibid*, p. 15.
34. Gajarajan, C.S., "Planned Rehabilitation and Economic Change – A Case Study of Tungabhadra Project Rehabilitation Colonies at H.B. Halli". 1970.
35. Tungabhadra Project, The Economic Weekly, August 15, 1953, pp. 919-920.
36. Emergence of Villages in Raichur district, Hyderbad Today, Vol, III, No. 3, June 1953, p. 3.
37. *Ibid*, p. 6.
38. Rajesh Kumar Saxena, 1963, Financial Aspects of Nagarjuna Sagar Project (Memio).
39. Government of Andhra Pradesh, Rehabilitation Policy-Assignment of Land to the displaced Families, etc, orders issued by Revenue Department, G.O.Ms. No. 1295, July 3, 1959.
40. Government of Andhra Pradesh, Nagarjunasagar Project – Rehabilitation Measures and Assignment Lands to the displaced Families, orders issued by Public Works Department, G.O. Ms.No.12, January 19, 1960.

41. Muthyam Reddy, K. "Some Aspects of Rehabilitation Policy of the State government with reference to Major Irrigation Projects – A Case Study of Sriramsagar and Srisailam", Ph.D, Thesis, Kakatiya University, Warangal, 1992.
42. Special collector, Pochampad Project, Brief Note on Land Acquisition and Rehabilitation under Sriram Sagar Project and Lower Maner Dam as on 15-9-1997.
43. Resettlement and Rehabilitation – Project Affected Families Economic Rehabilitation Plan (PAFERP) 2005, prepared for Irrigation and CAS Department, Government of Andhra Pradesh by Agricultural Finance Corporation Ltd.
44. Policy on Resettlement and rehabilitation for project Affected Families, 2005, G.O.Ms.No.68, April 8, 2005, Irrigation and CAD (Project Wing-LA IV-R&R) Department, Government of Andhra Pradesh.
45. Government of Andhra Pradesh, G.O.Ms.No. 141, April 19, 1968.
46. Documents on R&R: Commissioner for R&R, Government of Andhra Pradesh, 2012.
47. W Courtland Robinson, op. cit.
48. Bharathi, M., and R S Rao, op. cit.

Chapter 5

Resettlement and Rehabilitation Policy: Implementation and Impact on Scheduled Tribes

The present chapter has been divided into three parts. The first part deals with the demographical profile of the STs in Warangal District and the second part deals with the implementation and impact of R&R Policy and response of affected tribes in selected study area and the third part deals with few case studies.

Part-I

Warangal, one of the 10 districts of Telangana Region of Andhra Pradesh, is a place with a great historic past. It is the seat of the Vishnukundins and Kakatiya dynasties that ruled the region as early as pre-Buddhist period. Originally known as Orugallu - meaning a solitary cliff - Warangal was the capital of the Kakatiyas who have left their indelible stamp in the form of awe-inspiring architectural wonders. The Warangal Fort, the Thousand Pillar Temple, Ramappa Temple and Bhadrakali temple are fine remnants of the glorious bygone era. After the downfall of the Kakatiyas, the region was ruled by the Qutub Shahis, and the Nizam. The profile of Warangal district has been given in the following lines.[1]

History

Warangal was the capital of the Kakatiya kingdom ruled by the Kakatiya dynasty from the twelfth to the fourteenth centuries. Warangal is also known as Orugallu, Ekasila Nagaram and Andhra Naragram,

Andhra refers to Andhra Maha Vishnu. The old name of this newly formed city is *Orugallu*. *Oru* means one and *Kallu* means stone. The Kakatiyas left many monuments, including an impressive fortress, four massive stone gateways, the Swayambhu temple dedicated to Shiva, and the Ramappa temple situated near Ramappa Lake. The cultural and administrative distinction of the Kakatiyas was mentioned by the famous traveller Marco Polo. Famous or well-known rulers included Ganapathi Deva, Prathapa Rudra, and Rani (queen) Rudrama Devi. After the defeat of Pratapa Rudra, the Musunuri Nayaks united seventy two Nayak chieftains and captured Warangal from Delhi sultanate and ruled for fifty years. Jealousy and mutual rivalry between Nayaks ultimately led to the downfall of Hindus in 1370 A.D. and success of Bahmanis. Bahmani Sultanate later broke up into several smaller sultanates, of which the Golconda sultanate ruled Warangal. The Mughal emperor Aurangzeb conquered Golconda in 1687, and it remained part of the Mughal Empire until the southern provinces of the empire split away to become the state of Hyderabad in 1724 which included the Telangana region and some parts of Maharashtra and Karnataka. Hyderabad was annexed to India in 1948, and became an Indian state. In 1956, Hyderabad was partitioned as part of the states Reorganisation Act, and Telangana, the Telugu-speaking region of Hyderabad State which includes Warangal, became part of Andhra Pradesh.

Geographic location

Warangal district lies between 17° 19′ and 18° 36′ N latitude and 78° 49′ and 80o 43' East longitude. The district is bounded by Khammam district on the East, Karimnagar district on the North, Nalgonda on the South and Medak on the West. River Godavari serves as border on one side. The District Headquarters is Warangal, which lies about 150 kms away from the Capital city of Hyderabad.

Area

The geographic area of the district is 12834 Sq. Kms.

Topography

The topography of the district consists of isolated hills, rain fed tanks, lakes and shrubby forests. River Godavari forms the North Eastern border of the district, but is not yet tapped for irrigation.

The major soil types found in the district are red chalka (55 per cent), black cotton soil (22 per cent), loamy soil (14 per cent), and sandy loams (9 per cent).[2]

Climate

The climate in Warangal district is generally dry. Summers are hot, with mercury sometimes touching 50°C. The temperature dips to 13°C in winters, during the months of December and January.

Rainfall

Warangal district receives maximum rainfall through the South - West monsoon, during the months of July, August and September. Normal annual rainfall is 994 mm. The areas of Cherial, Maddur, and Bachannapet receive only upto 750 mm rainfalls and are classified as dry areas. Maximum rainfall is received in Mulug, Parkal, Mahabubabad and Narsampet Mandals. However, during the year 2002, many areas in the district have been facing drought-related problems. Rainfall received during the year 2001-2002 was only 820 mm. Rainfall received upto November 2002 was just 622 mm.

Demographic particulars

As per 2011 Census, the total population of the district is given in the following table:

Table 5.1: Demographic Profile of the Warangal District

Area	*Total Population*	*Female*	*Males*	*Families*
Urban	992333	493646	498687	241082
Rural	2520243	1259649	1260594	645197
Total	**3512576**	**1753295**	**1759281**	**886279**

Source: Census of 2011, Director for census operations, Government of India, Hyderabad.

Above table indicates that the population of the Warangal district, out of the total percentage majority of the people has consisting in rural area about 71.74 per cent and remaining in urban area i.e., 28.25 per cent. Out of the total population male and female are consisted about 50.08 per cent and 49.91 per cent. In urban area, the male and female population consisting about 50.25 per cent and 49.74 per cent, while in rural area 49.98 per cent and 50.01 per cent respectively. Refer to families out of the total families majority of the families are residing in rural areas 72.79 per cent and in urban area is 27.20 per cent.

Table 5.2: Literacy Rate in the Warangal District

Population	*Literates*	*Percentage*
Female Male	885233 1179790	50.49 67.06
Total	**2065023**	**58.79**

Source: Census of 2011, Director for census operations, Government of India, Hyderabad.

According to the 2011 census, the literacy rate in Warangal district is 58.79 per cent, out of these male and female found with 67.06 per cent and 50.49 per cent respectively.

Table 5.3: SC Population in Warangal District

Population	*Literates*	*Percentage*
Female Male	307709 308393	49.94 50.05
Total	**616102**	**17.53**

Source: Census of 2011, Director for census operations, Government of India, Hyderabad.

Table 5.3 represents about the scheduled caste population in Warangal district, out of the total population 17.53 per cent of SC population is consisting in the district, among these 50.05 per cent are males and 49.94 per cent are females.

Table 5.4: ST Population in Warangal District

Population	*Literates*	*Percentage*
Female Male	261680 268976	49.31 50.68
Total	**530656**	**15.10**

Source: Census of 2011, Director for census operations, Government of India, Hyderabad.

Above table disclosed about the scheduled tribe population in Warangal district, out of the total population 15.10 per cent of ST population is consisting in the district, among these 50.68 per cent are males and 49.31 per cent are females.

Avatars in Warangal District

There are eight reservoirs in Warangal District those are Gangarm, Bheemghnapur, Salivagu, Dharmasagar, Gandiramaram, Bommakur, Ashwaraopally and Rjavaram Ghanpur (Station) and these tanks are upgraded as reservoirs. In the above mentioned all reservoirs the following reservoirs affected to the Scheduled Tribes Villages/Thandas. Those are:

1. Ashwaraopally Tank: Cherla Thanda
2. Rajawaram Tank: Desai Thanda
3. Gandi Ramaram Tank: Dongala Chelma Thanda

The above mentioned tanks which are based on the Lift Irrigation Projects. On the other hand, there are some tanks are upgraded as balancing reservoirs based on canals. Those are Jamasthanpuram, Yllandu, Rangapuram, Mailaram and Parvathagiri tanks.

In the above mentioned projects only a few projects have been completed and remaining some projects have been completed partially.

I. **Mailaram Tank**[3] has been constructed as Balancing Reservoir in the Village limits of Mylaram, Rayaparthy (Tahsil) Warangal District, under Kakatiya Main Canal of Sri Ramsagar Project Stage-II between 296.00 to 301.00 Kms. The capacity of old tank was 0.350 TMC with Full Reservoir Level (FRL) + 247.850, Mean Water Level (MWL) + 248.450 to serve an ayacut of 1200 acres. It is modified as Balancing Reservoir with a capacity of 0.867 Thousand Million Cubic Feet (TMC) with FRL + 250.500. Muripirala is one of the major villages having 663 houses out of them 56 houses are coming under submergence within FRL + 250.500, 191 houses are coming within 100 meters surface distance FRL + 250.500 water line have completed. Out of these total houses, 27 houses in Janakamma Thanda are submerged within 100 meters surface distance from FRL +250.500 and

31 houses in Vidyanagar Thanda (Hamlet of Rayaparthy Village and Tahsil) are submerged within 100 meters surface distance from FRL + 250.500. Consequently, 12 Acres – 6 Guntas of land was allotted for PAF under R&R Policy. Out of these 2 Acres – 2 Guntas of land was allotted for PAF of Janakamma Banda Thanda near Zaffargadh to Muripirala B.T. Road and 2 Acres – 2 Guntas of land was allotted for PAF of near Rayaparthy to Kondoor B.T. Road. Regarding the agricultural land 50 acres in Vidyanagar Thanda and 49 acres in Janakamma Banda Thanda has acquired for the Reservoir.

II. Gandi Ramaram Tank[4] has been constructed as Reservoir in the Village limits of Gandi Ramavaram Village, Narmetta (Tahsil) Warangal District, under J. Chokka Rao Godavari Lift Irrigation Project Phase-II in 2007 year. The capacity of old tank was 0.023 TMC has been improved upto 0.40 TMC to serve an ayacut of 4000 acres of 422 Mts. with Full Reservoir Level + 250.500. Dongachelimi Thanda Hamlet of Gandiramram village having 73 houses, 83 families and 600 acres (Total 624 Acres) are coming under submergence within FRL + 250.500. Consequently 4 Acres – 31 Guntas (Government Assign Land) and 3 Acres – 20 Guntas (Patta land) of land was allotted for PAFs nearby displaced Thanda on the road of manchupla to Gandi Ramaram in Narmetta (tahsil) Warangal district under R&R Policy.

III. Ashwaraopally Tank[5] has been constructed as Reservoir in the Village limits of Jarrargudem Village, Raghunathpally (Tahsil) Warangal District, under J. Chokka Rao Godavari Lift Irrigation Project Phase-II in 2007 year. The capacity of tank was 0.71 TMC to serve an ayacut of 4000 acres of 400.500 Mts. with Full Reservoir Level 400.000. Cherla Thanda Hamlet of Jaffergudem village having 84 families and 232 acres, 38 guntas (Total 403.13 Acres) are coming under submergence within Full Reservoir Level + 250.500. Consequently nine Acres of land was allotted for PAFs nearby displaced thanda on the road of Jaffergudem to Ragunathpalli in Raghunathpalli (tahsil) Warangal district under R&R Policy.

IV. **Rajawaram Tank**[6] has been constructed as Reservoir in the Village limits of Rajawaram Village, Ghanpur (Tahsil) Warangal District, under J. Chokka Rao Godavari Lift Irrigation Project Phase-II in 2007 year. The capacity of the tank is 0.86 TMC to serve an ayacut of 10000 acres of with FRL 338.215 Desai Thanda Hamlet of Ganpur village having 104 houses, 200 families and 900 acres are coming under submergence within FRL. Consequently 15 Acres of land was allotted for PAFs nearby displaced thanda at Talakaya Gutta on the road of Phathepoor to Ghanpur in Ghanpur (tahsil) Warangal district under R&R Policy.

V. **Parvathagiri Tank (Pedda Cheruvu)**[7] has been improved as Summer Storage Tank-cum- Balancing Reservoir in the Village limits of Gandi Ramavaram Village, Narmetta (Tahsil) Warangal District, under J. Chokka Rao Godavari Lift Irrigation Project Phase-II in 2005-06 year. The Capacity of Pedda Cheruvu increased to 220 Mcft from existing 25.57 Mcft with Full Tank Level (FTL) + 243.500, MWL + 244.250, Tank Balance Level (TBL) + 245.75 for the stabilisation of existing ayacut of 1150.00 Acres. Gugulothi Bondalu Thanda Hamlet of Parvathagiri village having 20 houses, 26 families and 50 acres agricultural land has coming submergence within Full Reservoir Level and Gyama Thanda Hamlet of Parvathagiri village having 10 houses, 15 families and 25 acres agricultural land was coming under submergence within FRL. But the government authorities are not considering these 30 houses, 41 families under R&R Policy and they are going to be displaced very soon when the reservoir will be fulfilled with water.

In the above mentioned reservoirs Desai Thanda in Rajawaram and Cherla Thanda in Jaffargudem are the PAAs and these PAAs have come under the R&R Policy but the policy was not implemented till now, but the process is under progress. Consequently, I could not select these two PAAs. On the other hand, Guguloth Bondalu Thanda and Gyma Thanda in Parvathagiri are not considered under the R&R Policy. Even this area is not considered as PAA but the impact of this area is very high on both the thandas' tribals' life rather than their welfare.

According to these reasons I was selected, for the purpose of the present study, the following areas:

1. Parvathagiri Reservoir: Gugulothu Bondalu Thanda and Gyama Thanda.
2. Gandiramaram Reservoir: Dongalachelima Thanda.
3. Mailaram Reservoir: Vidyanagar Thanda and Janakamma Banda Thanda.

Part-II

Implementation and Impact of R&R Policy – Response of the Projects Affected Tribes

Restoration of livelihoods of the affected households is dependent on the R&R package, so the project authorities design to address the problem of displacement. Degrees of marginalisation of PAFs are related to the ingredients of compensation and take off assistance as well as the degree of collective action of the PAFs. Often PAFs do engage in a variety of measures seeking redressal or resisting displacement itself as it threatens their daily life and social basis. Marginalisation, as well as its intensity, is mainly due to lack of response from the project authorities in addressing the R&R. Problem of marginalisation is an outcome of the differences in perceiving the process of displacement - while the project authorities view it as one time activity ending with eviction and shifting their focus henceforth to the completion of the project but the PAFs view it as a continuous process starting with dislocation till their livelihoods are restored.[8]

Resettlement and Rehabilitation policies and packages tend to become "acts of reluctant charity" when project authorities present mental frames of "doing development" and refuse to make the entire process of displacement and rehabilitation a transparent and participatory process. Effectiveness of R&R policies is ensured by making it an inalienable part of the project design itself, rather than designing the R&R as a separate measure for addressing the painful outcomes of a project. Making R&R an integral component of the project design ensures participation of those who might be affected by it and also enable searching of alternatives to reduce displacement hardship. Participatory decision-making process of the project design cannot ignore displacement because it is becoming a premise of inevitability.

Participation, consultation and transparency with regard to the PAFs are essential to reduce displacement hardship and to evolve relevant as well as effective R&R packages. The major factors responsible for "primitive approaches being prevalent in addressing displacement issues world over", outlined by Michael Cernea[9] refer to:

(a) Policy being inadequate or narrow. Expropriation laws (land acquisition legislations) providing compensation for condemned assets, fail to aim at or promise re-establishment of prior levels. They fail to compensate the losses adequately, as they are designed to underplay both the number of displaced and the magnitude of loss: "Most governments use the might of the law and their institutional instruments to forcibly displace people, but do not sufficiently use their institutional instruments to facilitate land for land alternatives".

(b) Finances allocated for R&R being inadequate or ignored altogether.

(c) Methodology adopted in economic analysis of the project "tuned towards externalising the costs of displacement/ relocation. It is the 'secret' of resettlement miss-planning and failure. These externalised costs affect the PAFs and the hosts adversely.

(d) Weak Institutions typically characterised by "lack of policy mandate, commensurate organisational capacity and professional social engineering skills".

(e) Authoritarianism scuttling the participation and empowerment of affected groups to negotiate viable solutions. Besides, "Effective legal mechanisms for negotiating and resolving grievances are often absent or subverted".

The R&R Packages vary both from project to project and also with regard to different categories of PAFs with each project. Firstly, it is Important to acknowledge some common patterns in the projects under study. Resettlement and Rehabilitation was a separate component, and displacement was taken for granted. There was no participation, consultation or dialogue either in regard to project design and decisions concerning displacement, or with regard to designing to R&R package. R&R package was a technical obligation or generosity of the executive authority, and is an act of charity by an estranged agency.

Resettlement sites and packages were designed exclusively by the executive authority. Intervention of the courts enabled covering assignment lands also for compensation in Milaram and Gandi Ramaram project areas. It is also important to note that R&R packages were an extension of the Land Acquisition Act rather than based on the legislation and policies aimed at protecting the interest of tribal communities. Lastly, the compensation was under-assessed and the payments are delayed.

Two out of six categories of affected people have been totally ignored from R&R packages; those categories considered eligible for R&R were subjected to hardships in delays of compensation.

All the above factors are responsible for the failures with regard to R&R of the affected persons which are observed in three projects of Telangana Tribal Areas. Before discussing the nature of response from the PAFs and the relationship between the PAFs and project authorities, it is necessary to examine briefly the essential ingredients of R&R package adopted by each of the projects. Table-18 presents details of the R&R packages as well as the difference in package with regard to different categories of PAFs within each project.

Table 5.5: Age-wise Particulars of the PAFs

Age Group	*Janakamma Banda Thanda*	*Vidynagar Thanda*	*Dongachelimi Thanda*	*Guguloth Bondalu Thanda*	*Gyama Thanda*	*Grand Total*
Up to 18 years	2 (25) (7.40)	-	5 (62.50) (6.09)	-	1 (12.50) (10)	8 (100) (4.67)
18 to 35 years	8 (19.04) (29.62)	7 (16.66) (22.58)	10 (23.80) (12.04)	12 (28.57) (60)	5 (11.90) (50)	42 (100) (24.56)
36 to 45 years	13 (15.85) (48.14)	17 (20.73) (54.83)	45 (54.87) (54.21)	5 (6.09) (25)	2 (2.43) (20)	82 (100) (47.95)
46 to 55 years	3 (9.09) (11.11)	5 (15.15) (16.12)	20 (60.60) (24.09)	3 (9.09) (15)	2 (6.06) (20)	33 (100) (19.29)
56 to 65 years	1 (16.66) (3.70)	2 (33.33) (6.45)	3 (50) (3.61)	-	-	6 (100) (3.50)
Total	**27 (15.78) (100)**	**31 (18.12) (100)**	**83 (48.53) (100)**	**20 (11.69) (100)**	**10 (5.84) (100)**	**171 (100)**

Source: Field Study, Warangal District, Telangana State, 2013.

The above table gives a clear picture of the PAFs in five Thandas. Out of the total percentage, the majority of the respondents belong to the age group between 36 to 45 years with the 48 per cent. And the lowest of the respondents belong to the age groups between 56 and 65 years with the three per cent and 4.67 per cent of below 18 year it means children also displaced along with their families respectively.

Table 5.6: Gender-wise Particulars of the PAFs

Gender	*Janakamma Banda Thanda*	*Vidynagar Thanda*	*Dongachelimi Thanda*	*Guguloth Bondalu Thanda*	*Gyama Thanda*	*Grand Total*
Male headed	27 (16.26) (100)	29 (17.46) (93.54)	82 (49.39) (98.79)	18 (10.84) (90)	10 (6.02) (100)	166 (100)
Female headed		2 (40) (6.45)	1(20) (1.20)	2 (40) (10)		5 (100) (2.92)
Total	**27 (15.78) (100)**	**31 (18.12) (100)**	**83 (48.53) (100)**	**20 (11.69) (100)**	**10 (5.84) (100)**	**171 (100)**

Source: Field Study, Warangal District, Telangana State, 2013.

The Table 5.6 indicates the gender wise particulars of the PAFs in the five Thandas. Out of the total percentage, majority of the displaced families are held by the male with the 97 per cent and remaining three per cent of the families are held by widows.

Table 5.7: Educational Particulars of the PAFs

Educational Status	*Janakamma Banda Thanda*	*Vidynagar Thanda*	*Dongachelimi Thanda*	*Guguloth Bondalu Thanda*	*Gyama Thanda*	*Grand Total*
Illiterate	20 (15.38) (74.07)	25 (19.23) (80.64)	55 (42.30) (66.26)	20 (15.38) (100)	10 (7.69) (100)	130 (100)
Primary Level	5 (26.31) (18.51)	4 (21.05) (12.90)	10 (52.63) (12.04)			19 (100) (11.11)
High School	2 (11.76) (7.40)	2 (11.76) (6.45)	13 (76.47) (15.66)			17 (100) (9.94)
Intermediate			3 (100) (3.61)			3 (100) (1.75)
Degree			2 (100) (2.40)			2 (100) (1.16)
Total	**27 (15.78) (100)**	**31 (18.12) (100)**	**83 (48.53) (100)**	**20 (11.69) (100)**	**10 (5.84) (100)**	**171 (100)**

Source: Field Study, Warangal District, Telangana State, 2013.

The Table 5.7 reveals the educational status of the PAFs in five Thandas. Out of the total percentage, majority of the respondents' illiterates with the 76.02 per cent and the very meagre percentage of the respondents are educated up to intermediate level with 1.75 per cent and degree level with one per cent respectively and regarding to the school level 21.05 per cent are schooling, out of this percentage 11.11 per cent of primary level and 9.94 per cent of high school level stopped their education due to financial problems of the family.

Table 5.8: Household Particulars of the PAFs

Item	*Janakamma Banda Thanda*	*Vidynagar Thanda*	*Dongachelimi Thanda*	*Guguloth Bondalu Thanda*	*Gyama Thanda*	*Grand Total*
Pacca House	1 (11.11) (3.70)	5 (55.55) (16.12)	3 (33.33) (3.61)	-	-	9 (100) (5.26)
Tails/ Shed	20 (23.52) (74.07)	15 (17.64) (48.38	50 (58.82) (60.24)	-	-	85 (100) (49.70)
Hut	6 (7.79) (22.22)	11 (14.28) (35.48)	30 (38.93) (36.14)	20 (25.97) (100)	10 12.98) (100)	77 (100) (45.02)
Total	**27 (15.78) (100)**	**31 (18.12) (100)**	**83 (48.53) (100)**	**20 (11.69) (100)**	**10 (5.84) (100)**	**171 (100)**

Source: Field Study, Warangal District, Telangana State, 2013.

Table 5.8 reveals about the household particulars of the displaced families of the five Thandas. Out of the total percentage the majority of the respondents resided in Tiled or Shed roofed houses with the 50 per cent and it is followed by the resident in Huts with 46 per cent and the remaining four per cent of the respondents lived in Pacca Houses.

The above table gives a clear picture about the land holding particulars of the respondents. Out of the total percentage, majority of the respondents, about 61.40 per cent belong to Semi-medium farmers and the lowest belong to marginal farmers with the five per cent respectively.

Table 5.9: Landholding Particulars of the PAFs

Category	*Janakamma Banda Thanda*	*Vidynagar Thanda*	*Dongachelimi Thanda*	*Guguloth Bondalu Thanda*	*Gyama Thanda*	*Grand Total*
Marginal (<1 ha)	3 (37.50) (11.11)	5 (62.50) (16.12)	-			8 (100) (4.67)
Small (1-2 ha)	4 (19.04) (14.81)	2 (9.52) (6.45)	15 (71.42) (18.07)			21 (100) (12.28)
Semi Medium (2-4 ha)	19 (18.09) (70.37)	11 (10.47) (35.48)	45 (42.85) (54.51)	20 (19.04) (100)	10 (9.52) (100)	105 (100) (61.40)
Medium (4-10 ha)	-	8 (44.44) (25.80)	10 (55.55) (12.04)			18 (100) (10.52)
Big (>10 ha)	1 (5.26) (3.70)	5 (26.31) (16.12)	13 (68.42) (15.66)			19 (100) (11.11)
Total	**27 (15.78) (100)**	**31 (18.12) (100)**	**83 (48.53) (100)**	**20 (11.69) (100)**	**10 (5.84) (100)**	**171 (100)**

Source: Field Study, Warangal District, Telangana State, 2013.

Table 5.10: Awareness about Land Acquisition Act, 1894 and R&R Policy 2005 to PAFs

Item	*Janakamma Banda Thanda*	*Vidynagar Thanda*	*Dongachelimi Thanda*	*Guguloth Bondalu Thanda*	*Gyama Thanda*	*Grand Total*
Yes	1 (20) (3.70)	1 (20) (3.22)	3 (60) (3.61)	-	-	5 (100) (2.92)
No	26 (15.66) (96.29	30 (18.07) (96.77)	80 (48.19) (96.38)	20 (12.04) (100)	10 (6.02) (100)	166 (100) (97.07)
Total	**27 (15.78) (100)**	**31 (18.12) (100)**	**83 (48.53) (100)**	**20 (11.69) (100)**	**10 (5.84) (100)**	**171 (100)**

Source: Field Study, Warangal District, Telangana State, 2013.

The Table 5.10 gives a clear picture about the awareness about the Land Acquisition Act 1894 and R&R Policy 2005 to the project affected families in the five Thandas. Out of the total percentage, 97 per cent of respondents could not have the awareness and remaining three per cent of respondents merely have the knowledge about the Land Acquisition Act 1894 and R&R Policy 2005, because the three per cent are educated and also they are working as mediators in various works between the government officials and tribals. Owing to the delays in litigations for claims, a considerable section of respondents were still not paid compensation and all as their lands were considered mere encroachments. In the observation their houses are also indirectly considered encroached by the project; it will happen only after the reservoir level is fully filled by the water. After the filling of the water the Gugulothu Bondalu Thands and Gyama Thanda, 30 families are indirectly bounded by the reservoir and they will lose their livelihood and communication with the world. Yet, there is no full-fledged root to go to their Thandas and they could not have the minimum civic amenities at their Thandas. It is interesting to see the pattern of responses given by the respondents on the land acquisition process. A few of them who said that they know about law to the extent of the appeal like in the Value assessment. Many of the respondents informed that they only know to oblige the need of the government. A few of them have felt that they will be punished, Lambada tribes do not know anything about the acquisition process and innocently they took that news of evacuating the habitat which came as "sudden shock" to them, unfamiliar legality, unknown administrative procedures, the unilateral decision-making process on finalisations of the project proposals and take over the tribal lands and habitat that have led to a one sidedness in the acceptability of the displacement process. Principles of persuasion and consensus over the proposed ventures are least attempted for application. Hence, the respondents' views on the aspects of the land acquisition remain mostly less knowledgeable.

Table 5.11: Distribution of R&R Packages across Different Categories of PAFs

Affected Thandas	*Loss of*			*Rehabilitation Package*
	Land and House	*Only land*	*Only House*	
Jankamma Banda Thanda	F			B
Vidynagar Thanda	F			B
Dongachelimi Thanda	F			B
Gugulothu Bondalu Thanda	F			C & E
Gyma Thanda	F			C & E

Source: Field Study, Warangal District, Telangana State, 2013.

A = Built houses, land and cash grant

B = House sites, Built House and cash grant

C = Only cash grant for Land Acquired (Agricultural)

D = No compensation at all

E = Marked villages are displaced due to unplanned factors or "post project effect"

F = Compensation Item

House sites, Built House and cash grant policy was provided to all the PAFs of Milaram and Gandi Ramaram Projects. However, the package though relatively better compared to the package offered in Parvathagiri Project, it was disliked by PAFs as it failed to appreciate their lifestyles and livelihoods in consonance with the felt needs of the affected people and the designed priorities of the Resettlement Planners is seen clearly in the case of Lambadi tribes. It is again pointed out that the felt needs of the displaced are rarely taken into consideration of the policy. In the case of Lambadi tribes, a wide gap persists between their life experiences and the administrative programmes suggested by the government. By transition, these communities do not fit in to the settled cultivation of the land nor are they suited for any employment as the literacy among them is very low. Therefore, keeping the social transition in view, a community specific strategy for these tribal groups is to be evolved but the R&R strategy does not concentrate on these Intra-transitional and Inter-Community differentials. House sites and compensation of "assets lost" package has been the major R&R measure

Table 5.12: Distribution of Respondents by Resettlement Measures

Item	*Janakamma Banda Thanda*	*Vidynagar Thanda*	*Dongachelimi Thanda*	*Guguloth Bondalu Thanda*	*Gyama Thanda*	*Total*
House sites	27 (19.14) (25)	31 (21.98) (25)	83 (58.86) (25)	-	-	141 (100) (21.55)
Cash Compensation	27 (15.78) (25)	31 (18.12) (25)	83 (48.53) (25)	20 (11.69) (33.33)	10 (5.84) (33.33)	171 (100) (26.14)
House & Land compensation	27 (19.14) (25)	31 (21.98) (25)	83 (58.86) (25)	-	-	141 (100) (21.55)
Land Compensation	27 (15.78) (25)	31 (18.12) (25)	83 (48.53) (25)	20 (11.69) (33.33)	10 (5.84) (33.33)	171 (100) (26.14)
Awaiting	-	-	-	20 (11.69) (33.33)	10 (5.84) (33.33)	30 (100) (4.58)
Total	**108 (16.51) (100)**	**124 (18.96) (100)**	**332 (50.76) (100)**	**60 (9.17) (100)**	**30 (4.58) (100)**	**654 (100)**
Grand Total	**27 (15.78) (100)**	**31 (18.12) (100)**	**83 (48.53) (100)**	**20 (11.69) (100)**	**10 (5.84) (100)**	**171 (100)**

Source: Field Study, Warangal District, Telangana State, 2013.

in Gugulothu Bondalu Thanda and Guama Thanda. Around one-fourth of the respondents, mainly from the partly affected settlements, have not received any compensation, even after a lapse of one decade from the time of land acquisition. Details of the extent of R&R measure PAFs received are shown in Table 5.12.

The above table reveals the distribution of resettlement measures of the respondents in five Thandas in the mean of cumulative data. Out of the total percentage 21.55 per cent of respondents are received the house sites, 26.14 per cent received the cash compensation, 21.55 per cent of received house and land compensation, 26.14 per cent of received land compensation and 4.58 per cent of till waiting respective. Among the five Thandas, Guguloth Bondalu Tanda and Gyama Thnda families are not received the house sites, house and land compensation and they are received only cash compensation about 17.54 per cent and land compensation about 17.54 per cent; and they are waiting for house sites and land respectively.

Table 5.13: Utilisation Pattern of Compensation Money

Item	*Janakamma Banda Thanda*	*Vidyanagar Thanda*	*Dongachelimi Thanda*	*Guguloth Bondalu Thanda*	*Gyama Thanda*	*Grand Total*
Land Purchase	3 (11.53) (11.11)	5 (19.23) (16.12)	10 (38.46) (12.04)	3 (11.53) (15)	5 (19.23) (50)	26 (100) (15.20)
House Construction	15 (23.07) (55.55)	10 (15.38) (32.25)	40 (61.53) (48.19)	-		65 (100) (38.01)
Repayment of loans	5 (10.41) (18.51)	10 (20.83) (32.25)	20 (41.66) (24.09)	10 (20.83) (50)	3 (6.25) (30)	48 (100) (28.07)
House hold Goods	-	-	2 (100) (2.40)			2 (100) (1.16)
Children Marriage	3 (18.75) (11.11)	3 (18.75) (9.67)	5 (31.25) (6.02)	4 (25) (20)	1 (6.25) (10)	16 (100) (9.35)
Spent on Health	-		1 (33.33) (1.20)	1 (33.33) (5)	1 (33.33) (10)	3 (100) (1.75)
All	1 (9.09) (3.70)	3 (27.27) (9.67)	5 (45.45) (6.02)	2 (18.18) (10)		11 (100) (6.43)
Total	**27 (15.78) (100)**	**31 (18.12) (100)**	**83 (48.53) (100)**	**20 (11.69) (100)**	**10 (5.84) (100)**	**171 (100)**

Source: Field Study, Warangal District, Telangana State, 2013.

Table 5.13 reveals the utilisation pattern of compensation money by the respondents in the PAFs. Out of the total percentage of the respondents 15.20 per cent of respondents utilised the compensation money for purchase of land. 38.01 per cent of respondents on

House Construction, 28.07 per cent of respondents on Repayment of loans, 1.16 per cent on household goods, 9.35 per cent on their children marriage, 1.75 per cent of respondents on their health and remaining 6.43 per cent of respondents on all items respectively. According to the table, the majority of the respondents spent the compensation money on house construction, repayment of loans and land purchasing.

Table 5.14: Financial Assistance Received by PAF

Sl. No	*Item*	*Janakamma Banda Thanda*	*Vidyanagar Thanda*	*Dongachelimi Thanda*	*Guguloth Bondalu Thanda*	*Gyama Thanda*	*Grand Total*
1.	Daily Wage Provided for Agricultural Labour (625 days @ 170/-)	7 (9.45) (6.41)	7 (9.45) (11.86)	60 (81.08) (28.16)	-	-	74 (100) (19.17)
2.	Transportation Charges (5000/-)	27 (19.14) (23.68)	31 (21.98) (52.54)	83 (58.86) (38.96)		-	141 (100) (36.52)
3.	Construction of Houses with Old House materials (40000/-)	15 (17.64) (13.15)	10 (11.76) (16.94)	60 (70.58) (28.16)	-	-	85 (100) (22.02)
4.	Civic Amenities at the Rehabilitation Centre, Drinking Water supply, Hand bores, Electricity, Internal Roads, Drainages. (2000000/- Per one Centre)	27 (100) (23.368)	In Progress	In progress	-	-	27 (100) (6.99)
5.	Monthly substance allowance for 12 Months (170/- per day 250 Days)	11 (34.37) (9.64)	11 (34.37) (18.64)	10 (31.25) (4.69)	-	-	32 (100) (8.29)
6.	Community Hall	-	-	-	-	-	-
7.	Temple	27 (100) (23.68)	In Progress	In progress	-	-	27 (6.99)
8.	Cattle Shed Construction (3000/- per each)	-	-	-	-	-	-
Total		**114 (29.53) (100)**	**59 (15.28) (100)**	**213 (55.18) (100)**	-	-	**386 (100)**
Total		**27 (15.78) (100)**	**31 (18.12) (100)**	**83 (48.53) (100)**	**20 (11.69) (100)**	**10 (5.84) (100)**	**171 (100)**

Source: Field Study, Warangal District, Telangana State, 2013.

Table 5.14 gives a clear picture about the financial assistance to PAFs for their livelihood and providing the infrastructure facilities in the R&R Centres. Out of the total percentage, 19.17 per cent of the respondents are provided 625 days wage by government through Mahatma Gandhi National Rural Employment Guarantee Act (MGNREGA). These 19.17 per cent of respondents belong to those who encroached into their lands and those who have not purchased other land in the outside of the area. 36.52 per cent of the respondents opined that they are given financial assistance, 22.02 per cent of the respondents are given financial assistance to use old house materials in the new construction, only 6.99 per cent of the respondents expressed that civic amenities are provided by the government at the R&R Centre. In observance full-fledged civic amenities are provided at Janakamma Banda Thanda only and in the remaining areas the work is in progress. The 8.29 per cent of the respondents have opined that they are given monthly substance allowance for 12 Months (170/- per day 250 Days) by the government. Only 6.99 per cent of the respondents expressed that a temple has been constructed at their R&R Centre, in observance the temple has been constructed in only Janakamma Banda Thanda and in remaining centres it is in progress. Finally regarding to the community hall and cattle shed there is no response at all the R&R Centre. It can be observed that among the five Thandas Gugulothu Bondalu Thanda and Gyama Thanda displaced families are not getting any type of assistance.

Table 5.15: Land purchased from Respondents (Rs in thousands per acre)

Sl. No	*Item*	*Janakamma Banda Thanda*		*Vidyanagar Thnda*		*Dongalachelimi Thanda*		*Gugulothu Bondalu Thanda*		*Gyama Thanda*	
		A	*B*	*A*	*B*	*A*	*B*	*A*	*B*	*A*	*B*
1.	Wet Land	60	2.00	60	2.00	90	2.50	50	2.00	50	2.00
2.	Wet Land (which having Irrigation facility)	90	3.50	90	3.50	1.40	5.00	90	3.50	90	3.50
3.	Dry Land	50	1.50	50	1.50	70	3.50	-	-	-	-
4.	Dry Land (which having Irrigation facility)	70	2.50	70	2.50	90	5.00	-	-	-	-

A-Government Value; B-Market Value

Source: Field Study, Warangal District, Telangana State, 2013.

Table 5.16 gives a clear picture of the financial assistance given for construction of houses at R&R Centre of five Thandas. Out of the total percentage 100 per cent (the percentage excluded the Gugulothu Thanda and Gyama Thanda) of the respondents have taken financial assistance for construction of their houses from the government in the way of INDIRAMMA Scheme and R&R Policy, excluding the Gogulothu Bondalu Thanda and Gyama Thanda because these Thandas are not considered under R&R Policy. According to the INDIRAMMA and R&R policy before sanctioning the amount for construction of the houses, the beneficiaries of INDIRAMMA should construct the basement and should be shown to the sanctioning authority. Thus, 27 per cent (the percentage excluded the Gugulothu Thanda and Gyama Thanda) of the respondents have stopped their construction due to financial constraints, and 50 per cent (the percentage excluded the Gugulothu Thanda and Gyama Thanda) of the respondents have constructed their houses through taking the private loans.

The above table gives a clear picture about the land holding and encroached land by the projects and how they are converted to, before and after the project enhanced also. Out of the total percentage, the majority of the respondents, about 61.40 per cent, belong to Semi-medium farmers and the lowest belongs to marginal farmers with the 4.67 per cent and also it gives a logical statistical data about the land lost for the project. After the encroachment of the respondents' land, 13.45 per cent of the respondents lost their lands completely and they are getting their livelihood through daily wage, it means they are changed as daily wage workers in various sectors, 64.91 per cent of the respondents are converted as marginal farmers, 21.05 per cent of the respondents are quietly changed as Medium farmers and finally those who were land lords or big farmers they have still improved and secured their status (0.58 per cent).

Table 5.16: Financial Assistance for Construction of Houses at R&R Centre

Sl. No	*Item*	*Janakamma Banda Thanda*	*Vidyanagar Thnda*	*Dongalachelimi Thanda*	*Gugulothu Bondalu Thanda*	*Gyama Thanda*	*Total*
1.	By Government (including with INDIRAMMA and R & R Policy)	27 (19.14) (25.23)	31 (21.98) (54.38)	83 (58.86) (76.14)	-	-	141 (100) (51.64)
2.	Personal Loan (including with INDIRAMMA And R & R Policy)	50 (58.82) 46.72)	15 (17.64) (26.31)	20 (23.52) (18.34)	-	-	85 (100) (31.13)
3.	Houses stopped at the basement level	30 (63.82) (28.03)	11 (23.40) (19.29)	6 (12.76) (5.50)	-	-	47 (100) (17.21)
Total		**107 (39.19)**	**57 (20.87)**	**109 (39.92)**	-	-	**273 (100)**
		27 (15.78) (100)	**31 (18.12) (100)**	**83 (48.53) (100)**	**20 (11.69) (100)**	**10 (5.84) (100)**	**171 (100)**

Source: Field Study, Warangal District, Telangana State, 2013.

Table 5.17: Status of the Respondents before and after Displaced

Category	*Janakamma Banda Thanda*		*Vidyanagar Thanda*		*Dongachelimi Thanda*		*Guguloth Bondalu Thanda*		*Gyama Thanda*		*Grand Total*	
	Before	*After*	*Before*	*After*	*Before*	*After*	*Before*	*After*	*Before*	*After*	*Before*	*After*
Landless or daily wage works								18 (78.26) (90)		5 (21.73) (50)		23 (100) (13.45)
Marginal (<1 ha)	3 (37.50) (11.11)	26 (23.42) (96.29)	5 (62.50) (16.12)	18 (16.21) (58.06)	-	60 (54.05) (72.28)		2 (1.80) (10)		5 (4.50) (50)	8 (100) (4.67)	111 (100) (64.91)
Small (1-2 ha)	4 (19.04) (14.81)		2 (9.52) (6.45)		15 (71.42) (18.07)						21 (100) (12.28)	
Semi Medium (2-4 ha)	19 (18.09) (70.37)		11 (10.47) (35.48)		45 (42.85) (54.21)		20 (19.04) (100)		10 (9.52) (100)		105 (100) (61.40)	
Medium (4-10 ha)	-		8 (44.44) (25.80)	13 (36.11) (41.93)	10 (55.55) (12.04)	23 (63.88) (27.71)					18 (100) (10.52)	36 (100) (21.05)
Big (>10 ha)	1 (5.26) (3.70	1 (100) (3.70)	5 (26.31) (16.12)	-	13 (68.42) (15.66)						19 (100) (11.11)	1 (100) (0.58)
Total	**27**	**27**	**31**	**31**	**83**	**83**	**20**	**20**	**10**	**10**	**171**	**171**

Source: Field Study, Warangal District, Telangana State, 2013.

Table 5.18: Share of Compensation paid to middlemen

Sl. No	Amount Paid to Middlemen	Janakamma Banda Thanda	Vidyanagar Thnda	Dongalachelimi Thanda	Gugulothu Bondalu Thanda	Gyama Thanda	Total
1.	5 per cent	-	-	83 (100) (100)	-	-	83 (100) (48.53)
2.	6 to 15 Per cent	27 (30.68) (100)	31 (35.22) (100)		20 (22.72) (100)	10 (11.36) (100)	88 (100) (51.46)
Total		**27 (15.78) (100)**	**31 (18.12) (100)**	**83 (48.53) (100)**	**20 (11.69) (100)**	**10 (5.84) (100)**	**171 (100)**

Source: Field Study, Warangal District, Telangana State, 2013.

The Table 5.17 reveals about the share of compensation paid to middlemen by respondents. Out of the total percentage, 48.53 per cent of the respondents paid five per cent amount to middlemen and remaining 51.46 per cent of the respondents paid 6 to 15 per cent amount to the middlemen. This phenomenon reveals that corruption was involved in the sanctioning process of the compensation to the respondents.

Table 5.19: Distribution of respondents by their perception regarding Government or Project Authority interventions in R&R Policy

Sl. No	Opinion	Janakamma Banda Thanda	Vidyanagar Thnda	Dongalachelimi Thanda	Gugulothu Bondalu Thanda	Gyama Thanda	Total
1.	Helpful in quickening of compensation payments	7 (10.29) (25.92)	11 (16.17) (35.48)	50 (73.52) (60.24)	-	-	68 (100) (39.76)
2.	Ineffective ensuring adequate timely compensation.	15 (39.47) (55.55)	10 (26.31) (32.25)	13 (34.21) (15.66)	-	-	38 (100) (22.22)
3.	No implementation of promised R&R package	5 (14.28) (18.51)	10 (28.57) (32.25)	20 (57.14) (24.09)	-	-	35 (100) (20.46)
	Total	**27 (15.78) (100)**	**31 (18.12) (100)**	**83 (48.53) (100)**	**20 (11.69) (100)**	**10 (5.84) (100)**	**171 (100)**

Source: Field Study, Warangal District, Telangana State, 2013.

The above table reveals the interventions of the authority of government or R&R Policy. Out of the total percentage, 39.76 per cent of the respondents expressed their views that the authorities of the R&R Policy are helpful in quickening of compensation payment, 22.22 per cent of the respondents opined that the authorities of the R&R Policy are ineffective ensuring adequate timely compensation and remaining 20.46 per cent of the respondents opined that authorities of the R&R Policy have not implemented their promise of R&R package. It may observe that the, among the 5 Thandas Gugulothu Bondalu Thanda and Gyma Thanda respondents are not observed any intervention by the government authorities.

Part-III

Case Studies

I. Jathoth Bhulia:

Jathoth Bhulia is a 35 years aged lambada illiterate tribe person, who is a resident of Vidyanagar Thanda at Rayaparthy Thahsil of Warangal District. He is a victim of the Mylaram Reservoir and also his bad luck. He is living with his wife and two children at old Vidyanagar Thanda having two acres land. But unfortunately he was displaced by Mylaram Reservoir so he lost his land and house. Generally the government gives the land compensation if it is the registered land.

Old Vidyanagar Thanda

Bhulia has also registered his land but unfortunately he lost his land paper. Consequently, he has been displaced from his own land receiving an amount of 50 thousand as compensation from the government. The R&R authority has given two guntas land at R&R centre had given 2,40,000 rupees for the construction of house, but once again he is mocked by his luck. He has paid the total amount to private money lender and finally stood as a daily wage worker, and his wife with her son had migrated to district headquarter to work as maid servant. Ultimately, the reservoir stood to disturb his life and family. He has not completed his family responsibility and he has been facing lot of over burden to pull the cost of his family expenditure. He lost his credibility among his family members, kinship and relations. His wife and children are illiterate, thus, they are unable to do any literate's work. Consequently, they lived their lives as workers.

II. Nethawat Somla

Nethawat Somla is a 50 years old Lambada illiterate tribal person, resident of Vidyanagar Thanda of Rayaparthi Thahsil of Warangal District. He has two sons, these two children stopped their education at primary level and they are working in private service sector.

Nethawat Somla stayed at his own house at his birth place and surviving with his family by cultivating the three acreas of land. But his land and house submerged under the Mylaram Reservoir. The government has given Rs 1,80,000 (60 thousand amount per each acre) for his land, actually the land cost in the open market is Rs 150000 per acre. If he sell the same land in private market he may get Rs 450000 but he received Rs 1,80,000 thus, he lost nearly Rs 270000 rupees along with his house. The R&R authorities have given 1 lakh compensation for his house and allotted 2 guntas land for construction of the house at R&R Centre and Rs 240000 rupees has been given by the authority but with 15 per cent commission out of the total amount. At first, he started his house very happily, but his happiness did not long last. As he has taken private loan from money lenders on interest, and that began to increase many-fold and, consequently his house was stopped at walls level and he paid the remaining amount to them and he and his wife settled as daily wage workers in the old age.

III. Bhukya Laxmi

Bhukya Laxmi is a widow aged about 45 years and resident of Gugulothu Bondalu Thanda Hamlet of Parvathagiri Village and Thahsil of Warangal District is located between a small hill and Parvathagiri reservoir. Her husband died 10 years ago with ill health. She has five children (three Girls and two Boys) and she has got her three daughters

married and spent three lakh rupees, for this purpose. She approached a private money lender and of the two boys the younger one was going to school and the elder one was helping in agriculture to his mother. In the Laxmi's family no one has gone to school. All are illiterates. Laxmi's family migrated from Addabata Thada hamlet of Enugal village of Parvathagiri Tahsil 20 years ago to Gugulothu Bondalu Thanda. They purchased two acres land from local non-tribal about 30 thousand rupees per acre. But her husband did not identify that they purchased the government assigned land and innocently they did not register that land. If at that time they went for registration of that land they could have known that they cheated by the local non-tribal. Whatever it may be they constructed a small hut in that land and in the remaining land they were cultivating for their livelihood. So they are pulling their life-cot very easily with that land. But unfortunately, the Parvathagiri tank has been upgraded as balancing reservoir and so she lost her land and life source. The government authorities have given neither compensation nor land cost for her land and hut because she was living and cultivating the government land. Instead of giving money or compensation they threatened her if she had not vacated that land they might take legal action against her. Thus, Parvathagiri reservoir has an *avatar* and responsible for her family's problems and sorrow. If the reservoir was filled to its full level they might have been displaced from that place by nature without their permission. The government authority has not considered the Bondalu Thanda under the R&R Policy because they argued as their residences are located out of the range of Full Reservoir Level so there was no chance to consider them under the R&R Policy. But the truth is when the reservoir is filled with water they must lose communication with the world and they will be surrounded with water at one side and another side with hill. This situation has happened by unforeseen plans of the government authority. The rout to the Thandas and its condition has been shown in the following photographs.

IV. Bhukya Dharja

Bhukya Dharja is 55 years old citizen of the Gyma Thanda Hamlet of Parvathagiri village and Tahsil located at nearest of Gugulothu Bondalu Thanda. He has three female and two male children. Among these five children, three are female children, and got married and

Old Gyama Thanda

one younger son was depending on him, and he is studying in inter stand. The younger son was living himself as a nuclear family. Dharja was living with his wife alone. But his elder son was participating and helping him in agriculture. He migrated from Adabata Thanda hamlet of Yenugallu village of Parvathagiri tahsil of Warangal District from the last 25 years. When he migrated to here he purchased three acres of land from local non-tribal @ 35 thousand rupees per acre. The same situation was repeated to him as that which happened with Banoth Lakshi. But here a small change in their experience, that is, Dharja has purchased the registered land and he made the registration on his name. He has been living, depending on his three acres land for the last 25 years. But this land was encroached by the Parvathagiri reservoir. The government authority has given 30 thousand for his hut and 90 thousand per acre for his land and he gave 15 per cent commission to them. But his faith mocked at him in the way of heart attack and lungs infection to his younger son. He has consulted various doctors in various places; he spent all of the money which he received from the government cost and compensation for his land. Consequently, he neither purchased any land nor any house at any place. Ultimately, he lost his house and land and he was left as poorest of the poor. He lost his relationship with his kinship and neighbours. Generally, the Gayama Thanda consisted of 10 families but after the submergence of their land and residences only Dharja was living in that thanda as the remaining families shifted their residence to other village.

V. Korra Chander

Korra Chander is a 40 years old Lambada tribe of Dongachlima Thanda hamlet of Gandi Ramaram village of Narmetta Tahsil of Warangal District. He has been living with a small family of his wife and two female children. Chander's family is illiterate. Before the Gandi Ramaram tank was up graded as reservoir he was a big farmer with a land of 10 acres (four acres wet land and six acres dry land). His dry land valuated in open market @ 3 lakhs per acre of dry land and five lakhs per acre of wet land. He received 5.60 lakhs for wet land for four acres and 5.40 lakhs for dry land from government authority. Presently he is changed from large to small farmer because of Gandi Ramaram reservoir. His total land and residence submerged under the reservoir. At present he stands on the road. The government authority gave 90 thousand for dry land and 1.40 thousand for wet land. The R&R authorities gave one lakh compensation for his house and they are allotted two guntas of land for construction of his house at R&R Centre and Rs 240000 have been given by the authority with a 15 per cent commission out of the total amount to them and middlemen, because the sanctioning process was delayed. He purchased 32 acres of land at non-submerged area of the reservoir @ 5 lakhs per wet acre. When he started to build a pucca house with his own money, it was found to be very different, and so, he borrowed from the private money lenders. Even them, he could not complete the construction and finally, he stopped the construction of his house and is living in a hut. And he started to repay his private loan by selling his wife's gold. Ultimately, he lost his permanent assets and he was encircled by financial problems.

Gandi Ramaram Reservoir

Dongachelima R&R Centre

Submerged Old Dongachelima Thanda under Gandi Ramaram Reservoir

New problems in Project Areas

Relocation and project activity has made the PAFs and the neighbouring villages to suffer with different problems. While Gandiramaram Project is responsible for destruction of family and kinship network among the Lambadas, the disrupted access and interaction with neighbouring villages was a result of destruction of PAF approach roads.

The problems resulting from destruction of community life, loss of access to common property resources and health problems have greater implication to women folk. Women in the affected areas are worst hit due to the crisis of physiological aspects. Detailed examination of the major features of the officials' resettlement sites in three project areas reveals that they fall short of expectations both in quantitative and qualitative aspects. They lack basic amenities necessary for any community life, as the focus has been mainly on individuals of project affected families.

Summing Up

Enquiries in to the performance of the Governance and Administration of R&R Programmes in the study of Thandas provide a set of inter-related empirical findings. They are presented here:

1. A clear cut gap exists between the felt needs of the DP and the prioritisation of the project authorities and the orientation of the government on the content and mode of R&R programmes.
2. Rehabilitation and Resettlement strategies basically suffer from an elitist orientation of the dispensing the displaced rather than showing a genuine commitment to the amelioration of the conditions of the PAFs.
3. Considerable number of PAFs has been denied the compensation benefit. The enunciated legality as the conditioning criterion for eligibility and claims often do not exist in the case of tribal communities. The very notion of law is mostly alien to some of these primitive tribal groups. Lambadai have a different notion of habitat and the whole orientation of the government towards them was merely to reject on the pretext that their claims on habitat are not covered under the social law.
4. Compensation benefit extended to the oustees has been largely spent on the consumption purposes. Cash compensation as a major component of R&R policy is less suited option to the STs. Andhra Pradesh Government has agreed to provide land to the displaced if they are tribals. But this has not been put to effect. Further, in between the operationalisation of the claim and realisation of the benefit several middlemen exploited the tribals who have got compensation in five thandas. This makes the situation further worse, as the tribes have lost their earlier assets and lands and now do not get the full benefit of the newly extended help by the government.
5. Knowledge related to Land Acquisition Act among the tribes remains almost absent. A few have a value idea about the possible chances for appeal towards gaining the appropriate assessment.
6. The experience of the displaced tribal in approaching the Project Authorities for Grievance settlement is rarely met with an expected treatment by the project authorities. False promises of rehabilitation, threat of harassment by filing cases, legal litigations, long delays in communications, initiating evictions without resettlement and use of police

forces at times etc., are few negative responses of the government that are experienced by the displaced tribes. In certain cases, a few of the tribals after assertive agitations and repeated pleas were able to get employment opportunities as a part of R&R package. But their number is extremely limited.

7. The responsive character of the project authorities or government attitude towards the oustees is uncertain and disputable. Cash grants were quickly extended to non-tribals. Most of the tribes were rejected the collective infrastructural facilities in the respective habitats. Basic needs like fuel wood and individual electricity connections have been denied.
8. The very form of extending the welfare measures or rehabilitation package still remains highly one-sided and authoritarian. The role played by the Land Acquisition Officers and Revenue Officials is criticised by most of the displaced people. Project Authorities initial enquiries have been quoted as the falls promises and unattainable targets by the effected families. A sense of dejection is also prevailing among the displaced or PAP in all the study Thandas covered under the various projects.
9. Earmarking the resettlement sites handled by the officials mostly have been mechanical activities rather than treating it as a part of the official responsibility. The official orientation towards settling the oustees has not changed significantly.
10. Another aspect of the R&R Policy is that the cost of rehabilitation has been externalised, in the sense that it was not from project resources that the resettlement sites have been provided.

References

1. Hand Book, Chief Planning Officer, Government of Andhra Pradesh, 2013.
2. Status Report on J. Chokka Rao, Godavari Lift Irrigation Project, Warangal, Irrigation and Command Area Development Department, Government of Andhra Pradesh, 19-10-2005.
3. Status Report of R&R Plan under Mylaram Balancing Reservoir of SRSP, Stage-II, Warangal District, Irrigation and Command Area Development Department, Government of Andhra Pradesh, May, 2009.

4. Status Report of R&R Plan under Gandiramaram Balancing Reservoir of SRSP, under JCRDLIS Stage-II, Warangal District, Irrigation and Command Area Development Department, Government of Andhra Pradesh. 30-06-2011

5. Status Report of R&R Plan under Ashwaraopally Balancing Reservoir of SRSP, JCRDLIC Stage-II, Warangal District, Irrigation and Command Area Development Department, Government of Andhra Pradesh, May, 2012.

6. Status Report of R&R Plan under Rajavaram Balancing Reservoir of SRSP, JCRDLIC Stage-II, Warangal District, Irrigation and Command Area Development Department, Government of Andhra Pradesh, May, 2012.

7. Status Report of Parwathagiri Summer Storage Tank-cum-Balancing Reservoir, Warangal District, Irrigation and Command Area Development Department, Government of Andhra Pradesh, 11-08-2005.

8. Rehabilitation and Resettlement (R&R) Policy of Government of Andhra Pradesh, Government Order Ms. No. 68, Irrigation & Command Area Development (Project Wing–LA–IV– R&R) Department, Government of Andhra Pradesh, 05-04-2005.

9. Cernea, Michael M, Type of Projects that Cause Involuntary Resettlement, Involuntary Resettlement in Development Projects: Policy Guidelines in World Bank Financed Projects, Washington D.C., April, 1988, p. 15.

Chapter 6

Conclusion

Development is an extensive but amorphous concept that combines several definitions offered by social scientists. Development, in the dictionary context is closely related to "growth and quantitative attributes," gradual advance or growth through progressive changes. In other words development is also understood as the "act or process of progress". The main thrust of the present work is to examine the aspects of the Governance and the Welfare Programmes which were evolved to mitigate the problems of the displaced STs. This is very much pertinent as the tribal societies-in general and particularly in India has been subjected to a specific mode of development transition. Further, it is important that the very meaning and application of the development process to the tribal society throws different levels of impact. Therefore, study of the development in terms of process, policy and programmes is an appropriate method. And, the present study reflects the same.

Development has assumed major concern in the developing world. Progress and development are the main objectives of human life with regards to the dimensions, social, political, economical and national. There have been very few concepts in social sciences that are interpreted in multiple dimensions. Development has been often equated to refer to growth, social change, evolution, progress, advancement and modernisation. In all these senses, perhaps with the exception of social change that can also be in a negative direction, it implies a change in a specific direction which is for the users of positive values.

The Brandt Commission report also indicates that development is now widely recognised as involving a profound transformation of the entire economic and social structure. In brief, development is a process of improving the well being of the people. It is about raising the standards of living of the people, improving their education and health, and also opening out to them the new and equal opportunities for a richer and more varied life. Better health, a longer life with less sickness is crucial to a better standard of living. Thus, Brandt Commission brought new concepts and interpretation to the very concept of development.

The specific nature of the development transition of the tribal societies all over the world carved an interesting arena for the pursuit of social knowledge. This is particularly explicit in the Third World Societies where the development transition in twentieth century has acquired unevenness in its direction. Given the context of uneven development, tribal societies in these countries are also characterised as 'Fourth World' societies. The conception of the Fourth World was put forth by a group of scholars in late eighties to denote the very character of exploitation of the tribal regions of the third world by the advanced territories and native ruling elite adjusted with the international capital interests. These interests manifested through a series of systematic, institutional projects and programmatic components. According to this stand point, 'development' has a double edged effect. On one hand, as a process it is consciously introduced to create a new production apparatus which releases new economic and social relations. On the other hand, it results in a simultaneous process of integration and exclusion. The contradictory process of integration and exclusion becomes clear as the 'development process' begins to take place at a massive rate. Massive development activities have been escalated with the advent of liberalisation as a globalised economic relation.

The rapid changes that are introduced in India in the economic, industrial and agricultural sectors have an over reaching socio-cultural impact on a majority of the country's population. Wide-spread feelings are expressed time and again that the government is withdrawing from the civic sphere and the role of the international market forces is increasing. This is gradually paying a way for a process of impoverishment and marginalisation of majority people. Safeguarding elitist interests and the integration of the affluent elite of the country's population with the global market economy and life style seem to be the main political agenda for the development of the country. The implication of new economic changes is very directly impinges on the interests of the many poorer strata of society.

A country that, even after 69 years of Independence, is still unable to attend the basic needs like health, education, nutrition, drinking water, housing and sanitation to a majority of its people, is now being coerced to curtail its welfare programmes in the name of liberalisation' and 'structural adjustment'. In an economy where the majority of the farming community survives on the subsistence agriculture, is being pressurised into an agricultural setting that can only wipe out such farmers, a vast population of poor and tribal people. Further, it breaks the harmony of the community towards its relation with the resources and denies the rights to 'Forests', 'Land' and 'Water'. Therefore, the whole structure of social relations is normally molded by a system of governance and the levels of centralisation and decentralisation of the power. It means that greater the decentralised governance, the higher is the effective use of the resources for the benefit of larger section of people.

In India, there are more than 10.42 crores people designated as members of Scheduled Tribe. They constitute 8.61 per cent of the total population of India. The area in-habituated by them is about 20 per cent of the land mass of the country. They are among the weakest sections of the society. Although some of them have become assimilated into Indian culture, other maintains a traditional way of life, displacement.

Further the process of displacement has led to wide spread traumatic psychological and socio-cultural consequences to millions of poor people. These included the dismantling of their production system, desecration of ancestral sacred zones of graves and lands scattering of kinship groups and family systems, disorganisation of informal social networks that provide mutual support, weakening of self-management and social control of trade and market links by tribals etc. The accumulated evidence in the country suggests that except in the rarest of cases, forced displacement has resulted in, what Micheal Cernea Calls "a spiral of impoverishment".

Displacement in a broader sense is the destitutionalisation of the peoples, who have lost their "right to life" as an effect of an event of initiation of a programme or process in their socio-production sphere introduced or attempted by a competent government or firm or a company or an intended act of a powerful social group or one class against the other. The process more often aims, at exploiting human beings and nature to satisfy the unbridled consumerist demands of privileged sections of the society, deprivation is a condition of a forced inaccessibility to an opportunity resource and of an elimination process from an offing benefit legitimately extendable to human being. It is also a declining process from an existing condition. It acts through both the methods of in accessing and elimination. Prolonged deprivation may result in marginalisation and in displacement of the people from their earlier position. This decline of the actual position of the affected people also forms the major aspect of displacement.

In India, Hydroelectric and Irrigation Projects are the largest source of displacement and destruction of habitat although they might result in substantial contribution to the national economy and benefit the centralised national elite. Other major sources are mines (particularly open cast mines), super thermal and nuclear power plants, industrial complexes as well as military installations, weapon testing grounds, railway and road lines, the notification and expansion of-reserved forest areas, sanctuaries and parks and technological interventions which cause the large-scale displacement of tribals, people belonging to SCs and small marginal farmers. On certain occasions, a sizable number of large land holders also face the threat of evictions. But, tribes have traditionally different type of dependence on the common property resources and have survived by rendering services to the community as a whole. Even more poignant is the legalistic indifference at the overnight "pauperisation" of large populations of Sweden cultivators, hunters and food-gatherers or other subsistence seekers, who usually do not possess any legally enforceable occupation or usufructuory rights.

The founding fathers of the constitution were fully aware of the conditions of the tribal people and they considered that unless these people were provided with some safeguards in the constitution they would not be able to build up their inner strength meet the competitive situations prevailing in the country. It was precisely for this reason that special provisions were incorporated in the constitution to promote and also safeguard the legitimate interests of these weaker sections, namely the tribals.

A clear cut policy of the "positive discrimination" was pursued wherever necessary for which specific provisions were to be made in the Constitution itself. Added to the policy of positive discrimination, Land Acquisition Act of 1894 and Land Acquisition (Amendments) 1984 and 2013 are the three principal legal means with which the compensation is offered to reimburse the loss of displacement.

The Land Acquisition Act briefly consist three important phases namely, notification, verification and resolution. Although the Act considers the 'person interested' grievances as lawful, does not fully accord the needed space to the affected person. The Land Acquisition Act on many accounts is stated to be unilateral and the evolved machinery of land acquisition fully equipped with the one-sided powers denying the affected freedom for appeal and the displaced oustees do not get the appropriate justice to their claim. Following discussion will provide an opportunity to understand the Land Acquisition Act critically and there by provide insights into the public policy legislation related to compensation payment and rehabilitation aspects.

1. Land Acquisition Act does not empower the rehabilitation as the matter of right to the affected but treat as consolation.
2. The overwhelming provisions of the Land Acquisition Act are not known to most of the people except few educated people. This has given scope to legal manipulations by the influential people.
3. The survey and land value, assessment, are often done in a technical manner which is not properly explained among the affected, the whole process of survey and calculation of the loss still remains mystery to the affected people.
4. Grievance is redressed by the District Collector to whom the oustees' plea is to be forwarded. The District Collector is

excessively burdened with the normal District Administration functions and could not totally concentrate on these matters.

5. The Land Acquisition Act does not take the person "actual possession of the land" in to consideration but only takes the "legal position of the holder". As a result, many of the tribals and farmers who are not in possession of any guaranteed tenure rights on record and are precluded from the benefit of resettlement.
6. The Land Acquisition Act does not consider the non-land based asset loss of the affected persons for the extension of compensation benefit. For instance, many tribal communities in India depend upon common property resources (CPR), hunting and food gathering processes and collection of minor forest produce. Whenever these tribal groups are displaced, the loss of their survival resource value is not considered for any calculation leading to a denial of the compensation causing an infinite misery in their life.
7. Further, the government is also directly empowered to acquire the land for private companies. This clause is governed under the Part VII of the Land Acquisition Act of 1984. Large scale urban land speculation as well as violation of the land laws operating in the Scheduled Areas. In Andhra Pradesh Tribal areas which are Scheduled, Land cannot be possessed by anyone other than the tribals. This has been in vogue since 1959, most effectively 1970 onwards, Despite this Act, a huge number of acres of land has passed on to the non-tribals and private firms for whom the Land Acquisition Act, has been a handy legal way out to possess the lands in the Scheduled Areas. These legal stipulations have been constantly dishonoured by the vested interests. Under the various pretexts of launching ventures, approaching the government for granting the land in the Scheduled Areas by effective utilisation of this clause under the Land Acquisition Act has been in the offing.
8. The Assessment of the land value is a crucial aspect in the Land Acquisition process. The parameters adopted in the calculation of the loss are technically in the hands of the

officer, concerned. No where the role of affected is taken for prior determination of the initial price or fixation of the value of the land under proposed takeover. Thus, the farmer or tribal who are normally less equipped with the whole system have to accept the fixation with no choice of their own. In many cases, these affected have to approach Lawyers who in turn act as the legal mediators informally. Meantime, the affected is rarely the sole beneficiary as he has to pay huge amounts to the engaged Lawyers. Therefore, the mechanism involved in the land value assessment is elite oriented while giving no chance for the direct pay to the affected, although the existing market price is considered as the parameter for calculation.

9. The Act is also weighted in favour of the rich. Land can be acquired for the public purpose of hotels, Co-operative Societies of Lawyers, Government Servants and other Professionals. The speed with which the land is acquired under these clauses is phenomenal. The land to be acquired for the effected poor under the rehabilitation consist mostly inhabitable patches of land. Civic amenities and other equipped infrastructure are not extended to such acquired and resettled lands.
10. The underlying principle of the Land Acquisition Act is that cash, compensation alone is payable in lieu of deprivation. There is a provision under section 31(3) in the Land Acquisition Act for grant of land (applicable to *patta* holders only) in lieu of monetary compensation though it has seldom been used. Cash compensation is least preferred to a majority of the displaced persons or project affected persons, particularly tribals and the rural poor.
11. 'Rights' as defined in Land Acquisition Act revolve around the land. The whole Question of cultural rights is ignored in the act. Tribals who have an associational bond with the nature remain cut-half once they are out of their ancestral land if they are affected by any takeover or displacement by a project.

Thus, the Rehabilitation of these DPs as a consequence of the land acquisition has been quite inadequate due to various reasons.

The emphasis placed on cash compensation as a major component of the existing Rehabilitation Policy of the Coal India Policy etc. has proved to be not in the interests of tribals. The Land Acquisition Act of 1894 is thus less suited for the tribals as it does not take into account the loss of income from minor forest produce, though the tribals depend for more than half of their livelihood on CPRs like forests. The loss of livelihood incurred on these fronts are not compensated International Labour Organisation and World Bank too greatly had emphasised on these aspects of compensating the loss of the land by the tribals. International Labour Organisation had laid specific policy guidelines for protecting the socio-economic rights of the Indigenous and tribal communities. Among many specifications, two conventions namely, Convention No. 107 and Convention No. 169 are important in this context.

Despite the intensity of displacement and the untold misery that most of the oustees have faced in the last five decades since independence glaring and disturbing fact is that the successive governments have been still in the phase of evolving a model national policy of rehabilitation. As a result, till today, no NPRR for mitigating the grievances of the affected or tribals exist. Only project specific rehabilitation and resettlement package is offered in most of the States. The need for evolving a policy was aptly reminded by the Home Ministry a decade ago. The report of the Ministry said that in the tribal areas, where the displaced are given only cash compensation, the tendency to spend the compensation amount by buying consumer goods and becoming destitute are common". The Working Group on Development and Welfare of STs during the Eighth Five Year Plan mentions the need for a Comprehensive National Policy, which will provide for complete socio-economic rehabilitation of displaced tribals.

The working group felt that the Policy must aim at ensuring a better living standard to the displaced tribals' families at the relocation sites than what they had before displacement and that it must be backed by a Central Authority under legislation for its enforcement. In reality no such policy has been promulgated till now. A draft policy for displaced tribals was formulated in 1985. The Committee appointed to study the draft suggested that it should not be limited to tribals alone but should apply to all the displaced persons and that it should be legally binding. In 1992, two ministries, namely Industries and Welfare have announced that a policy has been finalised.

It is further noted that although the efforts to evolve a comprehensive National Rehabilitation Policy 2005 were in the stage of drafting for the last, five years by various ministries, recently Ministry of Rural Development prepared and proposed a NPRR as a consequence of Acquisition of Land for the consideration of the approval of the Cabinet, Government of India. It is still pending for the necessary approval of the Cabinet. Previous to such attempts the Coal India Policy, NTPC Policy has been evolved for attending the issue of R&R of the DPs. These policies have attempted to define and specify several aspects related to R&R.

A critical review of the proposed NPRR undoubtedly provides a departure of the attitude from an earlier rejecter orientation to a very receptive and open minded one.

There, despite acknowledged progressive aspect of the proposed NPRR the following few aspects need serious attention;

1. Although development as a matter of right of the displaced has been discussed in content, no concrete legal assurance to the infrastructural development of the displaced are extended.
2. Minimisation of resettlement which is an important issue of international development debate is least focused.
3. The issue of the right to Information in advance extended to the expected oustees is clearly underscored.
4. No specific emphasis is laid on the issue of setting up an Authority/Agency for implementation of the plan for resettlement. Instead, the less co-ordinate performance of the multiple government departments is continuous unabated.
5. The Bureaucratic attitude of the policy framers is also reflected in the section entitled "eligibility and compensation". The demand for producing the 'evidence' by the PAP to justify his claim will invariably put the claimants in legal and administrative difficulties.

Finally, the policy could not refer to the question of administrative accountability in administering the programmes of rehabilitation to the DPs. Non-performance of the programmes, non-compliancy of the assigned tasks and responsibilities by the functionaries while delivering the social and economic rehabilitative programmes could have been pointedly fixed. Non-specification and silence on the fixing of the administrative accountability with the functionaries perhaps once again contradict the spirited constitutional guarantees and basis of the welfare Governance.

An empirical study on displacement and rehabilitation among the tribal communities of Telangana is focused on developmental projects in three different areas on Lambadi tribes. The "sample of case studies facilitate taking stock a wide range of responses to the process of displacement and resettlement by the tribals in different projects as well as the varied forms of rehabilitation measures taken up by the project authorities.

The project affected tribal community present greater commonality rather than differences. Social reality shared in common by the tribes under study are in the areas of social organisation, CPR-based livelihoods, unique social and kinship networks, religion and ritual and community as a social resource for their livelihoods besides the essence of "Web of life". The differences among the displaced tribes refer to the variations in regard to their proximity to towns and market forces, share of returns of agriculture-forest produce related activities in their economy. Despite perceptible variations on the economic front, the similarity socio-cultural realm is relatively more significant. Their interaction with towns and markets (in Gandiramaram and Parvathagiri Projects) has been mainly the outcome of these projects in early.

The worst hit in the process of displacement is those without clear titles to land, artisans and landless labourers. They did not get any compensation for the losses incurred. Similarly, there are PAFs of four more villages who have not been compensated or rehabilitees as they are affected by threats such as submergence under water uncovered by the norms of the project specific rehabilitation.

Displacement among the tribals has been a continuous process not being an event taking place only once. While displacement as a consequence of land acquisition for commissioning of the project is common to all projects under the study, the tribals, "under some projects have been displaced as a result of hazards posed by the project in Warangal, and by alien environment of the relocated habitat in the case of Lambadi's in both the cases the project authorities left the tribals to own fates, as they had no legal obligation though it is project induced displacement. Thus, among the tribals it is evident that displacement assumes greater severity as it takes the form of perpetuating displacement or a series of displacements leading to destitution or impoverishment.

The process of impoverishment consists of several distinguishable patterns. Cernea presenting a model of the overall impoverishment process outlined eight typical interconnected trends viz., landlessness, joblessness, homelessness, marginalisation, increased morbidity, food insecurity, loss of access to common property, and social disarticulation articulation. This conceptual construct of impoverishment process based on "eight most important sub processes" does not exclude yet other processes that take place in specific cases. Affected tribals of the three projects have been subjected to most of the above consequences in varying intensities.

A schematic presentation of the process of impoverishment caused by involuntary displacement in three areas of Telangana reveals the interrelated sub-processes leading towards the crisis in affected families. In all categories of PAFs, there has been a decline in total access to common property resources which is their basic life style. Their livelihood opportunities have been significantly affected as a result of declining size of land holding. Marginalisation has been "further compounded as a result of investing money on construction of houses in the house sites provided by the project authorities. House construction activity among the evicted could not "be ignored even if compensation amounts were not received owing to delays or litigation disputes. Even among those who received compensation amounts, they had to invest most of their money on housing and land development. Indebtedness increased among most of the PAFs as they had to engage fully in "reconstructing livelihoods" when they were faced with lesser earning opportunities.

Empirical data collected under the micro analysis of the study of displacement Lambadi tribal communities of Warangal belonging to five sample Thandas provide a disturbing picture. The factual conditions with which these affected tribal and non-tribal groups experience a process of jeopardisation of life. If the project-wise affect on the clientele is analysed in detail, a few common findings emerge from the study. These common findings are:

1. The rise in socio-economic and non-tribal communities as an effect of the displacement is clearly found.
2. Increases in the incidence of joblessness, morbidity ratio and severe problem of food insecurity.
3. Ruination of the traditional sources of livelihood resulting in social disarticulation and rendering the Tribals disempowered.
4. Decline in the overall assets holding and increase in the landlessness.
5. Most of the displaced families experience greater economic stress and rise in the family debt-ratio.
6. Rise in the incident of health hazards and diseases.
7. Segmentation of the families and social disorganisation of the communities as an effect of the displacement.
8. Greater pressure of the induced development over the tribal families through the process of series of displacements.
9. Increase in the dependency by displacement process and reversal of the status from an independence living to a dependent status as most of them are less suited to the things offered to them under the resettlement packages. Thus, the impoverishments of the tribal communities due to the new changes introduced by the micro facts analysed in the study.

The empirical analysis of the administration of the rehabilitation programmes to the oustees in the study villages informs a series of insights and concrete findings. The R&R Package vary both from project to project and also with regard to different categories of PAF's with each project.

Firstly, it is important to acknowledge that R&R Package was a separate component, and displacement was taken for granted. There was no participation, consultation or dialogue either in regard to project design and decisions concerning displacement or with regard to designing and R&R Package. R&R package was a technical obligation or generosity of the executive authority, and is an act or charity by an estranged agency. Displacement and rehabilitation practices in there project areas have failed to appreciate the concerns of the affected people. Most of the respondents perceived response of project authorities as half-hearted or indifferent.

Resettlement sites and package, designed exclusively by the executive authority. The assigned lands are also covered an account or the intervention, of the, courts for eligibility for compensation in project areas. It is also important to note that R&R packages were an extension of the land acquisition. Act rather than based on the legislation and policies aimed protecting the interest of tribal communities. Lastly, the compensation amounts were under assessed and the payments, delayed.

It is interesting to note that the procedure involved in getting due compensation for asset loss through the legal process is not only time consuming but also highly expensive, it is a process of alienation of the claimant since it becomes a major source of illegal gratification to the entire palpable revenue bureaucracy, the lawyers and their middle men with every one becoming a beneficiary except the displaced person. Who the Lambadi of three projects do not have this experience, it common among a large number of PAFs in other two projects. PAFs have spent anything in the range of 15 per cent to one third of the money received through legal, procedure towards the gratification of middlemen.

R&R policies fail to be effective as they perceive the other as adversary, rather than as a significant partner in a collaborative process to ensure restoration of livelihoods with the development project being the centre of the whole process. A healthy environment for collective participation indesigning rehabilitation of the affected through the project becoming the very resource base has been "conspicuously absent in all three projects. It is a policy that distances the PAPs from the planning and implementation of R&R packages.

It is also revealed that most common features of the resettlement sites are provision of house sites and drinking for the dislocated PAFs. Other facilities include fair price shops/primary schools and housing, opportunities for economic restoration and access to basic amenities like medical care internal roads, grazing lands have been ignored. Basic needs like fuel wood and individual electricity connections have also been ignored. Broadly the orientation towards resettling the oustees seems to be mere providing a shelter rather than assuring a source for reconstructing individual and collective life. As a result, the PAFs have vacated the resettlement sites and joined villages neighbouring their earlier place of residence.

There are several factors that need to be taken in account making resettlement programme acceptable to the PAFs. Immediate deprivation of earlier facilities, lack of opportunities for improving livelihoods in new sites tends to push PAFs towards other familiar settlements in the nearby region. In resettlement sites the atmosphere conducive for permanent settlement is conspicuously inadequate. A detailed examination of the major features of the official resettlement sites in three project areas reveals that they fall short of expectations both in quantitative and qualitative aspects.

An enquiry in the performance of the governance and administration of resettlement programmes in the study villages provided a set of inter-related empirical finding. They are presented here:

1. A clear cut gap exists between the felt needs of the displaced people and the prioritisation of the project authorities and the orientation of the government on the content and mode of R&R programmes.
2. Rehabilitation and Resettlement strategies basically suffer from an elitist orientation of the dispensing the displaced rather than showing a genuine commitment to the amelioration of the conditions of PAFs.
3. Considerable numbers of PAFs have been denied the compensation benefit. The enunciated legality as the conditioning criterion for eligibility and claim often do not exist in the case of few tribal communities such as Chenchus. The very notion of law is mostly alien to some of these primitive tribal groups. Lambadi's have a different notion of habitat and the whole orientation of the government towards

the Chenchu tribals was merely to reject on the pretext that their claims on habitat are not covered under the specific law. This legal void leaves Lambadi tribes with not legal alternative available except quitting their ancestral lands and homes.

4. Compensation benefit extended to the oustees has been largely spent on the consumption purposes. Cash compensation as a major component of R&R policy is a less suited option to the STs. Andhra Pradesh Government has agreed to provide land to the displaced if they are tribals. But this has not been put effect. Further, in between the operationalisation of the claim and realisation of the benefit several middlemen exploited the tribals who have got compensation in three projects. This makes the situation further worse as the tribes have lost the earlier assets and lands and do not get the full benefit of the newly extended help by the government.
5. Knowledge related to Land Acquisition Act and R&R Policy among the tribes remains almost absent. Very few have a vague idea about the possible chances for appeal towards gaining the appropriate assessment in the Court of Law.
6. The experience of the displaced tribals in approaching the Project Authorities for Grievance Settlement is rarely met with an expected treatment by the project authorities. False promises of rehabilitation threat of harassment by filing cases, legal litigations, long delays in communications, initiating evictions without resettlement and use of police forces at times etc., are few negative responses of the government that are experienced by the displaced tribals. In certain cases, few of the tribals after an assertive agitations and repeated pleas were able to get employment opportunities as a part of R&R package. But their number is extremely limited.
7. The responsive character of the project authorities or government attitude towards the oustees or affected is uncertain and disputable. Cash grants were quickly extended, to non-tribals. Most of the tribes were rejected the collectively infrastructure facilities in the respective habitats. Basic needs

like fuel wood and individual electricity connections have been denied.

8. The very form of extending the welfare measures or rehabilitation package still remains highly one-sided and authoritarian. The role played by the Land Acquisition Organisation and Revenue Officials is criticised by most of the displaced people. Project Authorities initial enquiries have been quoted as the false promises and unattainable targets the effected families. A sense of dejection is also prevailing among the displaced or project affected people in all the study villages covered under the various projects.
9. Earmarking the resettlement sites handled by the officials mostly has been mechanical activity rather than treating it as a part of their official responsibility. The official; orientation towards settling the oustee has not changed significantly.

In the light of the above findings that the development process in the tribal habitations has resulted in exclusion of the tribals. It has failed in guaranteeing their basic rights to secure life and alternative survival which is found valid in the study.

The Constitutional and Administrative Machinery designed to act as the welfare mechanism is able to address the need of the displaced persons, thereby on tradition the very process of rehabilitation as an administrative policy and protecting the tribal interests which has also been found valid by the study.

Findings

On the basis of the empirical study conducted on the displaced families of various reservoirs, the following are some of the important impacts that have been revealed from the analysis of data:

***Decline in Joint Family System**:* The pre-displacement level of 40 nuclear and 60 joint families was changed into 74 and 26 respectively with tribal families showing the same trend of breaking down of joint family to nuclear families. This is a general feature noticed in most of the development projects.

***Landlessness**:* India being a farm dominated society with agriculture as the main occupation, displacement from land, removes the main foundation on which people's productive systems; commercial activities and livelihood are based. Unless this foundation is reconstructed elsewhere or replaced by steady income-generating employment, landlessness sets in and the affected families are impoverished. In most of the cases/projects, land for land, norm could not be followed. But cash compensation is inadequate to make up for the loss of land. This impact has serious implication in the current project under study and therefore needs special consideration by the project implementing agencies in general and the policy-makers formulating strategies for the impacted people of development projects at government level.

Joblessness and increase in the proportion of workers*:* When people were displaced from their habitat, they lose their means of livelihood. Creation of new jobs or alternative sources of income for them becomes very difficult since the oustees do not possess any skill to learn new methods of earning their livelihood. Hence, those who were owners of the means of production before displacement have now become daily wage earners.

Homelessness*:* Loss of house and shelter may be only temporary during the transition period for most of the displaced. But for some, homelessness remains a permanent feature. The project authorities only provided homestead plots while the displaced persons have themselves built their houses. Again when a split occurs in the family, those who leave the family become homeless.

Food insecurity*:* Forced displacement increases the risk of chronic food insecurity. If crops are grown to provide food to the family while vegetables are grown in the kitchen gardens that take care of the food needs of the family. Surplus is also sold in the market. But forced displacements deprive the oustees from their former resource of livelihood rendering them landless. Even when homestead land was provided, the oustees could not properly reclaim and level the plain area. In the projects, the displaced families have to buy everything including food items from the market.

Loss of access to common property*:* For the poor people, particularly, the landless and otherwise assetless people, loss of access to common property (forest lands, water bodies, grazing land, etc.)

leads to a major deterioration in their income and livelihood levels. Such lost resources are rarely compensated by the government in the relocation sites. There are also frequent conflicts between the host population and new settlers over the use of forest land and other government land. As a result, the resettled do not get fuel wood and other minor forest produce, which they used to collect from their old habitat.

Social Disintegration: Forced displacement tears apart the social fabric of the oustees. Production systems are dismantled, kinship groups and family systems are often scattered and cultural identity of the people is under threat. Social and community networks that help people to cope with poverty through exchange of food and clothing, mutual help with farming, building houses and caring children are disrupted. Social disintegration has been a major impoverishment risk in all the projects undertaken. In the projects, the mutual help arrangement and their socio-economic relationships have been totally disrupted.

Increased Morbidity and Mortality: Loss of ancestral and homestead land, less no access to healthcare facilities, the psychological trauma caused thereby and the food insecurity together often leads to serious diseases. There is also the danger of parasitic and vector born diseases in the relocated sites because of unsafe water, poor sewerage etc. In fact, lack of food, unhygienic living and environmental degradation in the new place were found in the project area to have a serious impact on the health of the oustees.

- The general socio-economic condition of the oustees has deteriorated significantly.
- Socio-economic inequalities have widened.
- The cropping pattern has changed drastically.
- Dependence on trees and livestock has reduced substantially.
- Increase in the proportion of agricultural labourers.
- Increasing trend towards nuclear family.
- Poor dwelling conditions of the oustees.
- Improper use of compensation money.
- Rise in the incidence of indebtedness.

- Drastic reduction in the socio-economic condition of women in the PAFs.

Critical Areas of Concern

The key findings of the empirical study on the impact of development project on the displaced socio-economic condition of the tribal families in the three projects clearly reveal that the vast majority of them live a life of penury and hardship in the post-displacement period. Development projects have made the life of the oustees in general and tribal displaced families in particular more miserable and they have been further impoverished and languishing in poverty. The following are some of the critical areas of concern which the researcher has flagged to be considered by the policy-makers and the project resettlement agencies to look into for improving the socio-economic condition of the displaced tribal families in particular in the project and in all take precautionary measures so that the such issues do not figure in case of the ongoing and pipe-line projects.

(a) ***Lack of basic amenities**:* - Most of the development projects failed to provide basic amenities to the displaced people, which is a critical area of concern.

(b) ***Non-availability of wage work**:* Avenues of wage work are severely restricted in the resettlement colonies, forcing many oustees to migrate to places outside the district and even the State.

(c) ***Decline in the Role of Women and Relationship in the Family**:* Women play a vital role in the family, community and society. But after displacement, their income has either dwindled or has come to a halt altogether. They have become totally dependent on their husbands or sons for household expenditure. This made their role and status very limited.

(d) The cordial and intimate relationship of the pre-displacement period is now disrupted. Decreases in family income have created conflicts and bitterness among them.

(e) ***Problems arising out of cash compensation***: Most of the project authorities pay cash compensation to the PAFs, which are often mis-utilised by the male members on consumer durable items or liquor. Increased alcoholism has led to a rise in crimes in these areas.

(f) ***Increasing difficulties in arranging marriage for Daughters***: Women oustees now face great difficulty in getting married because of the demand for more dowries. Use of cash compensation on the marriages leave the family pauperised.

In view of these effects of displacement, especially on the tribal's, it is necessary not only to identify, avoid and mitigate risks in each development project that entails displacement, but also to focus on benefits over and above compensation and rehabilitation for damages as well as benefit sharing arrangement. A prudent approach demands long-term commitments, financial and institutional guarantees and the use of professional approach in dealing with the issues of social development of indigenous people. Constant monitoring by technically competent independent observers can go a long way in ensuring more effective R&R arrangements in case of the displaced families which can end up in not only restoring the pre-displaced living condition of the millions of displaced families but also in substantially bringing in improvement in their socio-economic condition in the post-project period.

In the light of above findings the following suggestions assume importance:

1. Effective enforcement of the Constitutional privileges with a deep sense of administrative commitment may be the two principal solutions to offer for administration of the misery of the tribals displaced under the development process.
2. A host of administrative measures complimented by a single central agency endowed with the responsibility of rehabilitation will be of a relevant proposition.
3. Early enactment of the legislation on displacement will further dispel the number of hurdles encountered by the victims of the displacement mainly tribes of the study in Andhra Pradesh.
4. That the effects of 'displacement' extends not only to those directly affected but also to a much wider social and economic community; and that in the event of any displacement in any

given area, planning and provision must be made for this entire wider context, taking into account the interests of all these affected.

5. Modification in Laws:
   (a) Land Acquisition Act to take into cognizance CPRs, land for land compensation, villages as units of resettlement.
   (b) The Policy on displacement and rehabilitation and the Land Acquisition Act cannot go against existing, state or central laws that protect the interests of the disadvantaged groups and protected regions e.g., Land Transfer Regulation Act of Andhra Pradesh, Forest Conservation Act, etc.
6. Industrial/mining projects must make PAPs shareholders and partners in its management, irrigation/hydel projects must provide the benefits to the PAPs as individual households and villages collectively in the command area or in any region of their choice. Even irrigation projects must not exact from being its significant shareholders.
7. The criteria for compensation has been discussed extensively in various policies, namely National Working Group on Displacement, the first drafts of Ministry of Water Resources and Ministry of Rural Development. The compensation criteria in the above policies in principle should be land for land.

Finally, the desirable development pattern and project designing process should aim at minimisation displacement. The development strategy should concentrate on reducing the regional economic disparities, class and ethnic conflicts. Development projects need to be participatory and decentralised both in formation and implementation. The participatory operation with the decentralised conceptual basis will harmonise the social fabric and lead to an acountable welfare governance and people's development.

Bibliography

Reports

Amartya Sen or Prof. Martha Nussbaum, and even by Human Development Reports.

Sharma, B.D. Report of the sub-committee appointed by the Ministry of Panchayati Raj to draft Model Guidelines to vest Gram Sabhas with powers as envisaged in PESA, 2010.

'Displacement, Resettlement, Rehabilitation, Reparation, and Development' Final Version: November 2000.

Ethics of Development-Induced Displacement (EDID) research project, York University, Toronto, Canada.

European Commission, Green Paper: Promoting a European Framework for Corporate Social Responsibility, 2001.

Guiding Principles on Internal Displacement, United Nations.

Javir Singh, Working Paper Series Centre for the Study of Law and Governance, Jawaharlal Nehru University, New Delhi, 2004.

OECD, Development Assistance Committee, Guideline on Aid and Environment, Paris, 1992.

Report on India by Internal Displacement Monitoring Centre of U.N. Office of High Commissioner on Human Rights.

Shakti Shrama, Report of the National Commission on Self Employed Women and Women in the Informal Sector, New Delhi, 1988.

Tata Institute of Social Sciences (1993): 'The Sardar Sarovar Project: Experiences with Resettlement and Rehabilitation'.

Twelfth Annual Review of Project Performance Results, the World Bank, Washington D.C.

Documents

International Covenant on Civil and Political Rights.

International Covenant on Economic, Social and Cultural Rights.

International Labour Organisation Conventions and Recommendations Relating to Industry, 2013.

Regional Human Rights Instruments of Europe, Africa and the Americas.

The American Convention on Human Rights

The Constitution of India.

The Declaration of Human and Civil Rights of 26-8-1789.

The European Convention on Human Rights.

Universal Declaration of Human Rights, 1948.

Acts, Rules and Regulations

Land Acquisition Act, 1894.

Maharashtra Project Affected Persons Rehabilitation Act, 1986.

Panchayat (Extension to the Scheduled Areas) PESA Act 1996.

The Constitution (First Amendment) Act, 1951, The Constitution (Fourth Amendment) Act, 1956, The Constitution (Seventeenth Amendment) Act, 1964, The Constitution (Twenty-Fifth Amendment) Act, 191971, The Constitution (44th Amendment) Act, 1978.

The Constitution (Fourth Amendment) Act, 1956.

The Constitution of India (First Amendment) Act, 1951, IX Schedule.

The Environment (Protection) Act, 1986.

The Forest (Conservation) Act, 1980.

The Forest Act, 1927.

The Hindu Succession Act, 1956.

The Indian Stamp Act, 1899.

The Panchayat (Extension to the Scheduled Areas) PESA Act, 1996.

The Right to Fair Compensation and Transparency in Land Acquisition, Rehabilitation and Settlement Act, 2013.

The Scheduled Tribes and Other Traditional Forest Dwellers (Recognition of Forest Rights) Act, 2006.

The Scheduled Tribes and Other Traditional Forest Dwellers (Recognition of Forest Rights) Act, 2006.

The Sholapur Spinning and Weaving Company (Emergency Provision) Ordinance, 1950.

Books

Addo, M.(Ed.), Standards and the Responsibility of Transnational Corporations, 1999.

Aggarwal, Bina (Ed), Structures of Patriarchy, State, Community and Household in Modernizing Asia, Kali for Women, New Delhi.

Allen, Tim (Ed), In Search of Cool Ground: War, Flight and Homecoming in Northeast Africa, London: United Nations Research Institute for Social Development, Africa World Press.

Austin, Granville, The Indian Constitution Cornerstone of Nation, Oxford University Publication, New Delhi, 1966.

Bardhan, P. and T.N., Srinivasan (Ed.), Rural Poverty in South Asia, 1981.

Bentham, Jenney Theory of legislation- with an Introduction by Upendra Baxi, 1975.

Bentham, Jeremy, A Fragment on Government, Vol. 1, The Work of Jeremy Bentham, Bowring J. (Ed), New York, 1962.

Bernard, H. Siegan Property Rights: From Magna Carta to Fourteenth Amendment 5. 2001.

Bhattacharjee, Tanmoy (Ed.), Problems of Internally Displaced Persons in Assam with Special Reference to Barak Valley. Silchar, Department of Political Sciences, Assam University, March 2003.

Boyle, Alan E. and Michael R. Anderson (Ed.), Human Rights Approaches to Environmental Protection, Clarendon Press, Oxford, 1996.

Buxi, Upendra the Future of Human Rights. New Delhi: Oxford University Press.

Cernea M. (Ed.), Putting People First, Sociological Variables in Development, Oxford University Press, New York.

Cernea, Michael, (Ed.), The Economics of Involuntary Resettlement: Questions and Challenges, Washington, DC: World Bank.

Cernea, Michael Public Policy Responses to Development-Induced Population Displacements, Washington, DC: World Bank Reprint Series: Number 479, 1996.

Chimni, B.S., International Refugee Law: A Reader, Saga Publication, 2000.

Deogharia, Parkash Chandra Development, Displacement and Deprivation, New Delhi, 2012.

Dwyer Daisy and Bruce Judith, A Home Divided: Women and Income in the Third World, Stanford University Press, Stanford, 1988.

Fernades, Walter and S Anthony Raj, Development, Displacement and Rehabilitation in the Tribal Areas of Odisha, Indian Social Institute, New Delhi, 1992.

Fernandez Aloysius P (Ed.), Workshop on Rehabilitation of Persons Displaced by Development Projects, Institute of Social and Economic Change and MYRADA, Bangalore.

Gandhi, M.K. Hind Swaraj, Ahmedabad: Navjivan Publishing House, 1987.

Hopkins, Michael Corporate Social Responsibility: An Issues Paper International Labour Organisation (ILO) - Policy Integration Department, May 2004.

Huhua, Cao., Ethnic Minorities and Regional Development in Asia, Amsterdam University Press, 2009.

Jain, M.P., Indian Constitutional Law, VIth Ed., LexisNexis-Butterworth, Nagpur.

Kabir, Naila, Reversed Realities. Gender Hierarchies in Development Thought, Verso, London-New York, 1994.

Locke, John, Second Treatise of Government (an essay concerning the true, original, extent and of civil government) and a letter concerning toleration, 1966.

Mahapatra, L. K. Tribal Development in India: Myth or Reality, Vikas, New Delhi, 1994.

Menon, P. S. K. and Sinha, Bakshi D., Panchayati Raj in Scheduled Areas, New Delhi: Institute of Social Sciences, 2003.

Mishra, Nihar Rajan, Displacement and Rehabilitation-Solution for the Future, Bhopal, 2012.

Morris, S., and Sekhar Rajiv, India Infrastructure Report, Oxford University Press, New Delhi, 2004.

Morris, S., India Infrastructure report 2001: Issues and Regulation and Industry Structure, Oxford University Press, New Delhi, 2001.

Nair, R., Human Rights in India: Historical, Social and Political Perspectives, New Delhi: Oxford University Press, 2006.

Phillip, Nichols, Nichols on Eminent Domain, Lexis Nexis, Vol. I.

Poulter S., Ethnicity, Law and Human Rights: The English Experience, Oxford Clarendon Press, 1998.

Ray, B.N., Political Theory of Human Need Contemporary Political Thinking, Kanishka Publication, New Delhi, 2000.

Ray, S.N., Judicial Review & Fundamental Rights, Eastern Law House, Calcutta, 1974.

Rousseau, Jean, J., Discourse on the Origin and Basis of Inequality among Men, 1754.

Salomon, Sonya, Cultural Dimensions of Land Tenure in the United States, 1998.

Sarathi, V.P. Interpretation of Statutes, (Vth Edn), EBC, Lucknow.

Sarkar, P.K., 'Law of Acquisition of Land in India', (2nd Edn), Eastern Law House, 2007.

Schumacher, E.F., Small is Beautiful: A study of Economics as if people mattered, London, Vintage books, 1993.

Seervai, H.M., Constitutional Law of India: A Critical Commentary, (2nd Edn), Universal Law Publication, New Delhi, 2010.

Shah, G., Social movements in India: A review of literature, New Delhi: Sage Publications, 2004.

Sharma, G.S., Property Relations in Independent India: Constitutional and Legal Implication in India, ILI, New Delhi, 1956.

Sidgwick, Henery, The Methods of Ethics, Dover Publication, New York, 1966.

Thukral, Enakshi Ganguly, (Ed.), Big Dams Displaced People - Rivers of Sorrow, Rivers of Change, Sage, New Delhi.

Vask, Karl, (Ed.), The International Dimensions of Human Rights, Greenwood Press, Paris, 1982.

Ward, H., Public Sector roles in strengthening Corporate Social Responsibility: Taking Stock, working paper prepared for the World Bank, 2004.

Watts, Phil and Lord Holme, Corporate Social Responsibility: Meeting Changing Expectations, 1999.

White, Allen, 'Business Brief: Intangibles and CSR', Business for Social Responsibility, 2006.

William, H., Shaw Contemporary Ethics: Taking Account of Utilitarianism, Oxford, Blackwell, 1999.

Articles

Baxi, Upendra, 'The Constitutional Quicksand of Kesavanand Bharti and the twenty-fifth Amendment', 1 SCC 45, 1974.

Cernea, Michael, M, 'From Unused Social Knowledge to Policy Creation: The Case of Population Resettlement', Development Discussion Paper No. 342, Harvard Institute for International Development, Harvard University, USA, 1990.

Dam, Shubhankar and Vivek Tiwary, 'Polluting Environment, Pollution constitution: Is a 'Polluted' Constitution Worse Than a Polluted Environment?', Journal of Environmental Law 17, 2005.

Dana, David A, 'Reframing Eminent Domain: Unsupported Advocacy, Ambiguous Economics, and the Case for a New Public Use Test,' 32 Vt. L. Rev. 129.

Eyras Xavier, 'SEZ with Defiance?' Social Action, Vol. 58. July-Sept-2008, p. 272.

Fernades, Walter, 'Construction Workers, Powerlessness and Bondage: The Case of the Asian Games' Social Action, 36, No. 3, July-September, 1986.

Ghose, Soheli, 'A look into Corporate Social Responsibility in Indian and emerging economies', International Journal of Business and Management Invention, Volume 1, Issue 1, December, 2012.

Hazra, Anupam, 'Development at the Cost of Human Life', Social Action, Volume 60 April-June, 2010.

Kelly, A. Dhru, 'Displacement due to Land Acquisition for Development Projects in India: the Problems with Existing Legislative Policy', (Unpublished, NLSIU in Association with

NTPC, New Delhi, conducting training program.15th-17th December, 2010.

Mani Aiyar, S., 'Panchayat Raj: The Way Forward', Economic and Political Weekly, August 2002.

Marianus Kujur Joseph, 'Development Induced Displacement in Chhattisgarh: A Case Study from a Tribal Perspective', Social Action, Vol. 60, April -June, 2010.

Mehta, Pooja, 'Internally-Displaced Persons and the Sardar Sarovar Project: A Case for Rehabilitative Reform'.

Minz, N., 'Cultural Identity of Tribals in India' Social Action, Vol. 43, Jan-March, 1993.

Morris, S. and Pandey Ajay, 'Towards Reform in Land Acquisition Frame Work in India', Economic and Political Weekly, June, 2007.

Nagiah, C., 'Resettlement and Rehabilitation Upper Krishna Project, Special Deputy Commissioner UKP', (Unpublished), NLSIU in Association with NTPC, New Delhi conducting training program, 15th-17th December, 2010.

Negi, Nalin Singh and Sujata Ganguly, 'Development Projects vs. Internally Displaced Populations in India: A Literature Based Appraisal', Indian Institute of Technology Roorkee, February 2011.

Negi, Singh, Nalin and Ganguly, Sujata: Development Projects vs. Internally Displaced Populations in India: a Literature Based Appraisal, Bielefeld: COMCAD, 2011.

Nwete, Bede, 'The Equator Principles: How Far will it Affect Project Financing?' International Business Law Journals, 2005.

Ramanathan, Usha, 'Land Acquisition and Compensation in Involuntary Resettlement', EPW, Vol. 31, No. 24, June 15 1996.

Ramnathan, Usha, 'Displacement and the Law', Vol. 31 EPW, Issue No. 24, June 15, 1996.

Ramnathan, Usha, 'A Word of Eminent Domain', International Environmental Law Research.

Rao, K. Subba, 'Property Rights under the Constitution', 2 SCC 1, 1969.

Revathi, E., 'Adivasis and Telangana' The Hans India, August 27, 2013.

Sabar, Bhubanshwar, 'Development-Induced Displacement and Human Rights Violation of Odisha: An Anthropological Insight' Social Action, Vol. 60, April –June 2010.

Sahay, Ashok Kumar, Prabira Sethy, 'Tribal Displacement and Resettlement: effective safe guards?' Social Action, Volume 58, January-March 2008.

Sanpete Goyal, 'Economic Perspectives on Resettlement and Rehabilitation?' EPW, June 15, 1996.

Seshsayee, R., 'How Can Land Acquisition Be Made Human?' Economic Times, 16 June 2007.

Sharma, Kumud, 'National Policies for Natural Resources Management, Marginalisation of Poor Rural Women' (Occasional Paper No. 14), Centre for Women's Development Studies, New Delhi, 1989.

Sharma, Tannu, 'Public Purpose in Land Acquisition Act under SC Scrutiny' Indian Express, 11 May 2007.

Singh, Javir, 'Working Paper Series Centre for the Study of Law and Governance' Jawaharlal Nehru University, New Delhi, 2004 at Economic and Political Weekly, May 12, 2001.

Thipper, B., 'Right over forest land for tribals in the offing', The Indian Express, Feb 17, 2014.

University of Minnesota: Human Rights Resource Center, Justiciability of ESC Rights, The Indian Experience.

Viegas, Philip, 'The Hirakud Dam Oustees: Thirty Years After' in Enakshi Ganguly Thukral (Ed.), Big Dams Displaced People – Rivers of Sorrows, Rivers of Change, Sage, New Delhi.

Vikas, Nandal, 'Land Acquisition Law in India: A Historical Perspective' International Journal of Innovative Research & Studies, Vol. 3, Issue 5.

World Commission on Dams: Democratic means for Sustainable Ends, Economic and Political Weekly, May 26, 2001.

World Economic Forum, 'Global Corporate Citizen: The Leadership Challenge for CEOs and Boards' 2002.

Xaxa, Virginius, 'Tribes as Indigenous People' Economic and political Weekly, 1999.

Yadav, Kalpana, 'Eminent Domain: An Interrogation' 16 AIHCC, 2010.

Websites

http://documents.worldbank.org.
http://hdr.undp.org/en/humandev.
http://indiatoday.intoday.in
http://news.bbc.co.uk.
http://papers.ssrn.com.
http://reasonpapers.com
http://rru.worldbank.org
http://siteresources.worldbank.org
http://www.conseil-constitutionnel.fr
http://www.dams.org
http://www.deccanherald.com.
http://www.development-ethics.org/.
http://www.edid.yorku.ca/
http://www.ielrc.org.
http://www.ifc.org
http://www.ijbmi.org
http://www.indianexpress.com.
http://www.jnu.ac.in/cslg/.
http://www.oecd.org.
http://www.protectingpropertyrights.org
http://www.un.org.
http://www.unhcr.org
http://www.weforum.org
http://www.yorku.ca
http://www2.ohchr.org
http://www2.ohchr.org.
http://wwwl.umn.edu.
www.europa.eu.int
www.internal-displacement.org
www.internal-displacement.org.

Appendix

Government of Andhra Pradesh

ABSTRACT

Irrigation & CAD Department - Rehabilitation and Resettlement (R&R) Policy of Government of Andhra Pradesh - Issued.

Irrigation & CAD (Project Wing-LA-IV-R&R) Department

G.O. Ms. No. 68 Dated the 8thApril, 2005.

Order

Compulsory acquisition of land for implementation of development and infrastructure projects displaces people from their homes, land and/or their means of livelihood. Apart from depriving them of their land, livelihood and resources base, displacement has other psychological, social and cultural consequences also. The Government recognise the need to minimise large scale displacement to the extent possible and where displacement is inevitable, the need to address the issue of displacement with utmost care, human touch and forethought. Such an approach is especially necessary in respect of tribal, small and marginal farmers.

2. Various policies relating to the Resettlement and the Rehabilitation (R&R) of displaced persons have been in place from time to time, varying from project to project and district to district. The need has been felt for the evolution of a comprehensive policy on R& R to ensure uniformity of benefits across the State and also to ensure the delivery of benefits in a transparent manner.

3. A Committee was constituted by the Government vide G.O. Ms. No.70, Irrigation & CAD (Projects Wing) Department, dated 15-07-2004 for preparation of draft R&R Policy for Government of Andhra Pradesh. The recommendations of the Committee were discussed in a State Level meeting comprising of major stake holders in the policy like the Department of Energy, Industries, Roads & Buildings, Environment, Forest, Science & Technology, Finance, Tribal Welfare, Law and Revenue. The State Level Meeting endorsed the recommendations of the Committee.

4. Government after careful examination of the Committee recommendations as endorsed by State Level meeting hereby approve the Rehabilitation & Resettlement Policy for Government of Andhra Pradesh enclosed to this order for implementation by all the Departments for Government of Andhra Pradesh.

5. It is further ordered that as per Section 8.5 of this Policy the provisions of G.O. Ms. No. 98, Irrigation & CAD (ProjectsWing) Department, dated 15-04-1986 and G.O. Ms. No. 64, Social Welfare (T) Department, dated 18-04-1990 and any other Government order/ Memo/Instructions issued by any other Department of Government ofAndhra Pradesh shall cease to operate as far as those Projects are concerned that are notified under this Policy.

(BY ORDER AND IN THE NAME OF GOVERNOR OF ANDHRA PRADESH)

MOHAN KANDA
CHIEF SECRETARY TO GOVERNMENT

To : All the Departments of Secretariat

All the District Collectors in the State.
All the Special Collectors of Irrigation Projects.
The Engineer-in-Chief (AW)/(Irrigation), Errum Manzil, Hyderabad
All the Chief Engineers of the Projects.

Government of Andhra Pradesh Resettlement and Rehabilitation Policy 2005 gor Project Affected Families

Chapter – I: Policy

1.0 Preamble:

1.1 Compulsory acquisition of land for public purpose including infrastructure projects displaces people, forcing them to give up their home, assets and means of livelihood, a part from depriving them of their lands, livelihoods and resource-base, displacement has other traumatic psychological and socio-cultural consequences. The Government of Andhra Pradesh recognises the need to minimise large-scale displacement to the extent possible and, where displacement is inevitable, the need to handle with utmost care, human touch and forethought, issues relating to Resettlement and Rehabilitation of Project Affected Families. Such an approach is especially necessary in respect of tribal, small and marginal farmers and women.

1.2 The system of extending cash compensation does not, by itself, in most cases, enable the affected families to obtain cultivable agricultural land, homestead and other resources, which they have to surrender to the State. The difficulties are more acute for persons who are critically dependent on the acquired assets for their subsistence/ livelihoods, such as landless agricultural workers, forest dwellers, tenants and artisans, as their distress and destitution is more severe, and, yet they are not eligible for cash compensation.

1.3 The Policy essentially addresses the need to provide succour to the assetless rural poor, support the rehabilitation efforts of the resource poor sections, namely, small and marginal farmers, SCs/STs and women who have been displaced, besides, it seeks to provide a broad canvas for an effective dialogue between the Project Affected Families and Project Displaced Families and the Administration for Resettlement and Rehabilitation. Such a dialogue is expected to enable timely completion of projects with a sense of definiteness as regards costs and adequate attention to the needs of the displaced persons especially the resource poor sections. The intention is to impart greater flexibility for interaction and negotiation so that the resultant package gains all-round acceptability in the shape of a workable instrument providing satisfaction to all stakeholders/ requiring bodies.

1.4 The GOAP Policy on the Resettlement and Rehabilitation of Project Affected Families and Project Displaced Families will be applicable to the projects as defined in this policy and upon notification under this policy.

1.5 Administrator for Resettlement and Rehabilitation shall implement this Policy in letter and spirit in order to ensure that the benefits envisaged under the Policy reaches the Project Affected and Displaced Families, especially resource poor sections including SCs/STs.

Chapter – II

2.0 Objectives of the Policy

The objectives of the Policy are as follows:

2.1 To minimise displacement and to identify non-displacing or least-displacing alternatives;

2.2 To Plan the resettlement and rehabilitation of Project Affected and Displaced Families, (PAFs/ PDFs) including special needs of Tribals and vulnerable sections;

2.3 To provide better Standard of living to PAFs and PDF's; and

2.4 To facilitate harmonious relationship between the Requiring Body and PAFs through mutual cooperation.

Chapter – III

3.0 Definitions

The definition of various terms used in this Policy Document are as follows:

3.1 "Administrator for Resettlement and Rehabilitation" means an officer not below the rank of Joint Collector of the State

Government appointed by it for the purpose of resettlement and rehabilitation of the Project Affected Families of the Project concerned provided that if the appropriate Government in respect of the Project is the Central Government, Such appointment shall be made in consultation with the Central Government.

3.2 "Affected Zone", in relation to a project, means declaration under Para 5.1 of this policy by the appropriate Government area of Villages or locality under a project for which the Land is being acquired under Land Acquisition Act, 1894 or any other Act in force for the following areas:

(a) Area falling under FRL contour

(b) Dwelling House (S) falling within 100 meters of surface distance from FRL water line.

3.3 "Agricultural family" means a family whose primary mode of livelihood is agriculture and includes family of owners as well as tenants / sub-tenants of agricultural land, agricultural labourers, occupiers of forest lands and of Collectors of minor forest produce;

3.4 "Agricultural Labourers" means a person normally resident in the affected zone for a period of not less than three years immediately before the declaration of the affected zone who does not hold any land in the affected zone but who earns his livelihood principally by manual labour on agricultural land therein immediately before such declaration and who has been deprived of his livelihood as ascertained through enquiry in the Gram Sabha;

3.5 "Agricultural Land" includes lands used or capable of being used for the purpose of

(a) agriculture or horticulture;

(b) dairy farming, poultry farming, pisciculture, breeding or livestock and nursery growing medical herbs;

(c) raising of crops, grass or garden produce; and

(d) land used by an agriculturist for the grazing of cattle, but does not include land used for the cutting of wood only;

3.6 "Appropriate Government" means;

(a) in relation to acquisition of land for the purposes of the Union, the Central Government;

(b) in relation to a project which is executed by Central Government Agency/ Central Government Undertaking or by any other agency on the orders/ directions of Central Government, the Central Government, otherwise the State Government and

(c) in relation to acquisition of land for other purposes, the State Government.

3.7 "BPL Family": The Below Poverty Line Families shall be those as defined by the Planning Commission of India from time to time.

3.8 "Project" means the project(s) notified under this Policy and displacing

(a) 100 or more families en-mass in plain areas or

(b) 25 or more families en-mass in Tribal areas or in areas mentioned in Schedule V of the constitution

3.9 "Commissioner for Resettlement & Rehabilitation", means the Commissioner for Resettlement & Rehabilitation appointed by the State Government not below the rank of Commissioner/ Secretary of that Government.

3.10 (a) "Family includes a person, his or her spouse, minor sons, minor daughters, minor brothers or minor sisters and other members residing with him and dependent on him for their livelihood. Further each major son and major daughter residing with such person will be treated as a separate family and the cut off date for calculating their age of 18 years will be the date of notification issued under Section 4(i) of Land Acquisition Act, 1894 for acquisition of the village as notified under Pata 5.1 of this G.O.[1]

(b) [2]"Vulnerable persons" means the disabled, destitute, orphans, Widows, major unmarried daughter, abandoned/ divorced women or Persons above fifty years of age, who are not provided or can not Immediately be provided with alternative livelihood, and who are not otherwise covered as part of a family.[2]

3.11 "Holding" means the total land held by a person as an occupant or tenant or as both;

3.12 "Marginal farmer" means a cultivator with an un-irrigated land holding up to one hectare or irrigated land holding up to half hectare or combination of both on same principle;

3.13 "Non-agricultural Labourer" means a person who is not an agricultural labourer but is normally residing in the affected zone for a period of not less than three years immediately before the declaration of the affected zone and who does not hold any land under the affected zone but who earns his livelihood principally by manual labour or as a rural artisan immediately before such declaration and who has been deprived of earning his livelihood principally by manual labour or as such artisan in the affected zone;

3.14 "Notification" means a notification published in the Official Gazette;

3.15 "Occupiers" means members of the Scheduled Tribes/other Traditional forest dwellers in possession of forest land prior to the 13th Day of December, 2005.

3.15 (a) "Other traditional forest dweller" means any member of community who has for at least three generations (generation means a period of 25 years) prior to the 13th day of Dec' 2005 primarily resided in and who depend on the forest or forests land for bonafide livelihood needs.

3.16 "Project Affected Family" means

(a) a family whose source of livelihood are substantially affected by the process of acquisition of land for the project and who has been residing continuously for a period of not less than three years preceding the date of declaration of the affected zone or practicing any trade, occupation or vocation continuously for a period of not less than three years in the affected zone, preceding the date of declaration of the affected zone, regardless of the fact whether they owned land or not.

(b) family whose more than 50 per cent of land is acquired and left over land after acquisition is below Ac.5.0 dry or Ac. 2.5 wet or combination of both on above principle.

(c) AProject Displaced Family

(d) any tenure holder, tenant, lessee or owner of other property, who on account of acquisition of land (including plot in the abadi or other property) in the affected area or otherwise, has been involuntarily displaced from such land or other property.[3]

3.17 "Project Displaced Family" means any family, who on account of acquisition of his dwelling house in the village in the affected zone for the purpose of the project, has been displaced from such dwelling house.

3.18 "Resettlement Zone", in relation to a project, means the declaration of any area under Para 5.12 of this Policy by the appropriate Government acquired or proposed to be acquired for resettlement of Project Displaced Families as a resettlement zone:

3.19 "Requiring Body" shall mean any company, a body corporate, an institution, or any other Organisation for whom land is to be acquired by the appropriate Government, and includes the appropriate Government if the acquisition of land is for such Government either for its own use or for subsequent allotment of such land in public interest to a body corporate, institution, or any other organisation or to any company under lease, license or through any other system of transfer of land to such company, as the case may be;

3.20 "Small farmer" means a cultivator with an un-irrigated land holding of more than one hectare and up to two hectares or with an irrigated land holding of more than half hectare and up to one hectare or combination of both on same principle.

3.21 "Substantially affected" means where average annual income of PAF is likely to be reduced by more than 50 per cent and is likely to become BPL family due to acquisition of his land or other's land for the project, as compared to his average annual income in last three years preceding the date of notification, from land and or other sources of incomes.

3.22 "Tribal Areas" means areas as declared so by the Tribal Welfare Department, Government of Andhra Pradesh from time to time.

3.23 "Ombudsman" means the person appointed under Para 7.5 of this policy.[4]

Chapter – IV

4.0 APPOINTMENT OF ADMINISTRATOR AND COMMISSIONER FOR RESETTLEMENT AND REHABILITATION AND THEIR POWERS & FUNCTIONS.

4.1 Where the appropriate Government is satisfied that acquisition of land for any project involves displacement of families from their lands and or houses as a result of acquisition of land, it shall, by notification, appoint in respect of that project, an officer not below the rank of Joint Collector of the state Government to be the Administrator for R&R in respect of that project.

Provided that if the appropriate Government in respect of the project is the Central Government, such appointment shall be made in consultation with the Central Government.

4.2 The Administrator for Resettlement & Rehabilitation shall be assisted by such officers and employees as the appropriate Government may provide.

4.3 Subject to the superintendence, directions and control of the appropriate Government and Commissioner for R&R, the Administrator for Resettlement and Rehabilitation shall take all measures for the Rehabilitation and Resettlement of all Projects Affected Families (PAF's) in respect of that project.

4.4 The overall control and superintendence of the formulation of resettlement and rehabilitation plan and execution of the same Shall vest in the Administrator, Resettlement and Rehabilitation.

4.5 Subject to any general or special order of the appropriate Government, the Administrator for Resettlement and Rehabilitation shall perform the following functions / duties:-

(a) Minimise displacement of persons and identify non-displacing or least displacing alternatives in consultation with the requiring body;

(b) Hold consultation with the Project Affected Families while preparing a resettlement and rehabilitation scheme/ plan;

(c) Ensure that interest of the adversely Project Affected Families of Scheduled Tribes and weaker sections are protected.

(d) Prepare a draft plan/scheme of resettlement and rehabilitations as required under Chapter V and VI of this Policy. Wherever tribal PAPs are involved, the draft plan/scheme shall be prepared in consultation with respective area Project officer ITDA/DTWO.

(e) Prepare a budget including estimated expenditure of various components of acquisition of Land, Resettlement and Rehabilitation activities or programmes in consultation with representatives of the Project Affected Families and requiring body for whom the land is acquired;

(f) Acquire adequate land for the Project and also for Resettlement and Rehabilitation of the Project Affected Families;

(g) Allot Land and sanction benefits to Project Affected Families;

(h) Perform such other function as the appropriate Government may, from time to time, by order in writing, assign.

4.6 Administrator for Resettlement & Rehabilitation may, by order in writing, delegate such of the administrative powers conferred and duties imposed on him by or under this policy to any officer not below the rank of RDO/Sub-Collector or equivalent who will be called as R&R officer for the said project.

4.7 All officers and staff appointed by the appropriate Government under this policy shall be subordinate to the Administrator for Resettlement and Rehabilitation.

4.8 The State Government shall appoint an officer of the rank of Commissioner/ Secretary of that Government for Resettlement and Rehabilitation in respect of such projects to which this Policy applies to be called the Commissioner for Resettlement and Rehabilitation.

4.9 For the purposes of this Policy, the Administrator for Resettlement and Rehabilitation and other officers and employees appointed for the purposes of Resettlement and Rehabilitation of PAF shall be subordinate to the Commissioner for Resettlement and Rehabilitation.

4.10 The Commissioner shall be responsible for supervising the formulation of resettlement and rehabilitation plans/ schemes, proper implementation of such plans/ schemes and redressal of grievances as mentioned in Chapter VII of this Policy. Wherever tribal PAPs are involved, Commissioner, TW shall also be involved in above responsibilities and functions.

Chapter – V

5.0 SCHEMES/PLANS FOR RESETTLEMENT AND REHABILITATION;

The procedure mentioned in this Chapter shall be followed for declaration of Affected Zone, carrying out survey and census of Project Affected Families, Assessment of Government Land available and land to be acquired for the purpose of Resettlement and Rehabilitation, preparation of draft scheme/plan for R&R and its final publication.

5.1 The appropriate Government may, if it is of the opinion that acquisition of land for a project is likely to displace families from their lands and or houses, declare, by notification in the Official Gazette, area of villages or localities as an affected zone of the project and thereupon the contents of this Policy shall apply to the project involved.

5.2 Every declaration made under Para 5.1 of the Policy shall be published in at least two daily newspapers one of them should be in the local vernacular having circulation in villages or areas which are likely to be affected and also by affixing a copy of the notification on the Notice Board of the concerned Gram Panchayats and other prominent place or places in the affected zone.

5.3 Once the declaration is made under Para 5.1 of the Policy, the Administrator for Resettlement and Rehabilitation shall undertake a Socio-economic Survey for identification of the persons and their families likely to be affected by the project.

5.4 Every survey shall contain the following village-wise information of the project Affected Families:-

(a) members of families who are permanently residing, practicing any trade, occupation or vocation in the Project Affected Area.

(b) Project Affected Families who are likely to lose their house, agricultural land, employment or are alienated wholly or substantially from the main source of their trade/ occupation or vocation.

(c) Agricultural labourers and non-agriculture labourers.

(d) Project Affected Families who are or were having Possession of forest lands in the affected area prior to the 13th day of December, 2005.[5]

(e) Vulnerable persons such as the disabled, destitute, orphans, widows, unmarried girls, abandoned women, or persons above fifty years of age; who are not provided or cannot immediately be provided with alternative livelihood, and who are not otherwise covered as part of a family.

(f) Families that are landless (not having homestead land, agricultural land, or either homestead or agricultural land) and below poverty line, but residing continuously for a period of not less than three years in the affected area preceding the date of declaration of the affected area.[6]

5.5 Every survey undertaken under Para 5.4 shall be completed within a maximum period of ninety days from the date of declaration made under Para 5.1.

5.6 On the expiry of the period of ninety days as aforesaid or as earlier as possible, the Administrator for Resettlement and Rehabilitation shall publish a draft in the Gram Panchayat concerned the details of the findings of the survey conducted by him for inviting objections and suggestions from all persons likely to be affected thereby.

5.7 On the expiry of thirty days from the date of publication of the draft of the details of survey and after considering the objections and suggestions received by him in this behalf, the Administrator for Resettlement and Rehabilitation shall submit the final details of survey with his recommendations to the District Collector for approval. After approval by the District Collector necessary funds may be obtained from the relevant Head of Accounts from the Commissioner, Resettlement and Rehabilitation, AP.[7]

5.8 Within forty-five days from the date of receipt of recommendations of the Administrator for Resettlement and Rehabilitation, the District Administration shall publish the final details of survey in the District Gazette. A copy of such publication shall also be published in the Gram Panchayat concerned.[8]

5.9 The Administrator for Resettlement and Rehabilitation shall ensure that the Project Displaced Families may be settled preferably in group or groups and such sites should form a part of existing Gram Panchayat as far as possible. However it has to be ensured that the PDFs may be Resettled with the host community on the basis of equality and mutual understanding, consistent with the desire of each group to preserve its own identity and culture.

5.10 For the purposes of Para 5.9 above, the Administrator for Resettlement and Rehabilitation shall draw up a list of lands, which may be available in any existing Gram Panchayat or neighbouring Gram Panchayat for Resettlement of Project Displaced Families.

5.11 The Lands drawn up under para 5.10 shall consist of:-

(a) Government wastelands or any other land vesting in the Government available for Resettlement of Project Displaced Families.

(b) If sufficient Government land is not available there, then land to be acquired for the purposes of Resettlement (R&R centre) Scheme/Plan. However, the Administrator for R&R should ensue that such acquisition of land should not lead to another list of affected families.

5.12 The words "appropriate Government" occurring in the first line of Para 5.12 may be read as "District Collector".[9]

5.13 The Administrator for R&R or any other officer empowered by Government, on behalf of the appropriate Government, may compulsorily acquire lands required for re-settlement and rehabilitation of PAFs under the Provisions of Land Acquisition Act, 1894.

5.14 After completion of base line survey and census of Project Affected Families and Project Displaced Families and assessment of requirement of land for resettlement of land for resettlement and rehabilitation, the Administrator for R&R shall prepare a draft scheme/ plan for the Resettlement and Rehabilitation of the Project Affected Families and Project Displaced Families in consultation with representatives of Project Affected Families and Project Displaced Families including women, Chairpersons of elected Panchayati Raj Institutions within which the project area is situated.

(a) The draft rehabilitation and resettlement scheme or plan shall also be discussed in gram sabhas in rural areas and in public hearings in urban and rural areas where gram sabhas do not exist.[10]

(b) The consultation with the gram sabha or the panchayats at the appropriate level in the Scheduled Areas under Schedule V of the Constitution shall be in accordance with the provisions of the Panchayats (Extension to the Scheduled Areas) Act, 1996 (40 of 1996).[10]

(c) In cases of involuntary displacement of two hundred or more Scheduled Tribes families from their lands and houses in Scheduled Areas, the concerned Tribes Advisory Councils may also be consulted.[10]

5.15 While preparing a draft scheme/ Plan, the Administrator for R&R shall ensure that the cost of R&R scheme/ plan should be an integral part of the cost of the Project for which the land is being acquired and the entire expenditure for resettlement and rehabilitation of PAFs are to be borne by the requiring body for which the area is being acquired

5.16 It shall be the responsibility of the requiring body to provide sufficient funds to the Administrator for R&R for proper implementation of Resettlement and Rehabilitation scheme/ plan of Project Affected Families.

5.17 The Administrator for R&R shall keep proper books of accounts and records of the funds placed at his disposal and submit periodical returns to the Appropriate Government in this behalf.

5.18 Every draft Scheme/Plan of resettlement and rehabilitation prepared shall contain the following particulars, namely:-

(a) the extent of area to be acquired for the project and the name(s) of the corresponding village(s)

(b) a Village-wise list of Project Affected Families and likely number of displaced persons, family-wise and the extent and nature of land and immovable property in their possession indicating the survey numbers thereof held by such person in the affected Zone prior to acquisition of lands for the project and after acquisition of lands for the project;

(c) a list of agricultural labourers in such area and the names of such persons whose livelihood depend on agricultural activities;

(d) a list of persons who have lost or are likely to lose their employment or livelihood or who have been alienated wholly and substantially from their main sources of occupation or vocation consequent to the acquisition of land for the project;

(e) a list of occupiers, if any,

(f) a list of public utilities and government buildings which are likely to be affected;

(g) a comprehensive list of benefits and packages which are to be provided to project affected families;

(h) details of the extent of land available which may be acquired in settlement area for resettling of the project displaced families;

(i) Details of the extent of government land available which may be allotted to PAFs in lieu of land acquired for the project;

(j) Details of the extent of patta land available in project benefited area that can be acquired for allotment to PAFs in lieu of land acquired for the project;

(k) detailed of the basic amenities and infrastructure facilities which are to be provided for resettlement;

(l) the time schedule for shifting and resettling the displaced families in resettlement zones;

(m) such other particulars as the Administrator for Resettlement and Rehabilitation may think fit to include;

(n) a list of vulnerable affected persons, as defined at para 3 (ii) vide G.O.Ms.No.46, Irrigation & C.A.D.(PW:LA.IV-R&R) Department, dated 28-02-2009 read with G.O.Ms.No.77, Irrigation&C.A.D.(PW:LA.IV-R&R) Department, dated:10-07-2009;

(o) In case of a project involving land acquisition on behalf of a requiring body which involves involuntary displacement of two hundred or more Scheduled Tribes families, a Tribal Development Plan shall be prepared, in such from as may be prescribed, laying down the detailed procedure for settling land rights due but not settled and restoring titles of tribals on alienated land by undertaking a special drive together with land acquisition. The Plan shall also contain a programme for development of alternate fuel, fodder and non-timber forest produce (NTFP) resources on non-forest lands within period of five years sufficient to meet requirements of tribal communities who are denied access to forests;[11]

(p) Details of proposed training Programme for development of entrepreneurship, technical and professional skills for self employment;[11]

5.19 The Administrator for Resettlement and Rehabilitation shall submit the draft scheme/ plan for R&R to the District Administration for its approval. The draft scheme/ plan shall be published in the village/locality concerned. The draft scheme/plan may also be published in the District Gazette to give wide publicity to the same in the affected zone.[12]

5.20 Upon notification of such scheme/ plan, the same shall come into force.

Chapter – VI

6.0 R & R BENEFITS FOR PROJECT AFFECTED FAMILIES

6.1 The Resettlement and Rehabilitation (R&R) benefits shall be extended to all the Project Affected Families (PAF's) and Project Displaced Families (PDF's) whether belonging to below poverty line (BPL) or non-BPL except to the extent where specifically restrictions mentioned in the policy.

6.2 "Allotment of house site/ payment of exgratia

(a) Any Project Displaced Family (PDF) holding up to an area of 5 Cents of village site and whose site has been acquired shall be allotted house site of an extent of 202 square meters (5 Cents) of land in rural areas or 75 square meters of land in Urban areas in the Resettlement zone besides payment of compensation for the structures if any therein;[13]

(a1) Where any such PDF as defined above desires to migrate and settle at the place of his/her choice, cash of compensation in lieu of house site as applicable in the resettlement Zone shall be paid besides payment of compensation for the structures therein and in case the PDF belongs to BPL category, they shall be give suitable one time financial assistance for house construction including cost of sanitary latrine as fixed by the government from time to time.[14]

(b) In case if any Project Displaced Family (PDF) holds village site of more than 5 Cents, such holder shall be allotted village house site of an extent of 202 Square Meters (5 cents) of land in rural areas or 75 Square Meters of land in Urban areas in the Resettlement zone and also be paid exgratia for the site in excess of 5 Cents (for example if a family holds village site of 20 Cents in Project Affected Zone and have two major sons, residing with such person in case, they take 3 house sites of 5 Cents each in Resettlement zone, they will get exgratia for the balance of 5 Cents (20 Cents 3x5 cents=15 cents); and[13]

(c) The Compensation/ exgratia payable as above shall be on par with the package deal payable in case of acquisition of private / patta lands[14]

6.3 Grant for House construction:

Each PDF of BPL Category who has been allotted free house site under session 6.2 shall get a One time financial assistance of Rs 40,000 (Rupees Forty thousand only) shall be increased to Rs 50,000 (Rupees Fifty thousand only). This increase will have prospective effect. A sum of Rs 5,000 (Rupees Five thousand only) is granted to those who have already shifted houses from 8-4-2005 to 10-12-2007. Apart from the above, a sum of Rs 3,000 (Rupees Three thousand only) would be allowed in addition to the housing grant as per G.O. Ms. No. 68, dt:8-4-2005. The above increase shall come into force with retrospective effect i.e., the date of issue of G.O. Ms. No. 68, dt:8-4-2005.[15]

6.4 Allotment of Government land to PAFs, who become Small, or Marginal farmers or Landless after acquisition in lieu of Acquired land: in case of allotment of waste/ degraded or agricultural Government land, if available within the District, in lieu of acquired land and if agreed by PAF for allotment of such land, each such PAF shall also get financial assistance of Rs 10,000 per hectare or as fixed by Government from time to time for land development and in case of allotment of agricultural land, Rs 5,000 per PAF or as fixed by Government from time to time for agricultural production shall be given.

However such allotment of Government land will be restricted to an extent of land acquired from PAF or 2.5 Ha of dry or 1.25 Ha wet land whichever is lesser.

Provided further that in such cases,

(a) No compensation will be payable for the lands acquired from the PAF for the Project, to the extent of Government land is allotted.

(b) No exgratia will be payable for the lands resumed from PAF for the project, to the extent of Government land is allotted.

Land Acquisition officer shall pass the award for the lands acquired or resumed from PAF accordingly.

6.5 Allotment of land acquired by Government from the project benefited area to Scheduled Tribe PAFs, who become Small, or Marginal farmers or landless after acquisition, in lieu of Acquired land from them: Government shall acquire land within the project benefited area, as per guidelines issued by the Government from time to time such that no person should become small or marginal farmer or land less due to such acquisition, for allotment of such land to ST PAFs (who become small or marginal farmers or landless due to acquisition of their land for the project), if such PAFs so desire, in lieu of lands acquired from them.[16]

However, such allotment will be restricted to the extent of land acquired from such PAFs or 2.5 Ha dry land or 1.25 Ha wet land whichever is lower. Further provided that in such cases.

(a) no compensation will be payable for the lands acquired from the PAF for the project, to the extent of such land is allotted.

(b) No ex-gratia will be payable for the lands resumed from PAF for the project, to the extent of such land is allotted.

Land Acquisition officer shall pass the award for the lands acquired or resumed from PAF accordingly.

6.6 The land allotted under Para 6.2, 6.4 and 6.5 shall be free from all encumbrances. The land allotted may be in the joint names of wife and husband of PAP.

6.7 Grant for cattle shed: Each affected family that is displaced and has cattle, shall get financial assistance of such amount as the appropriate Government may decide but not less than Rs 15,000 (Rupees fifteen thousand only) for construction of cattle shed.[17]

6.8 Grant for Transporting materials: Each PAF shall get lump sum one time financial assistance of Rs 5000 or as fixed by Government from time to time for transportation / shifting of his building materials, belongings and cattle etc. from the affected zone to the resettlement zone.

6.9 Income Generating Scheme Grant: Each PAF comprising of rural artisan/ small trader and self employed person shall get one time lump sum financial assistance of Rs 25,000 or as fixed by Government from time to time for construction of working shed / shop.

6.9 (a) The affected persons shall be offered the necessary training for development of entrepreneurship, technical and professional skills for self employment.

6.10 Wages if after acquisition land owner becomes land less: Each PAF owning agricultural land in the affected zone and whose entire land has been acquired shall get one time financial assistance equivalent to 750 days minimum agricultural wages for loss of livelihood if no land is allotted in lieu of acquired land.

6.11 Wages if after acquisition land owner becomes marginal farmer "or continues to be a marginal farmer even after acquisition": Each PAF owning agriculture land in the affected zone and who consequently becomes a marginal farmer or continues to be a marginal farmer even after acquisition shall get one time financial assistance equivalent to 500 days minimum agriculture wages if no land is allotted in lieu of acquired land.[18]

6.12 Wages if after acquisition land owner becomes small farmer "or continues to be a small farmer even after acquisition": Each PAF owning agriculture land in this affected zone and who consequently becomes a small farmer or continuous to be a small farmer even after acquisition shall get one time financial assistance equivalent to 375 days minimum agricultural wages if no land is allotted in lieu of acquired land.[19]

6.13 Wages to Labourers: Each PAF belonging to the category of agricultural labourer' or non-agricultural labourer" shall be provided a onetime financial assistance equivalent to 625 days of the minimum agricultural wages.

6.14 (a) Subsistence allowance to displaced family: Each PAF who is also a project displaced family shall get a one time subsistence allowance equivalent to 240 days of minimum agricultural wages. It will be in addition to any other benefit available to him as PAF.

(b) Each vulnerable person as defined at Para -3.10(b) will be paid a pension of Rs 500 (Rupees Five hundred only) a month for life by arranging the necessary annuity policies by the Project Administrator at its cost.[20]

6.15 In the case of acquisition of land in emergent situation such as under Section 17 of the Land Acquisition Act 1894 or similar provision of other Act in force, each PAF shall be provided with transit accommodation, pending resettlement and rehabilitation scheme. Such families shall also get R&R benefits as mentioned in above Paras under the Policy.

6.16 The Project Affected Families who were in possession of forest lands in the affected area prior to the 13th day of December, 2005 shall also be eligible for the resettlement benefits under this policy.[21]

6.16 (a) In the case of irrigation or hydel projects, fishing rights in the reservoirs shall be given to the affected families, if such rights were enjoyed by them in the affected area;[21]

(b) In other cases also, unless there are special reasons, fishing rights shall be given preferentially to the affected families.[21]

(c) In the case of irrigation or hydel projects, the affected Scheduled Tribes, and members of other community having fishing rights in a river or pond or dam in the affected area shall be given fishing rights in the reservoir area of the irrigation or hydel projects.[21]

6.17 The PAFs enjoying reservation benefits in the affected zone shall be entitled to get the same reservation benefits at the resettlement zone.

6.18 BASIC AMENITIES TO BE PROVIDED AT RESETTLEMENT CENTRE FOR PROJECTS:

While shifting the population of the Affected zone to the Resettlement zone, the Administrator for R&R may as far as possible, ensure that:

(a) In case the entire population of the Village / area to be shifted belongs to a particular community, such population/ families may be resettled enmasse in a compact area so that socio-cultural relations (social harmony) amongst shifted families are not disturbed.

(b) The Re-settlement Centre shall be provided with the basic amenities and infrastructure facilities of drinking water, internal roads, Drainage Electricity, Primary School building, playground, Community Centre and access road to the resettlement site. In addition to these facilities, the other community centre and access road to the resettlement site. In addition to these facilities, the other community facilities which were available in the village, at the time of acquisition, shall also be provided.

6.19 R&R BENEFITS FOR PROJECT AFFECTED FAMILIES OF SCHEDULED TRIBES/FISHERMEN

(a) Each project Affected Family of ST category shall be given preference in allotment of land.

(b) Each Tribal PAF shall get additional Financial assistance equivalent to 500 days minimum agriculture wages for loss of customary rights/usage of forest produce.

   (i) Each non tribal PAF who is a member of a registered Fishermen Cooperative Society/Fishing license holders in the affected zone and who lost fishing rights and livelihood shall get additional financial assistance equivalent to 500 days minimum agricultural wages for loss of fishing rights.[22]

(c) Tribal PAFs will be re-settled close to their natural habitat of their choice, to the extent possible, in a compact block so that they can retain their ethnic, linguistic and cultural identify.

(d) Tribal PAFs resettled out of the district or out side tribal area will get 25 per cent higher R&R benefits in monetary terms.

(e) The Tribal land Alienated in violation of the laws and regulations in force on the subject would be treated as null and void and the R&R benefits would be available only to the original tribal landowner.

(f) The Tribal families residing in the Project Affected Area having fishing rights in the river/ Pond/ dam shall be given fishing rights in the reservoir area.

   (i) The Non tribal families residing in the project affected areas having fishing rights in the river /pond/dam who is a member of a registered Fishermen

Cooperative Society/Fishing license holders shall be given fishing rights in the reservoir area.[23]

(g) All the Fishermen PAFs will be accorded priority in extending benefits under various schemes/programmes being implemented by the state fisheries Department in consultation with R&R authorities.[23]

(h) Newly impounded/completed Reservoirs under jalayagnam shall be stocked with Fish Seed on priority basis by the state Fisheries Department by utilising funds available under different schemes with the Fisheries Department/DRDA/ITDA/SC Corporation/MADA/BC Corporation or by seeking provision of funds under R&R package as per requirement[23]

6.20 CONSTITUTIONAL BENEFITS TO ST/SC/BC PAPs AT THE RE-SETTLEMENT CENTRE:

The PAPs shall enjoy all the constitutional benefits at new settlement also to which they were entitled to at the village that was acquired for the project.

Chapter-VI-A

6-A[24] SOCIAL IMPACT ASSESSMENT (SIA) OF PROJECTS

6-A (1) Whenever it is desired to undertake a new project or expansion of an existing project, which involves involuntary displacement of four hundred or more families en masse in plain areas, or two hundred or more families en masse in tribal or hilly areas, DDP blocks or areas mentioned in the Schedule V or Schedule VI to the Constitution, the appropriate Government shall ensure that a Social Impact Assessment (SIA) study is carried out in the proposed affected areas in such manner as may be prescribed.

6-A (2.1) The above SIA report shall be prepared, in such proforma as may be prescribed, considering various alternatives, and using agencies accredited in the manner prescribed.

6-A (2.2) While undertaking a social impact assessment, the appropriate Government shall, *inter alia*, take into consideration the impact that the project will have on public and community properties, assets and infrastructure; particularly, roads, public transport, drainage, sanitation, sources of safe drinking water, sources of drinking water for cattle, community ponds, grazing land, plantations; public utilities, such as post offices, fair price shops, etc.; food storage godowns, electricity supply, healthcare facilities, schools and educational/training facilities, places of worship, land for traditional tribal institutions, burial and cremation grounds, etc.

6-A (2.3) The appropriate Government may specify that the ameliorative measures, which will need to be undertaken for addressing the said impact for a component, may not be less than what is provided in a scheme or programme, if any, of the Central Government or a State Government in operation in that area.

6-A (3.1) Where it is required as per the provisions of any law, rules, regulations or guidelines to undertake environmental impact assessment also, the SIA study shall be carried out simultaneously with the Environmental Impact Assessment (EIA) study.

6-A (3.2) In cases where both EIA and SIA are required, the public hearing done in the project affected area for EIA shall also cover issues related to SIA. Such public hearing shall be organised by the appropriate Government.

6-A (3.3) Where there is no requirement for EIA, the SIA report shall be made available to the public through public hearing to be organised by the appropriate Government in the affected area.

6-A (4.1) The SIA report shall be examined by an independent multi-disciplinary expert group constituted for the purpose by the appropriate Government. Two non-official social science and rehabilitation expert, the Secretary/Secretaries of the department(s) concerned with the welfare of Scheduled Castes and Scheduled Tribes of the appropriate Government or his (their) representative(s), and a representative of the requiring body shall be nominated by the appropriate Government to serve on this expert group.

6-A (4.2) Where both EIA and SIA are required, a copy of the SIA report shall be made available to the agency prescribed in respect of environmental impact assessment by the Ministry of Environment and Forests, and a copy of the EIA report shall be shared with the expert group mentioned in paragraph 4.1 above.

6-A (5) The SIA clearance shall be accorded as per the procedure and within the time limits as may be prescribed.

6-A (6) The SIA clearance shall be mandatory for all projects involving involuntary displacement of four hundred or more families en masse in plain areas, or two hundred or more families en masse in tribal or hilly areas, DDP blocks or areas mentioned in the Schedule V or Schedule VI to the Constitution, and the conditions laid down in the SIA clearance shall be duly followed by all concerned.

6-A (7) The Ministry of Defence, in respect of projects involving emergency acquisition of minimum area of land in connection with national security, may be exempted from the provisions of this Chapter, with due institutional safeguards, as may be prescribed, for protecting the interests of the affected families and achieving the broad objectives of this policy.[25]

CHAPTER – VII

7.0 DISPUTE REDRESSAL MECHANISM

7.1 R & R COMMITTEE AT PROJECT LEVEL:

(a) In respect of every project to which this Policy applies, the State Government shall constitute a Committee under the Chairmanship of the Administrator of that Project to be called the Resettlement and Rehabilitation Committee to monitor and review the progress of implementation of scheme/ plan of resettlement and rehabilitation of the Project Affected Families.

(b) The Resettlement and Rehabilitation Committee constituted as above shall *inter-alia* include as one of its members:

   (1) a representative of women PAP residing in the affected zone;

   (2) a representative each of the Scheduled Castes and Scheduled Tribes, PAPs residing in the affected zone;

   (3) a representative of a voluntary organisation;

   (4) a representative of the lead bank;

   (5) Chairperson of the PRIs located in the affected zone;

   (6) MPs/MLAs of the area included in the affected zone.

(c) Procedure regulating the business of the Resettlement and Rehabilitation Committee shall be framed by the Appropriate Government.

7.2 GRIEVANCE REDRESSAL CELL:

(a) In respect of every project to which this Policy applies, the State Government shall constitute a Grievance Redressal Mechanism under the Chairmanship of the Commissioner for Resettlement and Rehabilitation for redressal of grievances of the PAFs.

(b) The composition, powers, functions and other matters relating to the functioning of the Grievance Redressal Mechanism shall be such as may be prescribed by the Appropriate Government.

(c) Any Project Affected Family, if aggrieved, for not being offered the admissible R&R benefits as provided under this Policy, may move an appropriate petition for redressal of his grievances to the Grievance Redressal Mechanism.

(d) The form and manner in which and the time within which complaints may be made to the Grievance Redressal Mechanism and disposed of shall be such as may be prescribed by the appropriate Government.

7.3 The Grievance Redressal Mechanism shall have the power to consider and dispose of all complaints relating to resettlement and rehabilitation against the decision of the Administrator /

R&R Committee at Project Level and issue such directions to the Administrator for Resettlement and Rehabilitation as it may deem proper for the Redressal of such grievances.

7.4 Commissioner for Resettlement and Rehabilitation may, by order in writing, delegate such of the administrative powers conferred and duties imposed on him by or under this policy to any officer not below the rank of Joint Collector.

7.5 "Ombudsman":[26]

(a) An Ombudsman shall be appointed by the appropriate Government, in the manner as may be prescribed, for time-bound disposal of the grievances arising out of the matters covered by this policy.

(b) Any affected person, if aggrieved, for not being offered the admissible rehabilitation and resettlement benefits as provided under this policy, may move an appropriate petition for redressal of his or her grievances to the Ombudsman concerned.

(c) The form and manner in which and the time within which complaints may be made to the Ombudsman and disposed of shall be such as may be prescribed by the appropriate Government.

(d) The Ombudsman shall have the power to consider and dispose of all complaints relating to rehabilitation and resettlement against the decision of the Administrator for Rehabilitation and Resettlement or Rehabilitation and Resettlement Committee and issue such directions to the requiring body, the Administrator for Rehabilitation and Resettlement (where appointed, or the other senior Government official appointed for rehabilitation and resettlement, where the Administrator for Rehabilitation and Resettlement is not appointed; or the District Collector/Deputy Commissioner, as the case may be) as he may deem proper for the redressal of such grievances relating to implementation of this policy.

(e) In case of a project involving land acquisition on behalf of a requiring body, the disputes related to the compensation award for the land or other property acquired will be disposed of as per the provisions of the Land Acquisition Act, 1894 or any other Act of the Union or a State for the time being in force under which the acquisition of land is undertaken, and will be outside the purview of the functions of the Ombudsman.

7.6 INTER-STATE PROJECTS:

(a) In case a project covers an area in more than one state or Union territory where the Project Affected Families and Project Displaced Families are or had been residing, or proposed to be resettled, the states and or GOI in consultation with each other, may appoint the Administrator for Resettlement and Rehabilitation and the Commissioner for Resettlement and Rehabilitation for the purposes of this Policy.

(b) The method of implementation of plans schemes for resettlement and rehabilitation shall be mutually discussed by the State Governments and the Union territory administration and the common plan/ Schemes shall be notified by the Administrator for Resettlement and Rehabilitation in the State or Union territory administration, as agreed to, in Accordance with the procedure laid down in this policy.

(c) If any difficulty arises in the implementation of the scheme/ plans, the matter shall be referred to the Central Government in the ministry of Rural Development (Department of Land Resources) for its decision and the decision of the Central Government shall be binding on the concerned States and Union territory.[27]

CHAPTER – VIII

8.0 MONITORING MECHANISM AND APPLICABILITY

8.1 STATE LEVEL MONITORING COMMITTEE:

The GOAP, Department of Revenue, Shall constitute a State Level Monitoring Committee, to be chaired by the Principle Secretary/Secretary, Department of Revenue for reviewing and monitoring the progress of implementation of resettlement and rehabilitation scheme/plan relating to all projects to which this policy applies. The committee shall meet at lest once in three months to review and monitor the implementation of R&R plan in all projects. The committee will have the following or his nominee not below the rank of Joint Secretary as its Members:

1. Special C.S.& CCLA, Chairman
2. Commissioner for R&R & E.O.Secretary to Govt.
3. Prl. Secretary, Revenue
4. Secretary, Planning
5. Secretary, Social Welfare
6. Secretary, Tribal Welfare
7. Secretary, MA&UD
8. Secretary, PR&RD
9. Secretary, Housing
10. Secretary, Education
11. Secretary, Agriculture
12. Secretary, Women and Child Welfare
13. Secretary, Energy
14. Secretary, Law
15. Secretary, Finance
16. State Level NGO
17. Chief Engineer/ Project Administrator Special invitee
18. Secretary, Requisition Department[28]

8.2 THIRD PARTY CONCURRENT AUDIT OF IMPLEMENTATION:

Chairman State level committee shall put in place mechanism for each project for third party concurrent audit of implementation of R&R plan. The audit report of such concurrent audit shall be placed before state level committee form time to time.

8.3 PROJECT LEVEL MONITORING COMMITTEE:

The Administrative Department of the project for which land is being acquired, shall constitute a Project Level Monitoring

Committee, to be chaired by the District Collector of the district in whose jurisdiction the main component of the project lies, in case main component projects spreads over more than one district, senior most of the District Collectors shall chair the committee for reviewing and monitoring the progress of implementation of resettlement and rehabilitation scheme/ plan relating to the project to which this Policy applies. The committee shall meet at least once in two months to review and monitor the implementation of R&R plan The Committee will have following as its members

1. Joint Collector/ P.O ITDA- Convener
2. R&R officer- RDO/ Sub Collector of the division
3. SDC/ RDO/ Sub Collector, Land Acquisition
4. Project Director, DRDA
5. Chief Executive Officer, Zilla Parishad
6. District Panchayat Officer
7. District Education Officer
8. District Medical and Health Officer
9. District Level representative of DISCOM
10. Superintendent Engineer, RWS Panchayat Raj Department
11. Three members from PAPs, one at least women
12. One member from local NGO
13. Superintendent Engineer, Project site
14. Superintendent Engineer, Panchayat Raj
15. Superintendent Engineer, R&B
16. Executive Engineer, Social Welfare Department.[29]

APPLICABILITY OF POLICY:

8.3 THE POLICY ON THE RESETTLEMENT AND REHABILITATION OF PROJECT AFFECTED FAMILIES AND PROJECT DISPLACED FAMILIES (PRR-2005) SHALL COME INTO EFFECT FROM THE DATE OF ISSUE OF GOVERNEMNT ORDER.

8.4 The Project to which this policy is made applicable, the provisions of G.O. Ms 98 Irrigation (Project Wing) Department

Dated: 15.4.1986 and G.O.Ms.No.64 Social Welfare (T) Department, Dated: 18-4-1990 or any other order issued by any other department on this subject shall cease to operate from the date of commencement of this policy.

References

1. Added by vide G.O. Ms. No. 88, I & CAD (PW-LA-IV,R&R.I) Dept. dt:26-8-2010.
2. Added to Para 3.10 as 3.10(b) vide G.O. Ms. No. 46 I & CAD (PW: LA-IV-R&R) Dept., dt: 28-2-2009 and G.O. MS. No. 77 I & CAD (PW-LA-IV, R&R.I) Dept., dt: 10-7-2009. & Para 3.10 shall be treated as Para 3.10(a).
3. Substituted in place of para 3.15 vide G.O. Ms. No. 134, I & CAD (PW: LA-IV-R&R) Dept., dt:13-11-2009.
4. Added to para 3.16 vide G.O. Ms. No. 134, I & CAD (PW:LA- IV-R&R) Dept., dt:13-11-2009.
5. Added after para 3.22 vide G.O.Ms.No.134, I&CAD(PW: LA- IV-R&R) Dept. dt:13-11-2009.
6. Substituted in place of Para 5.4 (d) and added (e) & (f) vide G.O. Ms. No. 134, I & CAD (PW: LA- IV-R&R).
7. Substituted for para 5.7 vide G.O. Ms. No. 24, I& CAD (PW-LA-IV, R&R-) Dept., dt:18-3-2010.
8. Substituted for para 5.8 vide G.O. Ms. No. 120, I & CAD (PW-LA.IV, R&R-II) Dept., dt: 26.6.2006.
9. Amended vide G.O. Ms. No. 88, I & CAD (PW- LA.IV, R&R-II) Dept., dt: 26.8.2010.
10. Added after Para 5.14 vide G.O. Ms. No. 134, I & CAD (PW- LA.IV, R&R-II) Dept., dt: 13.11.2009.
11. Added after Para 5.18(m) vide G.O.Ms.No.134 I & CAD(PW-LA.IV, R&R-II) Dept., dt: 13.11.2009.
12. Substituted for Para 5.19 vide G.O. Ms. No. 120 I & CAD (PW-LA.IV, R&R-II) Dept., dt: 26.6.2006.
13. Substituted for Para 6.2 vide G.O. Ms. No. 76, I & CAD (PW.LA.IV- R&R.I) Dept., dt: 13-4-2006.
14. Added after Para 6.2a as 6.2a (1) and Para 6.2(c) Substituted Vide G.O. Ms. No. 134, I & CAD (PW.LA.IV- R&R.I) Dept., dt:13-11-2009.
15. Substituted for Para 6.3 vide G.O. MS. No. 271, I & CAD (PW.LA.IV-R&R)Dept., dt: 11-12-2007.
16. The word shall incorporated substituting the word may vide G.O. MS. No. 119, I & CAD (PW-LAIV, R&R.II) Dept., dt: 26-6-2006.

17. Substituted for Para 6.7 vide G.O. Ms. No. 134, I & CAD (PW.LA.IV-R&R.I) Dept., dt: 13-11-2009.
18. Added after Para 6.9 vide G.O. Ms. No. 134, I & CAD (PW.LA.IV- R&R.I) Dept., dt: 13-11-2009.
19. Added to Para 6.11 in the heading vide G.O. Ms. No. 46, I & CAD (PW:LA-IV-R&R) Dept., dt: 28-2-2009.
20. Added to Para 6.14 as Para 6.14(b) vide G.O. Ms. No. 46, I & CAD (PW:LA-IV-R&R) Dept., dt: 28-2-2009.
21. Substituted for Para 6.16 and Added after Para 6.16 vide G.O. Ms. No. 134, I & CAD (PW.LA.IV- R&R.I) Dept., dt: 13-11-2009.
22. Added vide G.O. Ms. No. 114 IRRIGATION & C.A.D. (PW: LA.IV-R&R) DEPARTMENT dt: 08-09-2009.
23. Added vide G.O. Ms. No. 114 IRRIGATION & C.A.D. (PW: LA. IV-R&R) DEPARTMENT dt: 08-09-2009.
24. Added a new chapter VI-A vide G.O. Ms. No. 134 IRRIGATION & C.A.D. (PW: LA.IV-R & R) DEPARTMENT dt:13-11-2009.
25. Added after chapter VI as chapter VI-A vide G.O. Ms. No. 134 IRRIGATION & C.A.D. (PW: LA.IV-R&R) DEPARTMENT dt:13-11-2009.
26. Added after Para 7.4 of chapter VII vide G.O. Ms. No. 134 IRRIGATION & C.A.D. (PW: LA.IV-R&R) DEPARTMENT dt:13-11-2009.
27. The existing para 7.5 shall be read as Para 7.6 of chapter VII vide G.O. Ms. No. 134 IRRIGATION & C.A.D. (PW: LA.IV-R&R) DEPARTMENT dt: 13-11-2009.
28. Substituted for Para 8.1 vide G.O. Ms. No. 184, I & CAD (PW: LA-IV-R&R) Dept, dt: 09-09-2008.
29. Added vide G.O. Ms. No. 101, I & CAD (PW: LA-IV- R&R) Dept, dt: 24-08-2009.

Index